Styles of Creation

STYLES OF CREATION

AESTHETIC TECHNIQUE AND

THE CREATION OF FICTIONAL WORLDS

Edited by George Slusser and Eric S. Rabkin

The University of Georgia Press   Athens and London

Designed by Louise OFarrell
Set in 10/13 Sabon by Tseng Information Systems, Inc.
Printed and bound by Thomson-Shore, Inc.
The paper in this book meets the guidelines for permanence
and durability of the Committee on Production Guidelines
for Book Longevity of the Council on Library Resources.

Printed in the United States of America

96 95 94 93 92   C   5   4   3   2   1
96 95 94 93 92   P   5   4   3   2   1

Library of Congress Cataloging in Publication Data
Styles of creation : aesthetic technique and
the creation of fictional worlds / edited by
George Slusser and Eric S. Rabkin.
p.   cm.
Includes bibliographical references and index.
ISBN 0-8203-1455-2 (alk. paper).
—ISBN 0-8203-1491-9 (pbk.: alk. paper)
1. Science fiction—History and criticism.
2. Fantastic fiction—History and criticism.
3. Style, Literary.   4. Creation (Literary,
artistic, etc.)   5. Literature—Aesthetics.
I. Slusser, George Edgar.   II. Rabkin, Eric S.
PN3433.5.S894   1992
809.3′876—dc20   91-40086
                                    CIP

British Library Cataloging in Publication Data available

"In the Palace of Green Porcelain: Artifacts from the
Museums of Science Fiction" was first published, in altered
form, in *Fictional Space: Essays on Contemporary Science
Fiction*, edited by Tom Shippey (Oxford, Eng.: Blackwell,
1991).

Contents

Preface

The question of style and aesthetic technique seems an important one for science fiction and fantasy. Stylistics may be one of the key aspects that distinguishes the poetics of these genres from the general poetics of literature, at least as that is defined today. Because it deals with language, stylistics acts on the level of *parole* more than on the level of *langue,* and it appears to play only a minimal role in structuralist and poststructuralist thinking. And yet science fiction and fantasy literature represents a proliferation of stylistic acts and experiments, each making a claim to world creation. Obviously, given the disparity between this style-oriented aesthetic and the structural or systemic bias of reigning literary theory, a new set of critical methods and models appears called for if the critic is to examine the role of style in science fiction and fantasy. This is the challenge, and the essays in this volume all address it from a variety of perspectives that represent the richness of the forms with which they deal.

All these essays are original, and all were originally presented at the Eleventh J. Lloyd Eaton Conference, held April 14–16, 1989, at the University of California, Riverside.

Part I

CREATION AND STYLE:

NATURE AND FUNCTION

Chapter 1

Reflections on Style
in Science Fiction

George Slusser

Style may be the man. But a term like *styles of creation* applied to a form like science fiction causes us to ask whether style can be the world as well, and SF worlds creations of style. This conjunction of style and world creation raises some interesting questions. Indeed, how can the "creation" of a fictional world be an act of style when style is traditionally seen as belonging to the realm of the individual rather than collective utterance? The very idea of *world* implies a complex set of laws and relationships— something that operates on the level of a general linguistic system and can only be articulated by means of such a system. The stylistic utterance, then, defined in relation to this idea of world, can be little more than idiomatic, an exception to the rule. Despite these traditional expectations, however, style plays a significant role in SF world creation. It may in fact be central to the process many see as the primary function of SF and what gives it its generic identity: the creation not just of narrative worlds but of *new* narrative worlds. And these new worlds, conversely, reveal a new role for style. The function of style here reinforces the possibility that SF may be effecting a quiet revolution in narrative priorities, inverting now-consecrated categories and allowing devices designated "minor" to reclaim prominence.

But before finding a new function for style, we must determine its place in the narrative system, both traditionally and in terms of contemporary

3

poetics. Today the role of style is clearly secondary—style is a matter of *parole* rather than *langue,* of individual utterance rather than general rhetorical structure. And this role is clearly reinforced by traditional poetics. Let us go back to the two great "poeticists"—Aristotle and Plato. The former gives credence to style, but only as species of a genus. Style refers to epithets like "Homeric age" that act as individual qualifiers to some general category. The Platonic view, in Pater's famous definition of style, is "the finer accommodation of speech to that vision within." This "vision within" is the ideal, or logos. In relation to it, however, style retains the subordinate position, it remains a part of the whole. Style is the necessary increment wrought by an individual on the gradient scale of ideality—the possibility in each personal utterance of approaching the ideal, of effecting speech's "finer accommodation." Modern poetics is more Aristotelian in the sense that it purports to dispense with metaphysics and ranks the category of rhetoric, on a scale that measures general structural function, higher than the more specific and subgeneric utterances of style. It is no accident that style is seen by some structuralists as a sign of the Platonic heresy, an excuse for acts of logocentric hubris.

Indeed, the few structuralists who have deigned to consider SF have been all too eager to define it as a literature of style in this secondary sense of the term. This is the gist of Gerald Prince's essay "How New Is New?" in which he argues that SF, in terms of narrative structures, is at best little more than a literature of stylistic idioms.[1] Despite claims to "newness," Prince argues, the forms or structures of SF, in their relation to the grammar or langue that necessarily governs all acts of story telling, are clearly little more than individual or idiomatic variations on the general system. Thus they are—and individual writers' often assertive claims to "originality" are proof of this—essentially stylistic acts.

The stylistic argument is also central (likewise in submerged form) to Michel Butor's article "Science Fiction: The Crisis of Its Growth."[2] Butor describes SF's potential for what we might call stylistic anarchy, the proliferation of "worlds" ungoverned by any narrative grammar or system. And this seems to trouble him deeply. Butor considers that SF can "grow" only when it agrees to access a general system or narrative structure, even if that structure, because we must abide by the rules of the SF game, is said to lie in a not-yet-existent future. Such a future can only be, as work of imagination, the product of a "great collective dream." In demanding this he is simply transposing Balzac's view of nineteenth-century Paris to the future world of SF. Balzac hoped to legislate the structures of what, for him, was the unique and only world imaginable. Using this same absolutizing process as standard, Butor faults SF authors for perpetrating acts of "world creation" that, because they are individual visions, can never achieve the unity necessary to become a world: "The result is an infinity of variously sketched futures, all independent of one another and generally contradictory. We shall have, in the same way, an infinity of Venuses, each of which diminishes the plausibility of the rest" (601).

Butor does not say so openly, but underlying his argument is a need to consider each act of SF world creation an act of style in the traditional sense; that is, an individual variation on a preestablished system. And not only does style not make a world here, but it constitutes the "human," or individual, vision only to the degree that it reveals the relationship of its particular voice to that general "grammatical" structure that allows any voice to speak meaningfully in the first place. In order to make his argument, Butor equates the science in "science fiction" with the language of science. This in turn he sees (a strangely monolithic view for a writer living in the age of relativity and probability theory) as a language that, ideally, must eschew all idiomatic and stylistic utterance if it is to achieve the clarity and precision it supposedly seeks. SF must cease to cultivate paratactic forms—its "infinity" of possible and parallel speech worlds—and create a syntax instead. The basis of this syntax, he proposes, might be a single city:

Now let us imagine that a certain number of authors, instead of describing at random and quite rapidly certain more or less interchangeable cities, were to take as the setting of their stories a single city, named and situated with some precision in space and in future time. . . . This city would become a common possession to the same degree as an ancient city that has vanished; gradually, all readers would give its name to the city of their dreams and would model that city in its image. (602)

Butor's point is that no single voice speaking as an arbiter of SF futures can legislate the ways of this city. For it is the city instead, seen as a system that precedes and hence presumes the individual, that provides the structural ground for all possible action. But to accept the rules of this totalitarian system is, in essence, to curtail the extrapolative capacity of SF, which invites individual writers, who share little more than a need to expand our collective sense of the nature of things and a common set of technological devices to do so, to put *their* mark on the territory they discover. Furthermore, to accept this city is to turn one's back on the methods of modern science. In the eyes of science, if the unified field is to be conceived of at all, it can only emerge from a plurality of hypotheses. This collective activity, in other words, construes individual statement as something more than simple reiteration of a basic structure. Scientific investigation and postulation today involve a complex interaction between individual, group, and natural world. Expressed in Butor's linguistic categories, such a relation has both syntactic and stylistic aspects. And within this relation, the individual utterance is entitled to claim status as a performative and finally an experimental act. The relation of individual to world no longer implies (as for Butor) a single nature but a potential infinity of perceptual natures or worlds, each one comprising a specific set of relations between perceiver and thing perceived. Despite Butor's dismissal, if we accept this experiential activity as proper to the science that subtends the compound *science fiction* and accord style its full potential as experiential act, then style may play a primary, not a secondary, role in SF. Of all today's literary forms, SF may be the one most informed by concerns that are stylistic rather than syntactic in nature. But the question is: What are the formal consequences of SF's propensity for acts of style? If the worlds SF creates are not Butor's single city, then what exactly is their nature and function?

One of the most interesting recent theories of style, in its implications for SF, is Richard Ohmann's. In his essay "Prolegomena to the Analysis of Prose Style," he offers, in contrast to the old manuals of rhetoric, an expanded role for style.[3] In statements such as "style is the hidden thoughts which accompany overt propositions," Ohmann defines style as the point at which acts of thought separate from the hegemony of propositional or formal aspects of language. To Ohmann, language is, ultimately, a system that permits the individual speaker to explore his or her natural world, making this latter a realm of experiential referents rather than simply one of signs and codes. His emphasis, therefore, is on what he calls (in a more classical sense) an epistemological rather than a structuralist approach to the function of language. The ancillary role to which rhetoric has traditionally relegated style has in a sense hidden its true potential, which is in reality a means for individual speakers of a given language to explore and understand realities that lie on the fringes of, or just beyond, its syntactical limits. It is important to note that Ohmann sees such acts of style not merely as epistemological acts but as "temporary epistemologies." Style is not merely something personal or idiomatic, though this is its point of departure. On the contrary, these "hidden thoughts" are not only tentative but also hypothetical in nature. This connection allows Ohmann to suggest a possible affinity between stylistic acts and scientific investigation itself.

In Ohmann's eyes, style obeys a different impetus altogether than rhetoric does, the impetus of *experience:* "The stream of experience is the background against which 'choice' is a meaningful concept, in terms of which the phrase 'way of saying it' makes sense, though 'it' is no longer a variable" (41). Ohmann, in still wanting to see the "it," or referential "world," as something constant and not variable, perhaps does not conceive of experience in the fully participatory sense that the modern scientist might. Nevertheless, by speaking of "way of saying it" he raises the question of choice, in this case the relation of personal act to systemic resistance. To Ohmann, the extent to which a language imposes its "world" on a speaker is understood less in terms of the syntactical tyranny of a Butor than in those of Benjamin Whorf's metalinguistics. Whorf describes the ways in which a given language may shape the cosmological view of its speakers, to the point of providing the medium, or "way," in which these speakers "see" or conceive what they see as their world. This structure, however, is never so rigid as to close a speaker's acts totally off from any genuine and transformatory interaction with experience. For Ohmann, language only limits the *possibilities* of choice for a given writer. He even, it seems, is encouraging the writer to seek stylistic escape from the limits of his or her given language: "A writer cannot escape the boundaries set by his tongue, except by creating new words, by uprooting normal syntax, or by building metaphors, each of which is a new ontological discovery" (43). Ohmann's three exceptions deserve to be discussed at length, for experientially or scientifically vectored as they are, they seem crucial to understanding the role of style in SF.

This sense of stretching or expanding boundaries is precisely the sense of extrapolation, the defining characteristic of SF. Ohmann can be said, then, to offer three modes of stylistic extrapolation. In relation to the actual practices and techniques of SF, however, these three modes need to be reranked in order of their relevance to the form.

The function of style least relevant to SF, it seems, is what Ohmann calls the *uprooting of syntax.* This may be, generally, a characteristic of twentieth-century fiction, but it is a preoccupation SF does not seem particularly to share. Walter Meyers, for instance, in his book *Aliens and Linguists,* notes little interest, at least in English-language SF, in personal experiments with syntax and grammar.[4] What was stylistic obsession in Joyce or Faulkner is, with so-called new wave stylists like Bester, Ellison, and Delany, at best a belated activity. More significant, and perhaps more ironic, these new wave experiments may actually divert the language of SF narrative away from the experiential function Ohmann describes, and toward a series of Butor-like meditations, reflections not on a scientific use of language but on a science of language, on a grammar of extrapolation that constrains rather than broadens its systemic activity. Delany's career is an example. Even in early works such as *Babel-17* we see Delany challenging linguistic relativism. And in subsequent novels such as *Nova* and *Triton* he deepens his search for a single structure that can be shared by languages and science fictions alike. Ironically, Delany the stylist, pursuing this search, has relinquished his own personal stylistic voice to the meta-discourse of theory in his most recent work. He follows in the wake of Joyce and the many scholars who have elucidated Joyce's structures—and thus demonstrates that this fictional exploration of syntax does not, any more for the modern than for the ancient Ulysses, lead to new worlds. It is not an uprooting but a homecoming, a return via the theory that reinforces it, to the comfortable complexities of rhetorical embellishment.

If syntactical experiment seems the least proper to SF alone of Ohmann's three categories, the *neologism* would seem to be its most distinctive stylistic aspect. For neologism, to the average SF reader, most characterizes the demiurgic (and anti-Butorian) power of the individual writer to conjure up new things and worlds simply by naming them. But what exactly is meant by this act? Ostensibly, the neologism can be an absolutely new word. Or it can be a new use for an existing word. But more commonly it is a combination of already existing words. In English-language SF the root words are most frequently taken from Greek or Latin. But is there here, any more than with syntax, any real uprooting of the language system that still seems to encompass the use of neologisms? SF abounds with new, made-up words. Indeed, at the fantasy end of its spectrum, many such words are simply phonetic recombinations, words whose very purpose is not to refer to anything specific but to suggest, in the manner of French symbolism, something inexpressible and ineffable. Some, of course, such as Le Guin's *kemmer,* are phonemes made to refer to something precisely defined. On grounds of newness, however, we are tempted to quibble with a neologism like *kemmer.* The word promises a process wondrously new. But when we read the description of that process, we find that the "new" word refers quite specifically to current, and even commonplace, ethnographic norms.

Gernsback would no doubt have quibbled with Le Guin's use of the word in this manner. And indeed, it is the Gernsback tradition that has lavished on the SF reader a profusion of words that, while making claim to a "sense of wonder," nevertheless claim for their new namings the more solid ground of recombined root words with prefixes and suffixes, of combined morphemes rather than mere phonetic sound structures. But a counter-quibble is possible. The Gernsbackian stylist as world creator is perhaps just as deluded as the new wave syntax bender. For rather than uprooting words, he is more than ever captive to their roots, in this case not only to morphemes but to semantic roots, to etymologies. The systemic base of this word-world creation is so apparent, in fact, that a writer like Stanislaw Lem can systematically parody SF's learned, and eminently rhetorical, coinage of neologisms in his novel *Futurological Congress*.

Webster's Dictionary, in support of its definition of *neologism*, offers the following statement: "All neologisms begin as slang, except in those branches of terminology where . . . there is an established tradition of word coinage or redefinition." [5] This marks a span—from slang to science—that the SF neologism seeks to negotiate. The concept of slang implies deviation from a norm, and thus fiction in slang traditionally exists at the edge (but never over the edge) of the mainstream sense of literature as closed system. This is the case with Anthony Burgess's *A Clockwork Orange*, an "SF" novel that the author finally, in a belated introduction, claims is actually a bildungsroman in which little Alex's *nadsat* slang is just another adolescent excess to be outgrown.[6] And yet Alex's style, as a product of its very minimal SF future, proves recalcitrant to this reduction. Most readers, including Stanley Kubrick, are more attracted by the exception than the rule, and in fact are captivated by the stylish manner in which Alex uses his neologisms. But how new are his words? Underlying his very skillful speech is a clearly identifiable amalgam of Cockney and Gypsy slang with Russian calques, simple replacement of the English *word* with *slovo,* and so on. The system of semantic substitution is paralleled by a syntactic one, which in like manner gives us quasi-Germanic inversions like: "Do watch that, O Dim, if to continue to be on live thou dost wish." Alex is less a stylist in Ohmann's sense—an uprooter of old worlds and generator of new ones—than a creature of eloquence in the traditional sense. In fact, the only neologisms that are not substitutions here result from what we might call phonetic irony—such coinages as *horrorshow* for *xorosho* (good) used by a speaker such as Alex without a full sense of the implications of this shift. Ignorance on the individual or style level must be supplemented by a general or structural sense of language as system. And this reveals Alex to be, despite his violent, rebellious manner, in terms of neologisms still an inhabitant of Butor's single city.

At the opposite extreme from slang, of course, is science—a "branch of terminology" in which Greek and Latin roots are manipulated and recombined with the stated purpose not simply of redefining the old but actually of describing new things. In fact, in the scientific sense this act of description, insofar as it involves a dynamic interaction between word system and world experience, also hopes to be an act of discovery. The neologisms of science are neither rhetoric nor slang. They are neither acts of conjuring nor of expression, but (at least ostensibly) attempts at knowing. They are extrapolations, or more precisely what Dedre Gentner calls structure mappings.[7] What the scientist does, according to Gentner, when he takes a word like *molecule* and applies it to a new area of experience is to extend a system of relations, rather than any literal similarity, from a base to a target domain—from the known to the unknown. For the scientist, the neologism is an analogy, a device for extending the scope of comparison and predictability, and even one of serendipitous discovery. What is more, it is an epistemological device that aspires to ontological validity. For in the ongoing search to find increasingly accurate verbal models for nonverbal phenomena, the scientist may even aspire to break through the barrier of language and make literal contact with the nonlinguistic physical world. Gentner calls this scientific neologism or analogy metaphor. And *metaphor* is Ohmann's third category of style. Conflating these insights, might we not consider scientific neologism and analogy alike as acts of style? In a very real sense both neologism and analogy are for the scientist an individual model, or "mapping," that is subsequently offered to the scientific community for verification and possible validification. To realize this urges us to make a serious assessment of the role of style in SF. For it is by a similar process that the SF writer offers up his or her world creations to a community of readers, who in turn share similar extrapolative premises and similar needs to validate and verify, but now in the literary context of thought "experiment."

    In itself, Ohmann's sense of metaphor as an epistemological device, operating within a literary rhetorical system whose comparisons have been traditionally what Gentner calls expressive in nature, is unorthodox. But when he connects both metaphor and epistemology to the traditionally individual, hence heavily "policed," realm of style, the implications are enormous. This connection proves crucial to understanding the SF activity Butor so greatly mistrusts. For this activity gives license to the SF writer, as "stylist" in the word's expanded sense, to do as the scientist does and strive to bring metaphor into contact with the physical world. Butor's mistrust, therefore, a mistrust that lies at the center of the SF "problem" and of SF's acceptance as a serious form of literary expression, is less concerned with the epistemological or even scientific pretensions of its use of metaphor than with the fact that epistemology here, claiming to be a stylistic act, represents an *individual* pretension to effect, within the general linguistic system, a desire to restore some "natural" relation between the sign and the thing signified.

Modern thought has been quite willing to extend the sense of the traditional rhetorical term *metaphor* to describe a general mode of cognition. Nietzsche, for instance, considered metaphor to be the basic means by which the human mind deals with the experience of the senses.[8] But Nietzsche saw metaphor as radically opposed to scientific "knowledge," which in his eyes was not the creation of analogies and hypotheses but rather science's ontological claims to abolish the figurative ambiguities of language in order to make direct contact with material "reality." To Nietzsche, such pretense at unmediated knowledge was illusion. The insurmountable barrier to science's claims to know the *Ding an sich* is metaphor. And metaphor tells us we can never know things directly, in themselves, but only know comparisons between things. The unknown is only understood through comparison with the known, and at best we substitute this mental category of comparison—or metaphor—for the structures of a physical world we can never directly apprehend.

"Science" as Nietzsche conceived it is very different in its epistemological method from science today. As opposed to the scientism of his time, modern science accepts the fact that the search to know must proceed by analogy. It proceeds by what Gentner calls explanatory metaphor. In relation to traditional rhetoric, Nietzsche may, on one hand, have made innovative claims for an epistemology of metaphor. But in terms of modern science, his view is restrictive. Nietzsche's sense of metaphor has had a strong influence on many contemporary literary theoreticians—and in a particular sense. The price for giving epistemological weight to language acts makes it imperative, it seems, that such acts be subject to a system of figurative relationships that controls them. The individual or "stylistic" act, therefore, can only derive from, and be understood in relation to, the preexisting structure of language. Given this view, neologisms can never be more than renamings. And metaphors are simply the reframing of potentially new experiences in preexistent mental forms. In Nietzsche's philosophy of metaphor, epistemology is always an intransitive process. In this context, ontological pretensions are necessarily reflexive, ontology as tautology. Not only must style, as individual idiomatic inflection on the general grammar, play a minimal role in this new rhetoric, but style seen as the means of what Ohmann calls ontological discovery is patently impossible.

The following equation, it seems, is possible here: Ohmann's idea of metaphorical discovery is to Nietzsche's epistemology of metaphorical closure as SF is to so-called modern experimental literature. By this I mean that Nietzsche and experimental fiction alike share a sense of the impossibility of reference. Both reduce conventional acts—be they ontological or narrative—to products of a system of mind forms. By doing this they deny these acts direct contact with "things," and even the possibility of making direct reference to things. On the other hand, Ohmann's idea of metaphor and SF share a claim to stretch systemic boundaries, making both metaphor and extrapolation devices for pushing outward the boundaries of the known or possible. Nietzsche's philosophy reduces science to tautology. Extreme experimental modernism views fiction the same way. It is against reductions like these that we must consider Ohmann's metaphor of discovery and its fictional analogue in SF world creation. The Nietzschean metaphor and structuralist fiction both seize and hold the systemic center. All else, outside, is declared to be idiomatic, an exception to grammatical norms. Given this division, SF writers can be said to explore and create worlds the same way Ohmann's writers use metaphor—as stylistic statement. In contrast to such legislated stasis, any act of style, individual and thus potentially unpredictable, assumes an unprecedented responsibility: that of enabling a direct (if not necessarily unmediated) relationship between human intelligence and the material world.

Paul de Man's essay "The Epistemology of Metaphor" is a good example of how this Nietzschean view has become, for today's critics, the motor of an expertly contrived rhetoric of ontological impossibility.[9] De Man merely assumes that the verb *to know* is neither transitive nor intransitive, but somehow treacherously reflexive. "Knowing" is not a process of transit between a subject and an object; it is confined, to use de Man's phrase, to "knowing about knowing." To Nietzsche, the proper sense of a science of knowing is to realize we can never know the thing itself but only the process whereby we would know that thing. This process is itself bound up in the endless generation of metaphors, which can never be more, if measured against the thing in itself, than *fictions* of knowing. Thus Nietzsche: "When we talk about trees, colors, snow and flowers, we believe we know something about the things themselves, and yet we only possess metaphors of the things, and these metaphors do not in the least correspond to the original essentials" (4).

In positing these mind loops of metaphorical language, Nietzsche was opposing demands by science in his time that language be used clearly—that is, without the distortions created by figures and tropes. For de Man, Locke is the source of this quest for a transparent language that will not impede the passage "between our understanding and the truth." De Man, however, does not contrast Locke with Nietzsche so much as he uses the Nietzschean sense of metaphor to demonstrate how Locke, in seeking to eschew metaphor, succumbs all the more to its lure. In a manner analogous to Butor's attempt to marginalize SF world creation as idiosyncratic in the blindness of its ontological hubris, de Man sees Locke's obsession with empirical "statement" as an aberration—an ultimately monstrous aberration, because it seeks to deny the "true" epistemological role of rhetoric. As with Butor, the grammar of figures must remain the center; to move beyond it, as Locke would do, is to isolate statement, increasingly, in that idiomatic realm we are calling style.

Locke seems to enjoin us, almost in the individualistic vein of the Cartesian *cogito*, to abandon figurative speech altogether "if we would speak of things as they are." In his eyes, rhetoric has become that deceitful "conduit that corrupts the fountains of knowledge that are in things themselves."[10] Each speaker is called upon to abandon the old medium of error and (in an act Ohmann today would call stylistic) direct language toward seeing into the heart of things. De Man would probably respond to this Wordsworth allusion by pointing out that it too is a metaphor, just as are Locke's "fountains" of knowledge. If no one escapes the metaphoric system, as de Man argues, then Locke's revolt becomes doubly perverse, for he cannot see that his prose is most eloquent in those very passages in which he most strongly condemns eloquence. Given this inescapability, Locke's search for a medium of ontological discovery becomes something dangerous, something that turns monstrously upon itself. Denial of the figurative "gap" between subject and object, de Man asserts, leads only to a deeper and deeper perversion of epistemology itself. This can be seen in Locke's unwitting fixation, as he proceeds in his denial of the figurative, on increasingly "abusive" tropes such as catachresis. De Man, in oddly animistic fashion, depicts Locke's denial of tropes as an act that summons this particular trope (as retribution almost) not only to figure but to actually incarnate this distorted relationship between knower and thing known that Locke's idiosyncrasy effects on the epistemological system. What Locke calls mixed modes are catechresis, but now the figure is placed in the service of Locke's perverse drive toward nonfigurative "contact." Because of this shift, what was originally only a mind form is now free to mutate into a thing. The appearance in Locke's text of changelings, monsters, and other physical manifestations of formerly figurative disparities between mind and body, inner and outer man, is a menacing sign to de Man that such a misguided attempt to know things can only result in an unknowing of self. The figure has taken flesh, but in a monstrous and unwanted way.

For de Man, the "thing in itself" can never be anything but a thing that is not. Things and "thingness" have no existence outside the metaphoric context that names them in comparison with something else; to claim they do de Man calls "fantasy." Such fantasy is dangerous because it is an ontological distortion, allowing "something to be if it is not necessarily the case that it is" (20). Fantasy has become an epistemological monster, metaphor on the rampage within the rhetorical system. And to de Man this monster, thrashing in the toils of its own ontological claims, increasingly takes on material presence within that system. Catachresis, as de Man sees it, generates the related figure of prosopopeia. As this occurs, the fantastic stylist, in his or her own divided being, undergoes an analogous "fall" in which his or her phantasms seem literally to take flesh, "and one begins to perceive a world of potential ghosts and monsters" (21). Thinking to discover the new, the stylist only generates a sport that gives monstrous form to the fatal initial distortion of the mind-body division, a sort of fall upon the fall. The stylist's utterance may indeed summon something new, but to de Man this is grotesque tautology, words "said to produce of and by itself the entity it signifies and that has no equivalence in nature." Just as catachresis precipitates into prosopopeia, so fantasy devolves into horror. A terrible equation is the result: rhetoric is to reality as style is to fantasy and, finally, horror. In light of this equation, those acts of SF world creation Butor so fears become exercises not in epistemology but in monster making—in the ontology of horror.

For de Man, apparently, it is better to be a monster than an inert thing. It is almost as if he erects his tropological view of language—centered on the circulation of metaphors and on the distortion worked on this pattern by acts of epistemological delusion—as a barrier against some real or imagined defection of the human subject to a condition of nonfigurative materiality, to inert thingness. Metaphor, for de Man, figures a resolutely dualistic vision. It is, however, a circumscribed duality, in which trope, now seen to operate in an area bounded by two radically absolute singularities, continues to exist only as some hybrid or monstrous product of the mind-matter division. One of these absolute poles of language function he calls "aestheticism," in which all speech arts are "purely symbolic and nothing else," "whereby nothing is seen as it is, not in practice either" (28). The other pole is "reification": "He who takes it for schematic and gives it the attributes of predictability and transcendental authority that pertain to the objective reality of entities unmediated by language is guilty of reification—the opposite of prosopopeia" (28).

Clearly, those who opt for Locke's materialist science are guilty of a sin against organicity in favor of the inorganic. Things are irrevocably dead, while even the prosopopoeic monster has life of sorts. De Man here is developing a Nietzschean misgiving. Nietzsche condemned materialist science for erecting a divinely sanctioned permanence of things in the face of an ephemeral human organicity. Yet, for him, not even science could push mind wholly into the realm of inanimate matter. At its worst science still produces metaphors, albeit "dead" metaphors. Against such total defection of living forms to lifeless ones, Nietzsche could only offer his pathological humanism. Seen through its eyes, scientific usage drains the vital force from the system of human discourse. The master metaphor of the Fall has now, in this light, become the hemorrhage.

From Nietzsche to de Man, an inexorable logic is working to stigmatize the role of style in contemporary poetics. In terms of a grammatical Eden, Adam's plucking of the apple becomes an act of stylistic disobedience. The initial metaphor, that of eating the apple of the tree of knowledge of good and evil, was circumscribed by moral, and hence human, boundaries. Nietzsche's science, however, aspires to go beyond these constraints, seeking truth and falsity in an *extramoral* sense. In this sense, epistemology would extend the process beyond the loop of metaphor and into realms of ontological discovery. Nietzsche, however, will not let the extramoral lead outside the moral organism, to something extrametaphorical. The figures of thought form a biofeedback system, one explainable perhaps by E. O. Wilson's concept of "biophilia," the innate human proclivity by which life is interested only in life. Nietzsche's version, however, is pathologically "fallen," the loop one of increasing sickness. Scientific discourse, for Nietzsche, produces only "coagulated" metaphor. Metaphor, from this point on, begins to act like an epistemological retrovirus in the organism of Western culture. Caught in this tropological loop, original sin becomes catachresis. Science, in its extramoral quest for knowledge, extends original sin, but only within the loop, causing the figure to mutate into disfigured prosopopoeia. But if the system is sick, the only way to health is the dictum "Physician, heal thyself." It is clearly this challenge of the singular that brings Locke to stress the role of the idiom in his epistemology of language. The same challenge lies behind the various "participatory" epistemologies of scientific hypothesis. And behind the analogous quest, through style, for discovery in literary creation, most particularly in SF "world creation."

SF emerges from this debate as that literary form in which the role of the stylist, user of metaphors in Ohmann's sense as temporary epistemologies, is crucial in uniting the two now-adversarial elements of rhetoric and science in a functioning whole. The SF stylist claims to explore new worlds, all the while recognizing, however, that at the same time these worlds are fictional constructs. Simultaneously there is scientific exploration and literary metaphor. The independent status of the stylist does not oblige him or her to see these as opposites, or force him or her to choose one or the other. On the contrary, they are allowed to be complementary rather than adversarial.

Let us take up these activities one by one, but now as aspects of SF style rather than as structures or ideologies. First, literary metaphor. SF does not deny (as a Nietzschean detractor might claim) that its creations are metaphors. In fact, it is precisely because it is so aware of their metaphorical status that it bestows on them an ontological status that is clearly *temporary,* a provisional material reality that is intended to be subsumed by future world creations. SF is fiction born of modern science. As such its metaphors are both individual statements and at the same time aware of an SF "community" of hypothetical statements centering on a common field of experience; and as part of this community subject to fictional analogues to scientific processes such as verification and correction. SF stories are independent creations insofar as each new writer reinvents a "trope" such as, say, Mars, but reinvents it within a rapidly expanding consensus of Martian features, including conventionally accepted paradigms such as the famous canals as well as currently known physical properties. SF, then, uses metaphor less in de Man's sense of "translation" than in the more open sense of "transfer." Both words share the same *etymon,* or origin. But the first derives from the past participle *latus.* And this implies that the activity of metaphorical extension, of reaching out for knowledge, remains controlled by its own sense of pastness—controlled by the anteriority of a text, both definitive and lost, in relation to which any metaphorical translation must remain a secondary version, a substitution. The second word, however, *trans-ferre,* highlights the infinitive. The implication here is that metaphor is, as speech act, something unconjugated, hence potentially always available to the individual, to the tentative epistemologies of his or her utterances. It is this dynamic figure that generates the continuous stream of individual future cities that challenge the existence of Butor's hegemonic edifice.

SF metaphors, then, originating as stylistic acts, are rich in epistemological possibility, not the sickly "metaphore blanche" of reigning literary theory.[11] In his graphocentric universe, no doubt Jacques Derrida would consider style little more than a "phonocentric" disruption to the hospital routine of working metaphor. But SF metaphor, by contrast, is an assertion of epistemological health, a figuring rather than disfiguring presence. It is not SF but the theoreticians who make this odd association of metaphor and sickness. Consider, for instance, the title of Roman Jakobson's famous essay "Two Aspects of Language and Two Types of Aphasic Disturbance." [12] If we compare Jakobson's approach to figuration with that of de Man or Derrida, we find a further nuance. To de Man, metaphor is assumed a priori to be a closed system. Any attempt to move beyond the trope in a speech act only leads to the generation of increasingly disfigured tropes. In Jakobson's view, if metaphor and tropes are generated by processes outside the grammatical system, it is explicitly by the physical disorder called aphasia.

Expressed in Jakobson's categories, what Butor describes as SF's lack of a single city is a "contiguity disorder." What is lacking in SF's endless generation of neologisms or metaphoric worlds is any sense of a coherent syntax by which these utterances can be controlled. What seems like variety is only a welter of *substitutions,* worlds upon worlds lacking any sense of general laws that control their interrelation. This syntax is assumed to precede any and all individual utterances, and the SF writer deludes himself if he thinks he explores when he only obeys preinscribed "laws." Jakobson's logic, however, rooted in a physical polarity rather than a metaphysical duality, works both ways. Seen through science fiction's eyes, could not Butor's city exemplify as well the opposite form of aphasia—the "similarity disorder"? For where Butor sees avoidance of metaphor, thus of the means of translating between individual worlds, we can reverse things and find too much metaphor, metaphor proliferating to the point where system has all but excluded the individual utterance, and with it the possibility of meaningful substitution. In this form of disorder there is an "erasure" of the stylist within the word system; therefore "words syntactically subordinated by grammatical agreement or government are more tenacious, whereas the main subordinating agent of the sentence, namely the subject, tends to be omitted" (Jakobson and Halle, 64).

Jakobson's article makes assumptions that are highly significant in terms of the nature and role of rhetoric in our contemporary age. Most curious of all, he claims his two forms of aphasia are the generic determinants for the two major forms of modern literary expression—prose narrative and poetry. He distinguishes the similarity-disorder system from the contiguity-disorder system by giving it a trope of its own: *metonymy*. Again reducing literary expression to a "tropology," Jakobson sees metonymy governing the epistemological system of realist prose fiction in Western culture. By the logic of metonymy, prose fiction develops horizontally through a seemingly limitless series of contiguous comparisons. Not really limitless, however, for the sum of these connections, determined as they are by the metonymic syntax of this network or "text," never goes beyond comparison between objects to any claim of ontological contact with objects in themselves. If anything, such a breakthrough seems more possible with metaphor, which in contradistinction to metonymy is seen to function on the vertical axis. If, for Jakobson, metonymy is the figure that governs prose, metaphor informs poetry. And the implications of this distinction are important both for the discussion of style and for qualifying the stylistic use of metaphor in SF. The poetry Jakobson is referring to is, clearly, lyrical poetry. If both prose and poetry are disorders, lyrical poetry is a disorder dominated not by the third-person "omniscience" of systemic similarities but by the counterexcesses of individual first-person "epiphanies." Style, in Ohmann's sense, has affinities (in its individualist emphasis) with this lyrical metaphor. Given this, metaphor can also, insofar as it creates temporary epistemologies, act to control Jakobson's tropological excesses on either axis. What is more, given style's further reach, in effecting temporary ontologies it can claim to participate in science's search for order as well. Indeed, there is a sense today in which scientific analogy itself could be called a lyrical act. For analogy offers to the scientist, beyond naïve claims to make "contact" with material things, the possibility of actually participating in their creation. There is a quasi-epiphanic ring to the fusion of observer and thing observed, for instance, in John Wheeler's description of participation: "May the universe in some strange sense be 'brought into being' by the participation of those who participate?" This process is demystified in science, however, precisely because of its particular "stylistic" sense of how metaphor operates.

What emerges from Jakobson's pathology of tropes is their distribution around central coordinates—here two forms of logic that remain basically metaphorical: similarity and contiguity. And placing what he calls metaphor on the vertical axis, Jakobson inches back toward the Lockean, or "scientific," sense of this figure as one in which language aspires to "break-through," to the naming of new things, or more precisely, new attributes of things. Historians of science are aware of this vertical tendency of sci-entific metaphor. But, like Mary Hesse, they tend to shun its excesses.[13] On one end, she warns against analogy aspiring to mathematical transcen-dence: "When we have climbed to the abstract mathematics by means of the analogy we can throw the analogical ladder away. But this account does not seem to be adequate, because we have seen that purely formal theories having no analogy to anything are scientifically useless" (177). On the other end of the scale, however, inverting Nietzsche, she sees analogy "degenerating" into metaphor. Her sense of analogy here derives from the Scholastics, who added to our two modern categories of logic—identity and difference—the third category of analogy. This allows her to distin-guish between phrases like *angry sky* and *angry dog.* Nietzsche's desire was to have metaphor "make the unequal equal." And the first phrase, *angry sky,* she sees as a metaphor in precisely Nietzsche's manner. There is no sense of transfer or passage from animate to inanimate terms, simply a desire to assimilate the inanimate to the animate, to indulge in the "pathetic fallacy." In contrast, the latter phrase, *angry dog,* is, as analogy, a true ex-ploratory extension of terms. In relation to humans, dogs are contiguous (they are animate and proximate beings). And insofar as the comparison asks whether dogs might also share something like human emotions, might they not be similar as well? But similar only in the sense that the result of comparison is an extension of our sense of what dogs might be; in other words, a new understanding of "dogness," and finally of the thing we call dog.

Hesse devalues metaphor just as Nietzsche values it. But the problem of metaphor remains, and it is one not really addressed either by the rhetori-cians or the Scholastics, but by the experimental scientists and the stylists. Hesse sees the problem as, fundamentally, the *description* of nature. And "when we have to consider descriptions of nature in terms of mathematics, we must deny that mathematical structure is ever predicated univocally of natural phenomena" (179). Not only this, she sees that, today, these de-scriptions are necessarily of unfamiliar, even "new," phenomena. Neither her Scholastics nor de Man's rhetoricians "have to cope with anything comparable to our modern problem of the analogical use of language to describe unfamiliar structures in nature which are brought to light by ex-perimental science" (179). Given this, a case can be made that metaphor is relevant here, and that the problem remains the classic one of tenor and vehicle. Scientific metaphor, contra Nietzsche, steadfastly insists on a particular inequality between its two terms. But instead of the tenor it favors the vehicle, extending it as far as possible beyond its point of comparison, until (ideally) it moves altogether beyond the retrieval pull of the original tenor.

This "stretching" need not be expressed in terms of horizontal or vertical pull. A better model, in fact, is Ralph Waldo Emerson's radial structure. De Man's tropology inscribes a circle, but as a two-dimensional network, a figure of structural containment whose generative center is evanescent, some now-lost origin in human pride and fall. Jakobson's axis is equally a place of sickness, where tropes and literary forms are generated out of speech disorder. Emerson's center, in contrast, expands circumferentially in all directions, offering at all moments the problem of power and form, of central energy and the growing edge. Extension is clearly from the animate to the inanimate, from mind to thing, but always in order that we may know more of the unknown. The vector here of scientific metaphor is Emerson's dictum that "fact is the end or last issue of spirit," and its issue is always the Emersonian hope that "by degrees we may come to know the primary sense of the permanent objects of nature." We neither dominate nor capitulate to the natural world; we gain facts. What is more, if we consider another famous Emerson utterance—that institutions are only lengthened shadows of men—we have metaphorical expansion generated by individual acts, by acts of style. Style's role in this process is, precisely, to make the equal unequal again, so that the extrapolative structure can stretch through myriad "degrees" or individual metaphorical acts until the old tenors lose their hold and we, piercing the rotten diction of Nietzschean denial, fasten words to things. Not just to visible things, as Emerson would have it, but also to things not yet seen, things new to the scientist.

Indeed, science's use of metaphor makes us think of reification in a very different, and ontologically positive, way. Lachman, Lachman, and Butterfield, for example, in their Cognitive Psychology and Information Processing, describe the process whereby independent scientific research in the twentieth century has converged, through a long series of theories and experiments which are originally metaphorical statements, toward a reification of the atom metaphor.[14] The result, they assert, is actual bestowal of ontological reality on the atom, the creation of a new thing that nevertheless remains unobservable to the five senses: "The atom of contemporary quantum theory and the molecule of turn-of-the-century physical chemistry have been reified to strong ontological claims about the subvisible microscopic structure of material things" (530). Nothing here is predetermined or predestined. The metaphorical structure that controls knowledge expands from within, through a series of ontological pinpricks that seek to fix a map of reality, to determine a field of activity rather than to define a system. Moreover, neither God nor a single individual has the authority to determine this field of reality, or to pronounce on our inability to achieve knowledge of it. Albert Einstein may have uttered the dominant theory, but not necessarily the decisive one. The extension of his metaphorical model to tentative ontological status is the product of a consensus. It is a "collective heuristic judgment" resulting from the convergence of what we might call individual stylistic acts:

A second important point about the Einsteinian resolution of the molecular hypothesis is that the theory, and the experiments that supported it, were not decisive in and of themselves. The end of the controversy reflected a collective heuristic judgment that, in the context of the cumulative data and theory of almost 50 years, Einstein's work supported an ontological claim.[15]

If SF makes ontological discoveries, it is in an analogous way, through a consensus of what are clearly stylistic statements, and not through Butor's legislation of a common system from without. What is unique in SF stories, I contend, is that they are, in a very fundamental sense, stylistic statements that make strong ontological claims. As such their aim is neither simply to teach nor to delight, but to provoke collective heuristic judgment on the part of those writers and readers who share this world-discovery enterprise. The stylistic act in SF is therefore a communal act of discovery (*heuristikon*, "to discover"), and it can be exemplified by the almost universal penchant in the genre for striking first lines—whose purpose, in the metaphorical sense, is to stretch to the breaking point the tyranny of familiar tenors. To conclude, I present a few such first lines, all taken from what is probably SF's most famous anthology, volume 1 of *The Science Fiction Hall of Fame*. Del Rey's "Helen O'Loy": "I am an old man now, and I can still see Helen as Dave unpacked her." Cordwainer Smith's "Scanners Live in Vain": "Martel was angry. He did not even adjust his blood away from anger." Bester's "Fondly Fahrenheit": "He doesn't know which of us I am these days, but they know one truth." Bixby's "It's a *Good* Life": "Perspiring under the afternoon 'sun,' Bill lifted the box of groceries out of the big basket over the front wheel of the bike."

By putting the word *sun* in quotation marks, Bixby is not simply taking it from its comfortable world of literal referents and returning it to metaphorical status. He is making it a term for which we the readers must now seek a new consensus reality. What might this "sun" be? The tenor becomes a vehicle that asks us, in a disquieting way, what should be substituted for it. Indeed, what sort of world is it where blood is "adjusted"? Or Helens are "unpacked"? Or as in Heinlein's famous story, roads "roll"? And what of the Bester story, in which the old metaphor of the split personality is now reified in a very ambiguous, but thoroughly present, speaking voice? Such examples of style as metaphor are legion in SF and perhaps represent its structural uniqueness, its unique mode of operating as a literature of thought experiment. In these first lines, style is the means not just of putting us in medias res but into the middle of new things as well.

I finish this essay with a sense of dismay, for it has taken some twenty pages of theoretical "sorting out" to reach the point where, exhausted, I can offer barely two pages of concrete examples of SF stylistics. This is indicative, sadly, of present-day academic discourse, in which the empirical need to engage the primary stuff of literature—physical books and works—finds itself interdicted in the same way that style as critical category is rejected simply because a theoretical establishment has legislated against parole in favor of langue, or for *metaphore blanche* instead of a fully active epistemology of metaphor. Yet, without the concept of style, it seems impossible to me to understand the tropology of a literary form like SF. Furthermore, deprived of this capacity for style, it seems impossible for our culture today, given its own sense of division between the sciences and humanities, to mediate between traditional figuration (as today's rhetoricians see it) and the scientific use of analogy. This division has become, in the wake of Locke and Nietzsche, a separation of two systems of "epistemology." Style, however, I hope I have shown, offers a means of ontological mediation between epistemologies. And therefore a way back, perhaps, to a sense that literature and science alike once again can offer a way to empirical knowledge, to a sense, if not of being, at least of discovery, of coming to know. Both through style and through SF, which today seems the literary form that most relies on style, we recover a sense of the tentative; that is, a sense of participation—not simply in the material world but in that interactive spatiotemporal transformation of mind and matter we call the future.

Notes

1. Gerald Prince, "How New Is New?" in *Coordinates: Placing Science Fiction and Fantasy*, ed. George E. Slusser, Eric S. Rabkin, and Robert Scholes (Carbondale: Southern Illinois University Press, 1983), pp. 23–31.

2. Michel Butor, "Science Fiction: The Crisis of Its Growth," *Partisan Review* 34 (Fall 1967): 595–602.

3. Richard M. Ohmann, "Prolegomena to the Analysis of Prose Style," in *Essays in Stylistic Analysis*, ed. Howard S. Babb (New York: Harcourt Brace Jovanovich, 1972), p. 45.

4. Walter E. Meyers, *Aliens and Linguists: Language Study and Science Fiction* (Athens: University of Georgia Press, 1980).

5. *Webster's New International Dictionary*, 2d ed. (Springfield, Mass.: G. and C. Merriam, 1958), p. 1640.

6. Anthony Burgess, "Introduction: A Clockwork Orange Resucked," in *A Clockwork Orange* (New York: Ballantine Books, 1988), p. v.

7. Dedre Gentner, "Are Scientific Analogies Metaphors?" in *Metaphor: Problems and Perspectives*, ed. David S. Miall (Sussex: Harvester Press, 1982), pp. 106–32.

8. Frederich Nietzsche, "On Truth and Falsity in Their Extramoral Sense," in *Essay on Metaphor*, ed. Warren Shibles (Whitewater, Wis.: Language Press, 1972), pp. 1–13.

9. Paul de Man, "The Epistomology of Metaphor," *Critical Inquiry* 5.1 (Autumn 1978): 13–31.

10. Cited in ibid., p. 16.

11. The term is Jacques Derrida's.

12. Roman Jakobson and Morris Halle, *Fundamentals of Language* (The Hague: Mouton, 1956), pp. 55–76.

13. Mary Hesse, "Scientific Models," in *Essays on Metaphor*, ed. Warren Shibles (Whitewater, Wisc.: Language Press, 1972), pp. 169–80.

14. Roy Lachman, Janet L. Lachman, and Earl C. Butterfield, *Cognitive Psychology and Information Processing: An Introduction* (Hilldale, N.J.: Lawrence Erlbaum Associates, 1979).

15. Ibid., p. 531.

Chapter 2

Waging War with Reality

David Brin

Consider poor Mr. Spock. He is strong, quick, handsome, and very, very smart. So why do we pity him?

Not just pity. A typical midnight viewing of "Star Trek" reruns is relieved by episodes of patronizing *amusement* whenever the pointy-eared science officer cries "that's illogical!" at yet another impulsive Kirkian coup. Insomnia gives way to a smug sense of superiority. Spock may be an icon of admirable maturity (e.g., Vulcans never lie), yet we come away from each episode relieved that we aren't like him . . . glad to have other, less laudable, but decidedly human traits.

"Star Trek" is hardly representative of high-end science fiction, of course. Even Spock's latter-day cousin, the android Data, is little more than Pinocchio updated to the twenty-fourth century. Like Gepetto's wooden son, he longs to learn all those indefinable human knacks like laughter and whimsy, for which he'd gladly trade all of his impressive powers. To the first order, these characters seem merely to convey one of Hollywood's classic propaganda campaigns—a fervently peddled myth that logic and emotions are forever incompatible. But there's more to this than just another dose of anti-reason indoctrination. Spock really *is* pitiable. He lacks something more valuable than strength, or raw intelligence, or even emotion. He is crippled by a basic inability to wage war with reality.

It is a war we all fight, nearly every waking hour. One might even define a human being as *the animal that's never satisfied with things as they are.*

Each of us, day in, day out, looks around and sees a version of the world relayed to us by our senses. In his allegory of the cave, Plato describes the dilemma as if each individual is, from birth, trapped inside a cavern, watching shadows cast upon the wall by objects outside, struggling to understand reality by subjective interpretation of imperfect images. What we name a chair is, in fact, only the set of sensations, or *phenomena*, elicited by a thing whose objective essence, or *nuomena*, we can never know.

Plato and Kant held that subjective models are doomed to be futile because they can never be perfect. Latter-day pragmatists, such as Jacques Ampère, countered that experiment and observation can isolate and characterize a thing's *properties*. Even incomplete maps and mental replicas can be good and useful tools—imperfect, but improvable with time and experience. We can use such models to *corner* Nature, forcing the world to surrender a little more predictability and make a little more sense with each passing year.

Whoever is right in a purely metaphysical sense, models and metaphors are what we're stuck with. Each morning, we wake up and start comparing the new day's reality with our internal picture of how the universe was before we went to bed. We also use mental models to speculate how the world *might* be if certain acts were performed.

This is an arrogant trait. No other creature is known to spend such a large part of its time scheming how to change things. Buddha and Jesus and Socrates are supposed to have said *don't do that*. Don't involve yourself in the world. Yet, the typical *Homo sapien* spends countless hours imagining what things may be like next week, or next year, or in five minutes, if only this or that event were to take place according to plan. From engineers designing a space probe to muggers lurking in an alley to a mother teaching her child the ABCs, we are all working to alter reality from what-is to what-we-want-it-to-be.

Internal models sketch out potential future chains of events—like computer simulations or trial runs in the lab. Often these extrapolations fail, but think how good they usually are! Consider driving through traffic. Day in, day out, we send two-ton behemoths of steel—packed with high-explosive vapors—swooping between other similarly careening monsters at high speeds. Evolution did not prepare or even preadapt humans for freeways, and yet our rapid-paced, constantly updated internal models of typical driver behavior work so well most of the time that we get upset if another car comes close to *touching* ours.

Metaphorical world models are attempts to work out in advance what mistakes to avoid, what strategies to use, so we'll get that promotion, that award, that date, that mate. While intelligence, strength, and all the other classic virtues often help us achieve our ends, they're futile if our models and guesses about the future are wrong. It's made even more difficult because people around us are trying to shift reality, too. The future is forever a moving target.

In other words, while reason and logic are good, it also helps to have an agile imagination.

Imagination was what I talked about in my presentation for the Ninth Eaton Conference.[1] At that time I spoke of my belief that SF authors have got to be among the greatest fibbers of all time.

Now straight-out lying is deservedly listed as one of society's Bad Things. Yet both the con man and the actor share an ability to portray what is not and make it seem true. A novelist has nothing on an excuse-making adulterer when it comes to inventing people and events that never happened. The engineer, the entrepreneur, and the Don Juan all cast their minds into the future, foresee things they desire to achieve, then actively persuade others to help them get what they want.

Earlier, I called this activity metaphorical drive. It is the unique human ability to create metaphors for reality—and other conceivable realities—by rearranging myriad alternate images of the world inside our heads. Occasionally, these reworked models are twisted, even sick. But they can also be prescient, inspired, or beautiful. They enable us to envision, and thereby possibly avoid, mistakes. They let us picture and convey—and therefore sometimes reify—portraits of possible tomorrows.

Spock has difficulty doing this because he cannot lie. He can make conjectures, but not wild, passionate hunches or far-out speculations. In other words, he really is crippled. No wonder we pity him, despite his brawn and brains. No wonder we cheer for him whenever he makes a move toward loosening up . . . toward becoming more human.

This is one reason why logic gets such a bad rap at times. Our civilization has profited immensely by unleashing imagination from the many constraints laid upon it by prior tribal and hidebound cultures. Judging by all the proimpulsiveness propaganda carried by popular media these days, it seems a great many people in the West fear that too much logic and reason will cramp us again. Perhaps they worry that stodgy reductionists will insist they justify every timid extrapolation, each tiny step into the future.[2]

How ironic such attitudes are. In truth, it was scientific, step-by-step reductionism that let us drive away so many ancient hobbles and superstitions and start learning how the world really works at last. Thanks to logic and experimentation, it has been proven that women aren't mentally deficient compared with males—even though it was common knowledge in nearly every civilization before ours. The Spock-like honesty that is the hallmark of science ripped through other age-old assumptions about disease and social class and life-style. We still have a long way to go.

Without modern skepticism we would almost certainly have remained trapped by the insidious, egotistic human tendency to smugly believe what we want to believe, whether it's true or not. For imagination has a dark side, lending power to our hatreds and prejudices. Prove-it-to-me science has saved us from much evil.

Yet science and honesty are themselves nothing *without* imagination, which provides the feedstock of notions, hunches, and ideas we need—new metaphors, maps, models, and theories—for science to test.[3] Imagination provides the ore, which rationality then grinds and sifts for rare, gleaming nuggets. In fields of endeavor experiencing vivid, creative times, this balance thrives. The brightest physicists play with Zen riddles, and some great engineers have also been noted artists or musicians.

Similar tension can be seen in art and literature, and especially in science fiction, the literature of alternate realities. Two powerful and apparently contradictory impulses have driven SF authors since the days of Verne and Wells. On the one hand, we appreciate vividness and boldness. We like the author to depict people and places as startlingly different from today's mundane world as possible.

On the other hand, we also enjoy extrapolations that make sense, that hold together logically, that project believably from today's world, and that possess both internal and external consistency. This tension pervades all levels of the art, from the macrocraft of basic plotting down to the sentence-by-sentence microcraft of aesthetic style, where use of metaphor is immediate and highly sensory. Ideally, the best novels and stories simultaneously display both flamboyance and discipline. Up close, each component paragraph can be its own *gedankenexperiment,* demanding that the reader abandon clichéd assumptions and test yet another new way of looking at things.

We're all familiar with examples where the balance fails. At one extreme are those yeomanly works composed of competent plot-smithing, uninspired gimmickry, and cardboard characters, which score high on consistency and basic readability but close to nil on inspiration or originality. Then there are flashy works that sparkle and scintillate with daring, brash imagery and actinic, skyrocketing prose—but which also often prove dense, impenetrable, self-indulgent, or simply impossible. We tend to feel strongly about such works; we argue vehemently about them. Rereading one can feel like puzzling over the notes you scrawled last night, after rousing from a dream with some exciting notion. It sounded great *then*, but alas, it makes less sense by daylight.

Cases of true synthesis, in which a balance is successfully struck, stand out. Joseph Heller's madcap *Catch-22* seems to be an example of imagination unleashed from any and all discipline. I remember being shocked to see copies of the detailed charts Heller used to keep track of his characters and the highly abstracted time line. Arrows traced flashback within nested flashback in exquisite detail. Not a plot line or foreshadowing hint was wasted. At the time I felt betrayed to learn it had been charted out so. It was more romantic to consider *Catch-22* a work of divine insanity that had erupted full-blown from some well of genius both ineffable and bottomless. So Hollywood teaches us to regard creativity—as something unconscious, guileless, and godlike.

As the years passed, I began to see how much inspiration owes to more mundane, worldly traits such as *skill* and *craftsmanship*. I realized that Heller's brilliance was completely undiminished by the fact that careful planning also played a role. Characters like Doc Daneeka and Clevinger are still products of a delightfully bizarre imagination. But that imagination probably spun out a hundred other characters and potential events for every one that was finally, carefully selected and honed by the author. Someone had to *choose* among all those metaphors—those cascading notions and images—mixing, matching, pruning.

Clearly we need both romance and reason, even in wholly creative arts such as fiction. They are siblings and would be lost without each other, no matter how much they appear to bicker.

Craft without imagination is like a mill without wheat.

Imagination without craft is little more than masturbation.

Where does this leave us, considering styles of creation? Free to do what we would anyway . . . point to what we like and come up with rationalizations for why we prefer it. Unlike science, in which all metaphors must eventually come up against the hard, objective test of experimental verification, literary aesthetics must and always will remain completely subjective. The experiments performed in literature—even in SF—will forever remain thought experiments.

I will continue to judge the works I read by how well they help me sketch out and live other realities, from the mundane musings of a grocer, to the funneling intensity of a black hole, to the bizarre glyph thoughts of an alien. Metaphorical explorations that are weird and different enough, or moving enough, may pass on that basis alone. Those which prove startlingly accurate or persuasive, also, need accomplish nothing else to be worth a bit of my time.

But on the whole, I will always prefer works that give me both—amazing notions and a willingness to test them against hard-nosed realism. From the level of the sentence all the way to the plot itself, that is what I'm really looking for.

Here is how I judge the style of any creation, especially a work of writing. Make me stop once, after reading some astonishing paragraph, so that I murmur "huh!" in amazement at a new thought. *Then* make me stop again, pages, chapters, *months* later, so that I think back on the same paragraph, in retrospect, and comment—"Wow. That really worked."

Notes

1. "Metaphorical Drive, or Why We're Such Good Liars."
2. Indeed, this is exactly what has happened to the U.S. space program!
3. Those patriarchs of science who try too hard to defend a specific model or theory and suppress opposition aren't being reasonable or logical at all, just egotists.

Chapter 3

Style, Fiction, Science Fiction:
The Case of Philip K. Dick

Carl Freedman

In an interesting essay on what we would today describe as the crisis of literary canonization, C. S. Lewis claims to know how "the plain man" distinguishes between texts that are "real Literature" and those that are not: the latter, it seems, " 'haven't got style' or 'style and all that.' " As a robustly neo-Christian critic and novelist, Lewis naturally maintains a rigorously antiformalist viewpoint, and he thus goes on to chastise his imaginary lowbrow friend for "a radically false conception of style." [1] But before we allow this apparently hapless plain man to sink too far beneath the weight of donnish contempt, it is worth noting that he, far more than Lewis, is supported by the most influential modern theories of literary form. The key reference here is surely to Russian Formalism, with its extremely various, detailed, and ingenious attempts to prove that the essence (or necessary and sufficient condition) of literature as such is a certain specifically "literary" use of language formally distinguishable from all nonliterary uses and definable in properly stylistic ways. Only relatively recently, to be sure, have the particular innovations of Viktor Shklovsky and his colleagues attained a worldwide impact commensurate to their intrinsic intellectual power. But ideas related directly or indirectly to Russian Formalism—especially with regard to its conviction that literature must be understood in terms internal and specific to itself, without necessary dependence on the referential status of the literary text—have resonated throughout most of the most prestigious Anglo-American literary theorizing of this century, from certain elements in the work of I. A. Richards, through much of American New Criticism, to such a relatively late epigone of Russian Formalism as Paul de Man—who, in one of his most widely known oracular gestures, proclaims that he does "not hesitate to equate the rhetorical, figural potentiality of language with literature itself." Indeed, it is in just this context that de Man significantly contrasts what he himself terms "the sub-literature of the mass media"[2] (specifically, an episode of "All in the Family") with *real* literature like À *la recherche du temps perdu*: the operative distinction is precisely that Proust's novel, unlike (or at least far more than) the dialogues of Archie and Edith Bunker, possesses style and all that.

Of course, the whole category of style must be historicized in order to be truly intelligible, and such historicization must first of all notice that the de-Manian use (like a great many other uses) of the term *rhetoric* involves a certain historical imprecision. For, as Fredric Jameson has suggested,[3] style is a specifically modern phenomenon, an effect of the bourgeois cultural revolution; and though it is in some ways the successor to rhetoric, it operates in a manner *antithetical* to that of rhetoric in the strict sense. The older term implies a storehouse of linguistic figures, each with its predetermined formal integrity and all available to all aspiring rhetoricians. Actual rhetorical practice must, of course, vary with the various aims and abilities of different practitioners, but the shared figural infrastructure of all rhetoric guarantees a considerable degree of pan-rhetorical community. Furthermore, those differences that do emerge among rhetorical performances are understood as rhetorical differences simply and solely, as variations in the practice of a common art; they are not taken to be outward embodiments of profound dissimilarities in character and personality, as indexes to the variety of human souls. But such is precisely the case with style. Style is the direct expression of the middle-class ego and must be created anew and almost ex nihilo by every stylist. Fundamentally, it has little in common with such a characteristically collective and transpersonal project of the precapitalist order as rhetoric. On the contrary, it is part and parcel of the whole celebration of personal subjectivity so typical of cultural modernity, not only in the sense that the individual stylist is personally and almost solely responsible for every act of stylistic production, but also in that every particular style—understood here as an overall pattern perceptible in the work of any given stylist—is taken to be profoundly revealing of the author not merely as producer of style but as a human subjectivity in toto. The style *is* the person, as the well-known French proverb has it.

Accordingly, it is not difficult to understand the primacy widely accorded to style in the formalist construction of literature. On the one hand, since style, in formalist stylistics, is taken to inhere in language itself, in the medium in which literature has its very existence, a stylistic emphasis enables the immense methodological economy of a quasi- (or pseudo-) scientific taxonomy of literature as an autonomous system sufficient unto itself and structurally describable without necessary reference to extraformal categories. On the other hand, the danger of a merely technicist aridity which such a stylistics might seem to imply is avoided through the considerable affective force and richness that derive from the privileged relationship assumed between style and the soul of the stylist. It is significant that the ultimate context of C. S. Lewis's rejection of formalist stylistics is nothing other than a considered *denial* of the viability of the distinction between literature, on the one hand, and, on the other hand, what Lewis's invented lowbrow says is not real Literature or what Paul de Man calls subliterature.[4] For Lewis's position is a minority—indeed almost an eccentric—one. More mainstream theorists (like de Man or Lewis's plain man) are convinced that the distinction is indeed viable and that its essence is style and all that.

The question of this distinction is, of course, a source of profound concern and anxiety in the fields of SF and SF criticism. On the most primitive, desperate level, those seriously interested in SF, especially academic critics, have still to contend with a considerable body of respectable opinion which would consign nearly the entirety of SF to the category of the subliterary. But the question retains some urgency even within those fields of discourse in which it is taken for granted that SF is and ought to be an object of serious critical scrutiny. Confining the discussion only to the SF of the past five decades or so in America, it is, for instance, possible to draw a comparatively distinct line between fairly recent work that is taken as unambiguously serious literature by most SF critics, and generally older (especially Golden Age) work, the literary status of which appears to be substantially more problematic. The more specific nature of this dichotomy can be illustrated with imperfect but tolerable clarity simply by citing two sets of names: on the one hand, Ursula K. Le Guin and Samuel Delany; on the other, Robert Heinlein and Isaac Asimov. I do not know that anyone has ever exactly said that Le Guin and Delany write real literature whereas Heinlein and Asimov write something different and lower.[5] But some such assumption (often, no doubt, in slightly weaker form) is implicit in much or perhaps even most of the best SF criticism. There is, of course, a powerful (and partly sociological) contrast between, on the one hand, the scientific, technical, military, and commercial orientations of the most typical Golden Age writers such as Heinlein and Asimov—with their technocratic identifications, their familiarity with popular science, and their general lack of interest in modern literature beyond the pulp SF magazines—and, on the other hand, the far more self-consciously literary vocations of the most representative writers of Le Guin's and Delany's generation, with their literary-academic leanings and awareness of Joycean and post-Joycean literary modernism, and their partly correlative interest in radical social theory, in sexuality and gender relations, and in philosophical speculation. But within SF as beyond it, the line between literature and subliterature is most confidently (and most *formally*) drawn on the basis of style. Though John W. Campbell, Jr., whose editorship at *Astounding* is generally credited with inaugurating the Golden Age itself, emphatically insisted on a putatively higher stylistic level than had prevailed in earlier pulp SF, the style of most Campbell-era SF (with some noteworthy exceptions, such as the best work of Alfred Bester and Theodore Sturgeon) has rarely been acclaimed as anything more than serviceable. SF writing of the Heinlein-Asimov sort seldom seems to register any stylistic aesthetic more complex or polished than that implied by the early fiction of Hemingway—and, it may be added, seldom measures up even to that standard. In sharp contrast, the most interesting work of the later generation—and in addition to Le Guin and Delany I would certainly name Joanna Russ, Thomas Disch, Marge Piercy, William Gibson, and such British kindred spirits as J. G. Ballard and Brian Aldiss—frequently attains the kind of style that is considered in seriously literary terms in the normative critical and academic forums.[6] And how proudly the SF criticism often highlights—to pick the most obvious examples—the literary fineness of Le Guin's prose or the intellectual depth of Delany's linguistic and stylistic concerns. Especially for those of us who study and teach SF in the academy, it is by pointing to such attainments that the status of SF as "real Literature" can be most readily and definitively established.

The SF of Philip K. Dick, however, seems to constitute something of an anomaly with respect to the conceptual scheme I have sketched above; and interrogating the scheme through a consideration of his work may result in some interesting modifications of the scheme itself. For Dick is in most respects surely to be counted in the same category as Le Guin and Delany; such a classification is assumed in most comparative SF criticism that touches on his work at all, and there is an increasing body of critical opinion that holds Dick's work not only to be serious literature but to constitute the most important and interesting corpus of fiction produced by any American author since Faulkner. Yet on what we have seen to be the most prestigious test of literary significance—style—Dick appears to fail. Older than most of the other American SF authors for whom comparable critical claims are routinely made, Dick is also—with respect to his publishing outlets and his general habits of work and productivity— more firmly rooted in the pulp magazine tradition of the Campbell era; and this lineage has a direct bearing on the quality of Dick's prose. Deeply influenced by Heinlein's dynamic narrative pacing (though not by the great Cold Warrior's politics or sensibility), Dick typically produces a style that is serviceable in what appears to be very much the Heinlein mode, a style functionally adequate to the movement of his fast-moving narratives but lacking the evident polish, syntactic elegance, and allusive resonance of incontestably literary prose. It would not normally occur to one to describe Dick—as one might easily describe Delany or Le Guin—as a stylist. If, then, Dick is an immensely finer writer—a writer of far greater radicalism, sensitivity, and intellectual complexity—than his stylistic precursor Heinlein, are we to conclude that his greatness is attained *despite* his style?

The following passage condenses the opening of *Ubik*, the novel I take to be Dick's finest:

At three-thirty a.m. on the night of June 5, 1992, the top telepath in the Sol System fell off the map in the offices of Runciter Associates in New York City. That started vidphones ringing. The Runciter organization had lost track of too many of Hollis' psis during the last two months; this added disappearance wouldn't do. . . .

Sleepily, Runciter grated, "Who? I can't keep in mind at all times which inertials are following what teep or precog. . . . What? Melipone's gone? . . . You're sure the teep was Melipone? Nobody seems to know what he looks like; he must use a different physiognomic template every month. What about his field?"

"We asked Joe Chip to go in there and run tests on the magnitude and minitude of the field being generated there at the Bonds of Erotic Polymorphic Experience Motel. Chip says it registered, at its height, 68.2 blr units of telepathic aura, which only Melipone, among all the known telepaths, can produce." . . .

Runciter said, "I'll consult my dead wife."

"It's the middle of the night. The moratoriums are closed now."[7]

The prose is not at all conspicuously "literary"; there does not appear to be any attempt, in the proper formalist manner, to use language in a state of intensified depth, density, and difficulty. On the contrary, the style seems to follow the predictable Heinlein (and sub-Hemingway) precedent of routine serviceability as it fluently adequates itself to the adventure narrative, not at all scorning the characteristic cliché formulations of the field: something "wouldn't do"; a character states that "nobody seems to know" something and asks "what about" something else; something is said to be true "among all the known" examples relevant. Such devices do convey a certain degree of urgency and breathlessness, but not, apparently, in a manner more complex than that attained by an action-adventure cartoon strip. The prose, it seems, is subliterary. Philip K. Dick is not a stylist.

Or is he? Since Delany's pioneering investigations,[8] it is hardly feasible to perform any stylistic analysis on a passage from an SF work without considering the specifically SF character of the style. From this point of view, the passage is an unusually decisive example of the way that SF tends to manifest its generic presence not only on the molar level of plot structure but also with regard to the molecular operations of language itself. The date in the opening clause suggests an SF framework temporally, and the solar perspective that opens up in the following clause does the same thing in spatial terms. There follow a flood of neologisms—this device being perhaps the most paradigmatic expression of SF diction—which suggest the new resources of a brave new world, whether technological ("vidphone," "moratoriums") or human ("psis," "inertials") or, indeed, in terms that implicitly offer to deconstruct that all-too-familiar binary opposition ("a different physiognomic template every month," "68.2 blr units of telepathic aura"). More generally, the passage clearly establishes, in strategically casual phrasing but also with noteworthy economy, that the setting of the novel is one in which such uncanny phenomena as extrasensory perception and communication with the dead—not to mention polymorphously perverse sexuality—have not only become routine but have been thoroughly integrated, economically, into the consumer capitalism of the 1990s. The language of the passage, in sum, emphatically establishes that which is the sine qua non of every SF text; namely, theoretical *difference*, a clear otherness vis-à-vis the mundane empirical world where the text was produced, which is, however, connected (at least in principle) to that world in rational, nonfantastic ways.[9]

A somewhat closer examination of the passage may, however, reveal the workings of otherness to be yet more complex than the foregoing analysis suggests. For what is at stake is not simply difference literally considered, "novelty" in the bald sense. More important is the way the style of the passage *manages* difference and differences, the way in which the unfamiliar and the familiar are held in suspension and related to one another through the operations of a radically heterogeneous and polyvalent prose. The overall agendum of *Ubik* as a whole—the satiric and rationally paranoid estrangement of the commodity structure of monopoly capitalism[10]—is here enforced through a complex multiaccentuality on the level of sentence production. For example: "We asked Joe Chip to go in there and run tests on the magnitude and minitude of the field being generated there at the Bonds of Erotic Polymorphic Experience Motel." On the simplest plane, this is a casual, serviceable, unadorned bit of adventure fiction, the loyally efficient report of Runciter's subordinate concerning the field operations of Runciter's top subordinate, Joe Chip. At the same time, the sentence introduces such novelties as the quantification of telepathic power and the institutionalization of polymorphic perversity, the air of things new and strange supported by the logical but striking coinage *minitude*. Even more complex and crucial, however, is the way that casualness and estrangement work together to suggest the routine commodification of telepathy, antitelepathy, and perversity—the assimilation of these moments of uncanniness to the quasi-familiar commercial structure that includes Runciter Associates, Hollis's competing organization, and the incidentally mentioned motel. The strange is to some degree thus de-estranged, but the more powerful tendency is the contrary one to estrange commodification itself, to evoke the fetishistic weirdness on which this superficially familiar process is based.[11] A similar stylistic heterogeneity may be detected in the seemingly very simple sentence that comes a few lines later: "Runciter said, 'I'll consult my dead wife.'" Again, the unadorned functionality of neo-Heinleinian prose—the boss is taking deliberate but fairly routine action to deal with a crisis—clashes with what is for the reader the intensely strange content of the action. Also again, however, this multiaccentuality problematizes the relation of familiar to unfamiliar in two directions at once: as the sentence introduces communication with the dead, but only in the context of corporate management, it suggests that the commodity structure can make even the reversal (or partial reversal) of the ultimate finality of death seem routine, while also reminding us that this structure is after all a fundamentally weird network in which dead and living labor interact with one another. It may be added that the point is reiterated almost immediately with the reference in the following line to moratoriums, which turn out to be commercial enterprises for the maintenance of "half-lifers" like Mrs. Runciter. In this passage, then, Dick's style not only moves his plot along and insinuates the estrangements that generically define SF, but even more important, the style, in its heterogeneous complexity, enacts on the molecular level the most searching theoretical juxtapositions and interrogations which the novel in toto is concerned to implement. If this style is "subliterary," then that category itself certainly needs to be rethought—especially, perhaps, in the general context of SF.

Such a rethinking is, in fact, implicit in the work of the Russian scholar who in recent years has emerged as the most eminent modern theorist of novelistic style. The essence of what I have tried to suggest concerning Dick's style can be conveniently expressed in the terms given critical currency by Mikhail Bakhtin: Dick's is a radically *dialogic* use of language, one that exploits to the utmost what Bakhtin calls heteroglossia; that is, the primacy of linguistic polyvalency, of the irreducible multiaccentuality of meaning, as against any concept of singular, closed, monologic discourse. Furthermore, the foregrounding in Dick of the interinanimation of form and content, of text and context, of sentence production and the economic realities of generalized commodity production strongly recalls Bakhtin's crucial insistence on the impossibility of detaching style from the sociality it registers and his correlative brilliance in relating the smallest linguistic turns to the most general movements of culture and society. For Dick and Bakhtin, style is an intrinsically *social* category.

This privileging of the contextual, however, this rejection of any attempt to construct literature as a self-sufficient autonomous system, is only one way in which both Dick and Bakhtin mount a powerful challenge to all formalist conceptions of style. For both, the internal structure of style is no less important than, while closely related to, its radical referentiality. With regard to the former, it has often been noticed that formalist accounts of a specifically literary use of language, from the Russian Formalists themselves onward, have tended to assume an unacknowledged synonymy between the literary and the *poetic,* and thus a putative superiority on the part of the older literary mode—an assumed superiority whose presence can be heard to this day in the eulogistic accent that almost invariably accompanies the descriptive use of terms like *poetry* and *poetic*. But Bakhtin—ever a respectful, unswerving opponent of the Formalists who were his own contemporaries and compatriots—reverses the conventional hierarchization of poetry over prose, arguing that poetic style, for all its apparent verbal richness, tends by its lyrical, rhythmic flow to repress otherness and to approximate to the authoritarian singularity of monologue: "The natural dialogization of the word is not put to artistic use, the word is sufficient unto itself and does not presume alien utterances beyond its own boundaries. Poetic style is by convention suspended from any mutual interaction with alien discourse." [12] In fundamental contrast, the style of the prose novel welcomes and glories in heteroglossia, highlighting and contextualizing rather than repressing otherness; the novelistic word "break[s] through to its own meaning and its own expression across an environment full of alien words . . . variously evaluating accents, harmonizing with some of the elements in this environment and striking a dissonance with others" (277). These words precisely describe the style of the opening of *Ubik*, with Bakhtin's stress on harmony and dissonance corresponding to the Dickian dialectic of familiarity and strangeness already discussed. It follows, then, that novelistic style, when most capable, most quintessentially novelistic (and in that sense, indeed, most *literary*), may eschew certain properties of polish, of well-roundedness, of fluently controlled density and resonance proper to the poetic. Correspondingly, novelistic prose that does display such qualities, however literary it may seem in normative terms, is perhaps to be suspected of contamination by the monologic authoritarianism of poetry.

To avoid possible misunderstanding, two important points about the Bakhtinian problematic must be stressed. In the first place, Bakhtin's exaltation of novelistic prose over poetry cannot be entirely separated from the general historical circumstances of early twentieth-century literary criticism, in which the supremacy of poetry among literary forms was still a commonplace and the novel was still widely regarded as something of a scruffy parvenu. The critical revolution that would partly overthrow this hierarchy had been launched as early as Turgenev, Flaubert, and Henry James, but it was still far from victorious. Though it is a matter of some controversy to what degree such victory has been achieved even now, it is certainly true that the binarism—the flat, somewhat reactive privileging of prose over verse—toward which Bakhtin's dialectic often tends must be seriously qualified in a critical universe where the "art novel" is a commonly accepted part of the landscape. But such an adjustment is unnecessary in the context of SF, whose scruffiness remains prominent; indeed, the place assigned to the SF novel by currently hegemonic critical ideology is in many ways remarkably comparable to the place of the novel generally during the period when Bakhtin's insurgent views were formed. The second point to be stressed is that the Bakhtinian problematic, for all its insurgency, does not require abandoning the formalist criterion of style as that which separates literature from other (non- or even subliterary) uses of language. Though there is perhaps some tension between such a discrimination and the egalitarian cast of Bakhtin's thought—his general distaste for "centripetal," or centralizing, forces—Bakhtin does not proceed to the extreme of a radicalism (spurious and self-defeating, in my view) that would dissolve the categories of literature and literary style altogether. But Bakhtin does, of course, require style to be understood in a radically social, referential way, attuned to the heterogeneous roughage of discourse and history so foregrounded by Dick. And he emphatically requires us to understand novelistic style as other than and even antithetical to the poetic model that haunts nearly all formalist concepts of literature and literary excellence—and which, it may be added, sometimes almost seems to haunt the stylistic intentionality of Le Guin and Delany.

Bakhtin's emphasis on the embracing of the *alien* in novelistic style has an obvious special relevance to the language of SF, and it is in this light that I will consider, very briefly, one more sample of Dick's prose. In the following passage of free indirect discourse from *A Scanner Darkly* (which Dick himself considered his masterpiece), the protagonist, undercover police drug agent Bob Arctor, muses on the installation of police scanning devices in his own home:

> To my own house, he thought. Arctor's house. Up the street at the house I am Bob Arctor, the heavy doper suspect being scanned without his knowledge, and then every couple of days I find a pretext to slip down the street and into the apartment where I am Fred replaying miles and miles of tape to see what I did, and this whole business, he thought, depresses me. Except for the protection—and valuable personal information—it will give me.
>
> Probably whoever's hunting me will be caught by the holo-scanners within the first week.
>
> Realizing that, he felt mellow.[13]

Like the passage from *Ubik*, this one seems, on the most evident level, to be little more than solidly competent. It differs in registering not much in the way of technological innovation, the only noteworthy item in that regard being the scanners (themselves only a revision and updating of the Orwellian telescreens in 1984, or, indeed, of the police listening devices so familiar in Dick's world and ours). But its style is nonetheless profoundly dialogic. As in the opening of *Ubik*, the play of heteroglossia, the presence of the alien and of alienation, involves both the conceptual structure of the novel as a whole and an elaborate network of extratextual referentiality—though the key historical reference here is less the economic reality of commodification than the political reality of conspiracy. Much of the complexity of the style derives from the ironic fine-tuning possible in free indirect discourse, an instrument Dick can at times play with something like Flaubertian precision. In the earlier sentences of the passage, the accent of the narrator and that of Arctor himself seem nearly at one, the evident identity wholly appropriate to the novel's sympathetic treatment of its hero. At the same time, however, the discourse is fissured by the paradox of self-alienation at the heart of the narrative: not only does Arctor possess a doubled self as both hippie and nark, but in these sentences he envisions the practically infinite replication of himself on holographic tape. The repressive state apparatus that employs Arctor assigns him to survey himself, and this assignment amounts to a splitting of the ego, a consideration of the very self as alien, which, in a more general sense, is to be understood as paradigmatic for the subjects of a conspiratorial bureaucratic regime. Arctor's musing thus has an estranging significance beyond his own intentions as a character, which are here limited to his personal situation.

The regime of conspiracy is estranged even more complexly, however, as the style switches gears, so to speak, with the last sentence of the first paragraph quoted above. At this point the narrator begins to withdraw his ratification of Arctor's viewpoint, not out of lack of sympathy but on account of superior knowledge. Arctor believes himself to be persecuted by a single enemy and hopes the scanning of his house will reveal the enemy's identity. The hope is naïve, and the text regards it ironically: it is Arctor, not the novel, who believes the information acquired from scanners to be valuable; and in the following two sentences the dialogic irony trained on Arctor intensifies, climaxing with the word *mellow*, scripted as if from within a drug haze in this deeply antidrug text. The irony thus powerfully anticipates the ultimate plot development of the novel; that is, the collusion of the highest levels of the police with the criminal drug syndicate and their conspiracy to destroy the mind of Bob Arctor. The shifting voices in this passage resonate strongly with Dick's overall attempt in *A Scanner Darkly* to estrange the bureaucratic conspiracies of both the state and the latter's nominal opponents, and to trace the connection between such conspiracy and the alienation (ultimately the obliteration) of the hapless individual subject.

I do not claim that the two passages of Dickian prose analyzed above are statistically typical of his style. On the contrary, they represent his style at what I consider to be its most complex and interesting; the passages are drawn from two of Dick's best novels and were not located by opening the volumes at random. Still, Dick does attain his best (or near best) with impressive frequency for a writer of such abundant productivity, and the passages I have chosen are sufficiently representative that it is possible to assert, with some confidence, Dick's brilliance at novelistic style. His work does not, after all, lack style and all that; and his justly exalted place in the pantheon of SF is not the anomaly it may seem.

The broader question remains, however, of the degree to which SF style in general needs to be reconsidered in the light of Bakhtinian theory. The task seems to me a considerable and important one. A field often stigmatized on stylistic grounds urgently requires a more intelligent and dialectical conception of style than any variety of formalism has to offer. In addition to appreciating with greater precision those SF authors generally regarded as stylists of distinction, we need to examine again such apparently undistinguished stylists as Asimov and Heinlein. We need not necessarily expect a great many rehabilitations of the sort I have just tried to suggest in Dick's case, since Bakhtin provocatively clarifies the relationship of prose to poetry but hardly denies that the great bulk of linguistic production belongs to *neither* category in any of the stronger senses. But the Bakhtinian approach—with its stress on clash, on difference, on the new and alien and strange—has a greater relevance to SF than to perhaps any other variety of fiction; and SF critics should not lag behind critics of fiction in general in exploiting Bakhtin's insights.[14]

Notes

1. C. S. Lewis, "High and Low Brows," in his *Selected Literary Essays*, ed. Walter Hooper (Cambridge: Cambridge University Press, 1969), pp. 270–71.
2. Paul de Man, *Allegories of Reading: Figural Language in Rousseau, Nietzsche, Rilke, and Proust* (New Haven: Yale University Press, 1979), pp. 9–10.
3. See Fredric Jameson, *Marxism and Form: Twentieth-Century Dialectical Theories of Literature* (Princeton: Princeton University Press, 1971), pp. 332–35.
4. The reference here is not only to the essay cited above but, even more important, to Lewis's later *Experiment in Criticism* (Cambridge: Cambridge University Press, 1961), in which he argues that the operative distinction ought to be between modes of reading rather than between texts.
5. In what is still probably the single most powerful full-length work of SF criti-

cism, Darko Suvin does, however, include four Americans in a list of those authors who have produced "the 5 to 10 percent of [current] SF that *is* aesthetically significant": predictably, Le Guin and Delany are mentioned (along with Dick and Disch), while Heinlein and Asimov are not. See Darko Suvin, *Metamorphoses of Science Fiction: On the Poetics and History of a Literary Genre* (New Haven: Yale University Press, 1979), p. vii.

6. There are obviously a great many other names that could be cited in this context and a great many differences among the writers named. But one general characteristic of the "stylistic" SF authors is especially worth noting: namely, the comparatively high percentage of *women* among them, especially as contrasted with the earlier authors of the Golden Age. There is an apparent paradox here, for the formalist exaltation of style has historically had strongly masculine connotations: the centrality of the metaphor of the *pen* need not be belabored or explicated, but the paradox can be at least partly resolved. Stylists or not, the most characteristic Golden Age writers retained their masculinity through identification with such fields as science and engineering, "hard" disciplines so thoroughly manly that literature as a whole is, compared with them, feminine. Correlatively, SF of the self-consciously "literary" variety has offered special opportunities for women writers, opportunities of a sort largely preempted by men in many other areas of fiction.

7. Philip K. Dick, *Ubik* (Garden City, N.Y.: Doubleday, 1969), pp. 1–2. My article cited below (n. 10) provides some specific reasons for the high place I give to this novel among Dick's fictions.

8. I am thinking, of course, primarily of Samuel R. Delany, *The Jewel-Hinged Jaw: Notes on the Language of Science Fiction* (New York: Berkley, 1977).

9. My debt here to the Suvinian theory of cognitive estrangement (see Suvin, pp. 4ff.) is evident but perhaps should be explicitly acknowledged.

10. See Carl Freedman, "Towards a Theory of Paranoia: The Science Fiction of Philip K. Dick," *Science-Fiction Studies* (March 1984): 15–24.

11. The main theoretical reference here is, of course, Marx. See especially Karl Marx, *Capital*, vol. 1, trans. Ben Fowkes (Harmondsworth: Penguin, 1976), pp. 163–77.

12. M. M. Bakhtin, *The Dialogic Imagination*, ed. Michael Holquist, trans. Caryl Emerson and Michael Holquist (Austin: University of Texas Press, 1981), p. 285. A further reference to this text is given parenthetically by page number.

13. Philip K. Dick, *A Scanner Darkly* (New York: Ballantine Books, 1977), p. 110.

14. An earlier version of this paper was presented orally at the Eleventh J. Lloyd Eaton Conference on Science Fiction and Fantasy, and I express my gratitude to George Slusser, co-coordinator and guiding spirit of the conference,

who made it possible for me to attend; to Robert Crossley, Peter Fitting, Frank McConnell, Patrick Parrinder, Robert Philmus, Gerald Prince, and Eric Rabkin, all participants at this unusually valuable conference, who made useful comments in response to my presentation; and to Robin Roberts and Jon Thompson, colleagues at Louisiana State University who supplied helpful criticism of the written text.

Part 2

STYLE AND GRAMMAR:

VOICE AND MOOD

Chapter 4

Style, Substance,
and Other Illusions

Gregory Benford

Listen. Here's a story.

There was a desert wind blowing that night. It was one of those hot dry Santa Anas that come down through the mountain passes and curl your hair and make your nerves jump and your skin itch. On nights like that every booze party ends in a fight. Meek little wives feel the edge of the carving knife and study their husbands' necks. Anything can happen. You can even get a full glass of beer at a cocktail lounge.

This is from Raymond Chandler's hard-boiled novelette "Red Wind." Here's another story: "The trunks of the trees too were dusty and the leaves fell early that year and we saw the troops marching along the road and the dust rising and leaves, stirred by the breeze, falling and the soldiers marching and afterward the road bare and white except for the leaves."

That's the fourth and concluding sentence in the first paragraph of Ernest Hemingway's *A Farewell to Arms,* with its curious catch midway through, *stirred by the breeze,* which defeats the monotony you have by now come to expect from the repeated *ands.* This last sentence finishes the work that paragraph had to do, calling our attention to the momentary stirring before the living leaves fall, yielding a premonition of early death. Fear of death drives the narrator to abandon combat, and in the end the early death comes not to him but to his beloved, in childbirth.

Listen. Here's another story: "The place stank. A queer, mingled stench that only the ice-buried cabins of the Antarctic camp know, compounded of reeking human sweat, and the heavy, fish-oil stench of melted seal blubber." Claustrophobia and revulsion at close contact, prevailing emotions in John W. Campbell, Jr.'s, "Who Goes There?" Now listen to an opposite, expansive encounter with the alien: "The ship came down from space. It came from the stars and the black velocities, and the shining movements, and the silent gulfs of space." Abstractions link lyrically with sensations in Bradbury's "Mars Is Heaven!" etherial and grand and doomed in its black velocities. Listen to Alfred Bester in "Fondly Fahrenheit" scramble your preconceptions immediately by fidgeting with grammar: "He doesn't know which of us I am these days, but they know one truth."

I submit that the essence of the story appears in the tone, the style, of these opening passages. One of the signatures of particularly effective fiction is just such implication-rich beginnings.

What of closings? Suppose you wish to evoke, at a story's recessional, the feelings of resignation: "It was years before he saw her again. But they spent the last days of '99 together, shooting dodos under the shadow of mighty Kilimanjaro." That is from Robert Silverberg's "Born with the Dead," and it echoes Raymond Chandler's ending for *The Big Sleep*, "All they did was make me think of Silver-Wig, and I never saw her again." And William Gibson used it again in *Neuromancer*: "He never saw Molly again." By now it has become a cliché genre signature that yanks the reader out of the narrative's world and back into his own.

Authors often concentrate their themes into stylistic turns. You can see the story implicit in the manner of telling. Substance dances with style, and the dance is what we see, seldom the dancers. To separate them is to falsify the reading experience.

I suspect authors often don't quite realize what they're doing; certainly I don't. Their styles tell us matters beyond their conscious control.

I contend that style is not just an important element in science fiction; it can be crucial in determining matters the author cannot say any other way—even in this supposedly analytical, science-based literature, its rational underpinnings so often displayed for all to see like a lady's scarlet bloomers. We might well agree with the opening of a great SF novel, Ursula K. Le Guin's *The Left Hand of Darkness*: "I'll make my report as if I told a story, for I was taught as a child on my homeworld that Truth is a matter of the imagination. The soundest fact may fail or prevail in the style of its telling: like that singular organic jewel of our seas, which grows brighter as one woman wears it and, worn by another, dulls and goes to dust."

George-Louis Buffon said that "style is the man himself," and indeed there is nothing more personal, no better way for our subconscious to gain its voice. For our words are chosen, all right, but not by "us"—that consensual, passing parliament of the mind we call consciousness. The subconscious lines up our words for us, so that even as I begin this sentence not all of me knows how it's going to end—hence, style samples the dark netherworlds, with Freudian slips on banana peels.

Discussing SF, indulge not in glossy generalities. We must *quote*. Voice is crucial, even in mere book reviews, and here we will not truly know what we're talking about unless we give examples. Let writers speak for themselves!

Styleless Style

Of course, for long decades the prevailing opinion among fans and even writers of SF was that the best style is one that appears to be no style whatever. The theory here was that the scientific ideas and wrenchings of social perceptions were so great that to mingle any of these with the flourishes, ambiguities, and outright flummery of stylistics demanded too much of the reader. This was the ideology of hard SF especially, and it largely remains so in the hands of Robert Forward, David Brin, and Charles Sheffield, for example. There is much to be said for this point of view, but the key words here are *appears to be*. No style is in fact transparent except to a certain kind of reader, with whom it shares plenty of assumptions. To become even translucent, a manner of telling must agree with the worldview of the reader; it must support his or her basic assumption about mechanism and roles, even defer to the most superficial, ordinary view of the objective labyrinth of sense impressions.

Take the sun, for example. We see it every day, and throughout human history we largely agreed to forget about what made it burn. It was so strange, if you thought about it, that everybody agreed to *not* think about it. A styleless style.

Nobody knew, so we slapped religious assumptions into place and, understanding nothing, nonetheless made possible such phrases as "as sure as the sunrise." After all, the sun might have gone out while we were on the other side of the earth from it. Worse, it might go nova, as in Larry Niven's "Inconstant Moon." Now we know pretty much how the sun works through nuclear fusion, so we forget it again. But suppose aliens should arrive who believe our sun is divine. The stylistics of dealing with this must be different. Gordon Eklund and I, in "If the Stars Are Gods," used Swiftian references and humor, combined with stylistic immersion in the actual experience of merging with the divine sun: "Colder than cold, more terrifying than hate, more sordid than fear, blacker than evil. The vast inner whole nothingness of everything that was anything, of all." This passage now seems to me rather overwritten. It is an example of effing the ineffable, a literary holy grail in SF, usually accomplished by what I call *stylistic blowout*. Overpower the reader with adjectives, throw apparently incompatible analogies at him, mingle senses ("he sounded green down the analytic corridors," to make up one on the spot). Give him rushes of prose, quiet pauses of apparent contradictions, tweaks and allusions to ideas he already knows but will find topsy-turvy here.

An opposite approach is the lofty Mandarin sentiments of Evelyn Waugh, who said, "Properly understood, style is not a seductive decoration added to a functional structure; it is of the essence of the work of art. The necessary elements of style are lucidity, elegance, and individuality." *Elegance* is a tricky word; Hemingway achieved it, but he said that "prose is architecture, not interior decoration"—which seems to contradict much of Waugh. Hemingway's elegance is that of Melville's "Call me Ishmael" and the Bible's "Jesus wept"—the short, declarative sentence, elegance in simplicity. Much emotional muscle behind few words.

English is the largest of all languages, and style depends on that immense vocabulary. We have only a few puny tools to manage all this. First, there is positioning on the page, which has severe limits. The odd uses of this, as in Harlan Ellison's patchwork compositions and a single, spiraling sentence, are typically used only once; we have a curious resistance to spatial invention. And there are a handful of punctuation marks, although some, such as the exclamation mark, are virtually unused. I remember a conversation with Samuel Delany and Quinn Yarbro about a new punctuation mark we'd like to have—the sarcasm mark. You could simply begin a sentence with it to denote sarcasm by yourself or your character, letting the voice be implicit. But we decided it probably wouldn't catch on.

One might think that genre authors pay less attention to style, relying on swift plots to enrapture their audiences, but I don't believe so. Witness Raymond Chandler:

In the long run, however little you talk or even think about it, the most durable thing in writing is style, and style is the most valuable investment a writer can make with his time. It pays off slowly, your agent will sneer at it, your publisher will misunderstand it, and it will take people you never heard of to convince them by slow degrees that the writer who puts his individual mark on the way he writes will always pay off. He can't do it by trying, because the kind of style I'm thinking of is a projection of personality and you have to have a personality before you can project it. But granted you have one, you can only project it on paper by thinking of something else. This is ironical in a way; it is the reason, I suppose, why in a generation of "made" writers I still say you can't make a writer. Preoccupation with style will not produce it. No amount of editing and polishing will have any appreciable effect on the flavor of how a man writes. It is the product of the quality of his emotion and perception; it is the ability to transfer these to paper which makes him a writer, in contrast to the great number of people who have just as good emotions and just as keen perceptions, but cannot come with a googol of miles of putting them on paper.

This given, what is special about style in science fiction?

The Constraints of the Fantastic

I feel that the essential task we face as writers is to enlist the devices of realism in the cause of the fantastic. Yet this is not so simple as it seemed to writers of SF before the 1960s.

We ground our flights in the reality we already see. So Joe Haldeman opened *The Forever War* with: " 'Tonight we're going to show you eight silent ways to kill a man.' The guy who said that was a sergeant who didn't look five years older than me"—and we are in boot camp, learning only when the word *brainwipes* comes along at the end of the third paragraph that something has changed; this is a future in which people can have their minds erased. But by then we've bought into the reality of this world.

Similarly, near the beginning of Sheila Finch's *Infinity's Web* the narrator announces, "She would never forgive herself for not being there when her son was born," and we know we are in a future open to new biotechnology.

Establishing that confidence is crucial. Hard SF has done it with a choice of voices, all suggesting possible postures toward the material. Most common is the distant, analytical tone. Arthur Clarke often uses a third-person point of view with the lead characters' reactions described from outside, so that the true intelligence of the story is often embodied in the narrative voice. Sometimes this is even a historian looking back on events. This mirrors the scientific literature, its disconnection, gathering strength from its association with the unbiased texture of scientific papers—but at times inheriting its dulling mannerisms, such as the passive voice. It can also convey quiet certainty, underplaying its lines, as in, "Overhead, without any fuss, the stars were going out" from Clarke's famous "The Nine Billion Names of God."

Another approach: James Blish, Arthur Clarke especially, Stapledon, Poul Anderson (*Tau Zero*), and myself, among others, have used the voice of cosmic mysticism. This voice assumes an even grander perspective, often with lofty sentiments untied to overt theology but paralleling the cool immensities of physical law. Clarke's *2001* opens: "The drought had lasted now for ten million years, and the reign of the terrible lizards had long since ended."

A third and opposite tone is the wiseguy insider. Heinlein used this extensively, as do Fred Pohl, John Varley, and Joe Haldeman. Its cocky savvy plays well to technophiles, who, I suspect, feel that they understand rather better than most just how the gritty, hard-edged, and unforgiving world works. Sometimes the propensity for one-liners compresses, as in Heinlein's *Notebooks of Lazarus Long*, which proposes this standard for Renaissance manhood:

A human being should be able to change a diaper, plan an invasion, butcher a hog, conn a ship, design a building, write a sonnet, balance accounts, build a wall, set a bone, comfort the dying, take orders, give orders, cooperate, act alone, solve equations, analyze a new problem, pitch manure, program a computer, cook a tasty meal, fight effectively, die gallantly. Specialization is for insects.

Even Roger Zelazny used an urban variant, as in *Isle of the Dead*: "I boosted the *Model T* into the sky and kept going until space and time ended for a space and a time. I continued."

Elizabeth Bowen has said of modern fiction generally, "We want the naturalistic surface, but with a kind of internal burning." I think we can describe the stylistic aims of many SF writers as seeking to make our sentences burn with an inner reality—often a changed one, not consensual, and often proceeding from an *idea*—our most persistent tribute to the idea as hero in SF, perhaps.

Henry James's dicta to the writer—select, contemplate, render—must contain also the vital infusion of imagination (notably not a strong trait in James). The *idea* must shine through. So when Bradbury conjured up his boyhood Midwest, he could not simply salt his sentences with the lore of times lost, musky memorabilia. He must cast the old into the new, as he did in *The Martian Chronicles*. Delany had a more difficult task, as we see in the opening of *Dhalgren*:

to wound the autumnal city.
> So howled out for the world to give him a name.
> The in-dark answered with wind.

These lines ride alone on the page, each one like a howl itself, lonely. Remember that style isn't simply word choice; it includes position of words on a page, always remembering that the eye proceeds forward in the linear universe of print. Then he hits you with specifics. One of the universals of style is *be concrete*. Smooth, general words conjure up little. Pick hairy words, words that arrive with a baggage of associations. *Chevy* is better than *car, brassy* is better than *metallic*. Delany continued:

> All you know I know: careening astronauts and bank clerks glancing at the clock before lunch; actresses scowling at light-ringed mirrors and freight elevator operators grinding a thumbful of grease on a steel handle; student riots; know that dark women in bodegas shook their heads last week because in six months prices have risen outlandishly; how coffee tastes after you've held it in your mouth, cold, a whole minute.

He loads all that fine description in one long paragraph burning with detail, a sinker below those high-riding opening lines. The novel ends with "I have come to"—and the seamless connection to the first phrase comes, a cyclic turn.

Or at least I believe I understand Delany's methods. In the end I can only speak for myself.

The Most Personal of Elements

Of all literary elements, style is the most personal and the hardest to analyze.

I don't subscribe to the ideology of transparent style. It seems to me to be another tool in the narrative game. I use style unremittingly, trying to get at elements not approachable with any of the tones I listed for the hard SF writer, though I am for the most part a member of that club.

I used Joycean rhythms and methods in an early novel, *In the Ocean of Night*, though for different purposes and without actually having read much Joyce. My point is that the inventions of modernism, particularly its shattering of consensual reality, now lie open to use by SF. But in using them we mean something quite different from the rather limited goals of the modernists. We really *do* talk about the grandly discordant, the truly alien. Stream of consciousness is now a technique that, taken over into a wildly different SF context, can mean very different things—the choice is up to the writer, who can trim his stylistic canvas and sail before these mainstream winds. That I have tried to do.

William Faulkner said that a writer who has plenty to say—"a great deal pushing to get out"—can't take time with style. Yet he mastered the most gnarled, surprising style of this century in English. His long sentences, connected by little *and*s which suggest the diction and authority of the King James Bible (a device Hemingway knew, too), seemed to me to arise not so much from a conscious working of voice but rather from a heritage: the story-telling arts of the Deep South, where I grew up as well. I heard stories told this way around the fire in my grandparents' house, on the Fish River, after the Grand Ol' Opry had been turned off and everybody was too zesty to go right to bed.

So when it came to mind to write a novel about the persistence of basic human modes, even in the face of vast, fresh, alien environments, prickly with bizarre technology, I naturally adopted that voice. But I knew the world thought of such oral constructions as a literary signature, so in employing them I made deliberate use of Faulkner himself, and especially of his novella "The Bear." I structured the first third of my novel *Against Infinity* after Faulkner because I was again telling the age-old hunting yarn, variants of which I had heard from my father and grandfather a decade before I ever read Faulkner.

Why? The truest answer lies in the pages of the novel, for I am acutely aware of how little I can truly say about my own book. Once it is written, I am free of its grip. Years have passed now. I trail the novel on a thin line, towing it behind my career, while critics have at it like the sharks in *The Old Man and the Sea*, and now it is hard for me to see through all the blood in the water. There is a further problem, a universal one in discussing style alone: the choices are made by your subconscious, and now my conscious, critical self fumbles at fathoming them.

Nevertheless, why? My devices evolved as I tried to use the emergence on far Ganymede of ancient human activities, the hunting and going out, the bond between animals and men. I glimpsed also that aliens would know these features of us, would see in us our true origins and play to them. Our modern theories of ourselves are as matchsticks to these great, lumbering truths.

I also wanted to talk about the frontier, which most SF is about, as in Heinlein—essentially a human stage. There has not yet been much SF about the wilderness, that territory we do not rule and which cannot be housed inside some human paradigm. Thoreau wrote of it, and Faulkner, sometimes. In SF, Stapledon and Clarke have sung of the grand, natural perspectives beyond humanity.

The encounter with that wilderness is a basic event (all too rare nowadays) that propagates through human history, shedding sparks into our literature and lives. SF brushes against that experience, and finding it unsettling, alien, usually turns away. Space opera is more like opera, an urban human activity, than like the huge spaces that wait only a hundred kilometers above our heads.

Critic Gary Wolfe examined my possible motives in deploying an ornate style, concluding that I was "adopting a heightened rhetoric that serves to distance us equally from both the mundane action of the novel (family relationships, economics, etc.) and the scientific adventure" (*Fantasy Review*, 1986).

Well, yes—and no. Using verbal story-telling cadences does "defamiliarize the iconography of hard SF without sacrificing its sense of wonder." That was indeed a crucial reason to choose such an unusual maneuver. Deliberately choosing a southern voice, one I learned as a boy but set aside when I entered the nawthern intellectu'l realm of university discourse, accomplished several tasks.

Personally, it got me back to the world of my own growing up—quite appropriate for a tale of maturation. Generally, it underlined the point that there are deep processes and rituals laid down in us, such as hunting, and these will emerge again in circumstances wildly different. The heart-stirring thrill of tracking in piney woods may be quite like the pursuit of the unknowable among icy wastes. In *Against Infinity* the alien Aleph which draws humans out may well be using this simple fact. To study us? We don't know. But we will go . . .

So I tried to use a Faulknerian perspective on the irreducibly alien, to see it as both strange and natural and unknowable, and to do it in a voice that recalled prior human encounters. So here is a single sentence:

Some Jew had given it that, a blank name that was the first letter of the Hebrew alphabet: a neutral vowel that bespoke the opaque nature of the blocky, gravid thing, the bulk that humans had tried to write upon with their cutters and tractors and on which they had left no mark. A neutral name, and yet it was the source of long legend of domes cracked open and rifled, of walker and crawlers and even whole outposts caught up and crushed and trampled as it moved forward on its own oblivious missions, or else homes and sheds ripped apart as the thing rose up out of the ice where it dwelt, walls split by the heaving of the land as it broke free of ice and poked its angular face—eyeless, with only sawtoothed openings to mark what men chose in their ignorance to call a face and so to take away some fragment of its strangeness—breaking freshly again into the dim sunlight, seeking, always seeking materials men also needed and had compacted into their homes and factories, and thus were forced to futilely defend against the legend that came for the metals and rare rock, the Aleph making no distinction between what men held and what the bare plains offered, so that it took where it found and thus engendered the continuing legend of alarms ignored and traps brushed aside and servo'd armaments smashed and animals mangled and men and women injured and laser and even electron-beam bolts delivered at point-blank range as though into nothing, the alien absorbing all and giving nothing, shrugging off the puny attempts of men to deliver death to it, and without pause it kept going— down a corridor of ruin and destruction starting back before Manuel's birth and even before Old Matt, the massive thing lumbered, not swift but with a ruthless determination, like a machine and yet like a man too; moving onward eternally on some course humans could not guess, it ran forever in the boy's dreams, a vast immemorial alabaster shape.

Of all my passages, this most nearly echoes Faulkner, pointing directly to a constellation of associations—to "modernism," to biblical story-telling rhythms, to science as a lived-in activity and not just metaphor (as in the new wave).

Though this sentence appears in the novel's first chapter, it attempts (among other aims) something I suspect much SF does, though perhaps unconsciously. In this literature we often live in the shadow of natural immensities. Our entire humanistic program dwindles in the perspectives of vast time and space. This is a central fact of our time, one that mainstream literature has reacted to by variously adopting postures of ennui, of numbing angst, of rage—but most often by ignoring it, retreating into the closed geometries of an obsessively human scale, otherwise known as "realism," and in its most reductionist form, "minimalism."

Contrast this quoted passage with the much more austere, impersonal voice used by Arthur C. Clarke. In his balanced, calm sentences we feel the cool, analytical view of science, gazing above the tumult of character and incident at the distant, lofty peaks of principle and great time. Which approach is better? All—and none. Like blind men grappling with an elephant, we bring back what impressions we can.

Yet I suspect that, in the end, any SF writer seeks to achieve a similar telling affect. In poignant moments, particularly near the conclusion, I often hear the tone of something utterly completed vying with a sense of something startled into scope and freedom. When a story functions well, one experiences a whole meaning, simultaneously clicking shut and popping open, a momentary illusion (or is it?) that the fulfillments one senses in the ear indeed do spell out completions available in the world—either the world to be or the one here and now. No matter how much an SF text may insist on humankind's trivial role in the universe, its fall toward a valueless limbo is arrested by the perfectly stretched safety net of literary form itself: which argues perpetually for meaning.

Works Cited

Benford, Gregory, and Gordon Eklund. *If the Stars Are Gods*. New York: Berkley, 1977.

Bester, Alfred. "Fondly Fahrenheit," in *Science Fiction Hall of Fame*. New York: Avon Books, 1971.

Bradbury, Ray. "Mars is Heaven," in *Science Fiction Hall of Fame*. New York: Avon Books, 1971.

Campbell, John. *Who Goes There? Seven Tales of Science Fiction*. Chicago: Shasta, 1948.

Chandler, Raymond. *Red Wind*. Cleveland: World, 1946.

———. *The Big Sleep*. New York: Vintage Books, 1976.

———. *Raymond Chandler Speaking*. New York: Doubleday, 1963.

Clarke, Arthur C. *The Nine Billion Names of God: The Best Short Stories of Arthur C. Clarke*. New York: Harcourt Brace Jovanovich, 1967.

———. *2001, a Space Odyssey*. New York: New American Library, 1968.

Delany, Samuel R. *Dhalgren*. New York: Bantam Books, 1975.

Finch, Sheila. *Infinity's Web*. New York: Bantam Books, 1985.

Gibson, William. *Neuromancer*. New York: Ace Books, 1984.

Haldeman, Joe W. *The Forever War*. New York: St. Martin's Press, 1975.

Heinlein, Robert A., and D. F. Vassallo. *The Notebooks of Lazarus Long*. New York: Putnam, 1978.

Hemingway, Ernest. *A Farewell to Arms*. New York: Scribners, 1929.

Hall, Oakley. *The Art and Craft of Novel Writing*. Cincinnati, Ohio: Writer's Digest Books, 1989.

Le Guin, Ursula K. *The Left Hand of Darkness*. New York: Ace Books, 1976.

Silverberg, Robert. *Born with the Dead*. New York: Random House, 1971.

Zelazny, Roger. *The Isles of the Dead*. London: Arrow Books, 1973.

Chapter 5

From "Nat" to "Nathan":
The Liberal Arts Odyssey of a Pulpster

Paul A. Carter

It is early on a winter morning . . . dark and bitterly cold; some four smoky candles, guttering and flaring, shed a dim illumination over the School. There is no central heating system, no stove, not even a fireplace. The sooty windows are rimed with frost; the breath of the attentive pupils ascends in clouds of steam.

The rich and well-born are enveloped in furs; the poor and the lowly draw their tattered cloaks about them; their lips are blue and pinched, their limbs almost numb with cold.

One and all, they squat on the straw-strewn floor . . . none higher or lower than his fellow. A democracy of straw!

Now our viewpoint shifts to that of one shivering student:

He sat cross-legged on the straw in the very forefront of the room, right under the master's nose. The mingled odor of unwashed human bodies and damp, long-strewn straw tickled his nostrils. Precious parchment fragments lay on the auditors' laps, with quills poised above them to take down the master's words.

The master, in the first of the foregoing passages, "is a man of dignity and substance; he and he alone is seated." His lecture to a cold, crowded room is "on the intricacies of the syllogism." The master in the second passage is an erstwhile twentieth-century Harvard professor who has been unwillingly warped through time to Paris in the year 1263. His subject is astronomy, and he is about to shock his hearers by telling them that Ptolemy's *Almagest*, their textbook, is in error. The first quotation is from the chapter on "Student Life and Customs" in *The Mediaeval Universities*, by *Nathan* Schachner; the second is from a novelette published in *Unknown*, that lamented and wonderful companion magazine to *Astounding Science Fiction*: "Master Gerald of Cambray," by *Nat* Schachner.[1] The first, in a book its author described the following year as "a deadly serious volume," looked toward a career in what used to be called polite letters—biography, history, the conventional novel; the second returned its author to the homely world of the pulps, where for half a decade he had been faring very well.

Yet of all the really prolific writers for the SF-fantasy pulps in the 1930s—before the Golden Age—Nat, or Nathan, Schachner is perhaps the most forgotten, although in his day he published some 350 stories of which approximately 100 were fantasy or science fiction. Unlike Clifford Simak, who was still turning out well-crafted and well-received tales well into the 1980s, or C. L. Moore, whose work from the 1930s many younger readers of SF and fantasy have discovered with delight, Schachner has virtually dropped out of sight—"known," as Peter Nicholls's SF encyclopedia puts it, "mainly for his work outside the SF field."[2] Science fiction has recently seen extensive discussion of its relationship to the so-called mainstream, and Schachner was in a sense its first "crossover." Beginning as a pulper, even a bit of a hack, he ended as the author not only of mainstream-type historical fiction but also of serious biographical studies accepted as legitimate by Ph.D.-wielding historians—a feat Schachner managed without first undergoing the ordeal of graduate school.

A "jack of all trades," Schachner once described himself. Having devoured "with avidity if not complete understanding" before the age of thirteen *The Divine Comedy*, *Faust*, the complete Shakespeare, Keats, Shelley, et cetera, he turned toward the sciences, graduated from City College in 1916 with a B.Sc., and worked for a time as a chemist; he earned a law degree from New York University and practiced law for sixteen years; and finally he turned to writing—"but all along what I really wanted to be was an astronomer."[3] Although he was a chemistry major in college, he had also taken classical Greek and never gotten over it. Schachner carried all his life the ideal of the well-rounded pursuer of the liberal arts—sometimes to ridiculous lengths, but that is part of his charm.

The viewpoint character in a Schachner story tends to be a man of action who is also an intellectual of the literary sort. Thus the hero of "The Return of Circe" (1941), a somewhat Thorne Smithish irruption of gods and goddesses from classical antiquity into modern America, has previously hazarded his life in the Antarctic and buzzed Alaska's peaks in a small plane—but when he needs to find the name of a flower once reputed to have magical powers, he remembers enough English literature that he can go into a library and look it up in the poetry section. So also Owen Crawford in "The Dragon of Iskander" (1934), blundering into a lost colony in central Asia that was originally founded by Alexander's Macedonians, is able to cope with their descendants because he speaks "the pure, ancient tongue, briny with Attic salt, the speech of Homer and Sophocles, of Sappho and Pindar."[4] And Sam Ward, who has knocked about with Chinese warlords, Bedouin bandits, and New York capitalists, when he meets a surviving ancient Greek warrior in "Past, Present, and Future" (1937), is able to converse with him; for "Sam had studied Greek at college and recognized the long surges, the mighty flow of that noblest of all languages"—though his new Hellenic friend chides him that the accent his professors taught him as "the true Attic Greek in all its purity" is wrong.[5]

Moreover, when Kleon, the Greek (who represents the "past" in the story's title), and Sam, the modern American (the "present"), meet up with Beltan, a denizen of the ninety-eighth century (thus representing "the future"), and exchange further conversation, Beltan dismisses both Kleon's "naive scientific conceptions" and Sam's vaunted march of twentieth-century science as "mere halting steps toward the future." But the concepts of Greek philosophy as explained by Kleon impress this man of the far future profoundly. Even in the ultra-advanced ninety-eighth century, it seems, Plato and Aristotle will still be taken seriously—the ultimate "Great Books" trip! However, we are not faced here with the forced choice of *either* science *or* the humanities; Schachner, stubbornly and admirably, insisted on having it both ways. This lifelong devotee of classical languages and literature was also a founder and the first secretary of the American Rocket Society, and he was injured in one of the society's early experiments.

Schachner wrote his first story in 1930 "on a bet," as he later stated, "and much to my surprise, it was accepted." For his first eleven science fiction stories he teamed with Arthur Leo Zagat, who had been one year behind him at City College of New York, and who, like Schachner, took a law degree (LLB, Fordham, 1929). Zagat, however, never entered law practice. Most of his time between 1930 and his death in 1949 was devoted to pulp fiction writing: detective, adventure, fantasy, SF—five hundred "short works" in these fields, including such remembered items as "Drink

We Deep," "Seven out of Time," and "The Lanson Screen." Unlike his collaborator, Schachner did stay with his legal practice for a time—"until," as he confided to his SF readers in 1939, "my stenographer objected. Typing manuscripts she had no time for law briefs. I decided therefore to drop the law."[6]

Unfortunately, the market for the first stories under the Schachner byline consisted of Hugo Gernsback's clunky, styleless *Wonder Stories*, T. O'Conor Sloane's rather dusty *Amazing*, and the rock 'em and sock 'em Clayton *Astounding*, plus some of the general adventure pulps. For the most part Schachner gave them what they expected, and for the most part his output from those early years is eminently forgettable. "What was a girl, dressed in ancient Greek costume, and responding to the sound of the pure Greek tongue, doing in the T'ien Shan ramparts between Turkestan and the Black Gobi?" the hero of "The Dragon of Iskander" asks. What, indeed?

But in 1933 Street & Smith, onetime publisher of dime novels, bought *Astounding* and installed F. Orlin Tremaine as its editor. Although overshadowed by the sweeping, idiosyncratic reforms of John Campbell later on, Tremaine's *Astounding* did break away considerably from the creaky "I've got you covered—No, *I've* got *you* covered" tradition, thereby opening the way to a greater variety of gambits, including sociopolitical satire. Nat Schachner swiftly adapted to the new regime, and in December 1933 *Astounding* published his "thought-variant" story (as Tremaine billed it) "Ancestral Voices," which can be considered the first shot fired in pulp science fiction's ragged but earnest crusade against Hitler and fascism.[7] That crusade assumed a context of international aggression and conquest: Mussolini's Mare Nostrum, Hitler's Thousand-Year Reich, Japan's Greater East Asia Co-Prosperity Sphere.

But the history of the twentieth century has also known the diametric opposite of that drive toward hegemony—political breakdown and fragmentation. The First World War ended, after all, not in imperial triumph but in collapse; centuries-old empires fell apart. Similarly, after the Second World War, alongside the undoubted expansion of U.S. and Soviet spheres of power came the carving up of former French and British domains in Africa while new microstates in the Indian Ocean and the Caribbean petitioned for admission to a not very United Nations.

H. G. Wells, still writing SF in the 1930s, although rarely with the evocative power of his early work, foresaw this dialectical contradiction between imperialism and chaos. In 1933, the year Hitler came to power (and was burlesqued by Schachner as "Herr Hellwig"),[8] Wells wrote a "history" of the next two hundred years, *The Shape of Things to Come*. He got in some remarkably accurate predictive shots: Japan invades China in the mid-1930s but bogs down in that nation's "great invertebrate body"; the American and Japanese battle fleets clash on the high seas and, as at Leyte Gulf in real time, separate "after two days of gunfire and heavy losses with the Americans going on to Manila"; the British Empire, rather than suffering a Rome-style decline and fall, is described as having "relaxed . . . to nothing"; Germany and Poland go to war in 1940 over Danzig. But Wells's imagined Second World War does not climax in Nazi hegemony that will need to be crushed by united effort. His scenario is rather one of collapse and dissolution—hardly what most of the Hitler alarmists were primarily worried about. To be sure, in this projected future Wells's lifelong dream of a unified, rational, cosmopolitan world order ultimately prevails; his predicted dark ages of pestilence, barbarism, and chaos last only one generation, and survivors from that downfall of civilization may indeed expect to live into the early years of a peaceful, prosperous, planetwide Modern State.[9]

Suppose, however, that the planetary reintegration never comes? Or if it does come, suppose that it in turn succumbs to inner centrifugal strains? One month after his backhanded tribute to Herr Hellwig in "Ancestral Voices," Nat Schachner rebounded to the opposite pole and created for *Astounding*'s readers the anarchic society of "Redmask of the Outlands." In that future, after "the final breakup that destroyed the world state" in the year 4250, North America has become a land of armed, sovereign cities, separated by wilderness tracts occupied by nomadic bands of outlaws. And as both the ancient Greek and the Renaissance Italian city-states had shown in their day, decentralization does not necessarily mean freedom. New York—"a huge cube of blackness" bounded on one side by "the interminable Atlantic, billowing and sun-bright," and on the other by "the almost as interminable forests of the Outlands"—is a hereditary oligarchy; Pittsburgh is a fascist prison with a dictator who physically cannot speak but uses a voice machine (shades of Darth Vader!); Chicago has fully planned and top-down-directed communism, to the point of total eugenic control. Only Washington, D.C., of all places, remains a free society, with no walls, no defenses, no great buildings, and a simple agrarian economy wherein each family grows its own food.

Wandering freely through these city-states and the wild Outlands is Stephen, the licensed jester. Weaponless, carrying his violin—the only violin still in existence; a Stradivarius made in 1715—he is permitted to go where he will. "Only a democrat, . . . he gives joy to those who understand and mirth to those who do not"; his rendition of the Waldweben from *Siegfried* moves even dictators' minions to tears. But Stephen is not what he seems. He turns out to be the archetype of adventure fiction, a diffident, wimpish poet by day and a dashing, macho outlaw by night, modeled no doubt on Red Shadow in Sigmund Romberg's operetta *The Desert Song*, and including among his literary kinsmen the Scarlet Pimpernel and Zorro. Those soulful violin songs go out on a directional beam, a code that transmits his orders to his merry men, an adroit blending of the humanities with high tech.[10]

The imagined history in the background of this story is sketchy. What, in cities that once made up part of a world state, has happened to leave them united "only in a common, mutual, ineradicable hatred"? Schachner did not explain. A year later, however, in "Mind of the World" (*Astounding*, March 1935), this relentless generalist proposed a societal collapse caused not by conflicting political ideologies but by a pathological exaggeration of Adam Smith's classic "division of labor": technical progress, which so often today is seen as a tyrannically unifying force, has instead *divided* humankind.

The tale begins in the Hall of Science, a survivor from an earlier epoch "when the people of the Earth were still divided into nations based upon the accident of contiguous birth rather than upon community of interest in work." Here the Tribes of the World, composed not of ethnic or religious or linguistic groupings but of specialists in different scientific or technical disciplines, have been called into session. The delegates in the back row can't see the proceedings except through view-glasses thoughtfully provided by the Optical delegates; and some representatives, "notably those from the Tribes devoted to subdivisions of the social sciences, could make neither head nor tail of these strange instruments." The Delegate of the Psychopaths explains that he has left an experiment on the effects of switched neuron paths on hallucination to walk five hundred miles to this conference; his neighbor, a Rocketor, has flown to the conference but does not know what neuron paths are. Both are starving, although their colleagues the Food Synthesizers know how to solve that problem.

"In our very heights of knowledge we have grown abysmally ignorant," says the Tropo-Chemist who has called this convention. Earth was happier and "more civilized and scientific" back in the twentieth century "when science was still a cooperative affair." Indeed, this tribalized world society has fewer of "the good things of life" or "the learning, attainments, or broad-mindedness" even of the benighted twentieth century, when people first realized it was impossible for any individual to have a thorough knowledge of more than one particular discipline.[11]

The provisional solution the tribal delegates attempt is to telepathically transfer all the different special kinds of knowledge into one person's brain, thereby putting Humpty Dumpty together again. As might be expected, that solution is a disaster. The chosen tribesman (his field is wave mechanics, presumed fundamental to all else) proceeds to solve all the immediate material problems—transportation, food, medical care—after which he establishes a police state and proclaims his godhead. Wearily the hero and his friends flee from and eventually overthrow the dictator. At the end of the story they establish a new tribe, called Coordinators, "to be trained from infancy in the ability to sense broad relationships, to pick unerringly essential facts out of a welter of data, and supply them to the construction of general theories"—the very model of the liberally educated.[12] Judging by some of Schachner's other fiction published over the next two years, this was an answer the author himself did not find entirely convincing.

Nor could he let go of his theme of politically malformed city-states surrounded by barbarian Outlands. He combined it with ecocatastrophe, for example, in his conservationist novel-sermon "Sterile Planet" (*Astounding*, July 1937), and with antifascism in his "Past, Present, and Future" sequence, which integrates the motif of hyperspecialized cities in a future wilderness with an urgent call to arms in the present. Hispan, the first of these isolationist burgs visited by Sam, Kleon, and Beltan, is a drabber version of *Brave New World*: a self-enclosed habitat shut off from the world above and built downward into the rock, with a population segregated by levels: Oligarchs at the top, under them ten grades of Technicians, and at the bottom the Workers, a far less spunky lot than Orwell's Proles:

They worked their shift, and they returned to the eating level, ate their pellets in silence in long community barracks, shifted to the mating quarters, performed their necessary acts, ascended next to the recreation level, where . . . they talked, quarreled, jested, saw selected audio visions of innocuous comedy at which they roared unthinkingly, and, by signal, shifted to the final sleeping unit, there to be awakened by further signal to continue the endless round.

Harg, the next city on this infernal itinerary, sorts its people into Overseers, Scientists, Providers, Hetarae, and Warriors: in short, Hispan plus militarism. "Evolution has its price," broods Beltan. "A single faculty expands, but only at the expense of others." On the remote Pacific isle of Asto, the expanded faculty is mind; big-headed, shrunken-bodied superthinkers sit, yoga-style, and contemplate the cosmos as isolated individuals. "Thought is a solitary process, not a community affair," one of them explains. Not so, Kleon points out; in his day philosophers had walked and talked together. Asto's intellect, Beltan concurs, is "thought that seeks the inner seeds of specialized decay." And Sam, the omnicompetent American, opines that "a little more of the old Greek ideal of a sound mind in a sound body—a happy balancing—would have worked wonders for these overemphasized States of the future." [13]

The initial story in this "Past, Present, and Future" series appeared in *Astounding* in September 1937, together with the first installment of "Doc" Smith's *Galactic Patrol*.[14] In October, while the Smith space opera was still running, notices appeared of Nathan (as distinguished from "Nat") Schachner's breakout into the literary mainstream, with a solid historical biography supported by manuscript sources quarried from the Library of Congress, the New York Historical Society, and other such archives, together with a choice array of newspapers and court records. Its subject was that somewhat science fictional character Aaron Burr.

Thick, even a bit prolix, though enlivened at times by striking phrases (e.g., as a subtitle for the fateful duel with Hamilton: "Pistols for two; coffee for one"), the book drew reviews which may tell us, Rorschach fashion, more about the reviewers' opinion of Burr than about Schachner's biography of him.[15] The book's greatest strength may lie in the acute, lawyerly way Schachner threaded the maze of the Burr conspiracy-treason trials in 1807, dissecting likely conjecture from the masses of sheer gossip. The book's point of view toward those trials—that Jefferson abused presidential authority in an effort to "get" Burr, in a case whose verdict should have been at most "not proven"—has lately been on the upswing among specialists in that period.[16] (As the Chief Justice of the United States put it early in 1989, "Historians simply have not made up their minds what Burr was doing all this time.")[17]

Why, then, if Aaron Burr was a responsible statesman rather than the absolute scoundrel of legend, is he not better remembered? "His greatest limitation was the lack of a rounded, well-organized philosophy applicable to the issues of the day," Schachner's biography concludes. "It is to Hamilton, to Jefferson, to Jackson, to John and Samuel Adams, that one looks for comprehensive plans, whether good or bad. . . . One looks in vain to Burr for such matters." Aaron Burr was, in short, not a member of the

Tribe of Coordinators, with their "ability to sense broad relationships, to pick unerringly essential facts out of a welter of data and apply them to the construction of general theories"; he was "one who viewed government in terms of men rather than in terms of ideals and philosophic concepts" after the fashion of his two great rivals, Thomas Jefferson and Alexander Hamilton.[18]

While Kleon, Sam, and Beltan were visiting (and then fleeing from) the militaristic City of the Rocket Horde and the exasperating Island of the Individualists in sequels to "Past, Present, and Future," Nathan Schachner was preparing to bring forth his second nonfiction work. Fascinated by the form the dialectic of order and disorder had taken in the Middle Ages, when a king of England could technically be a vassal of a king of France with whom he was at war, and when universities enjoyed a corporate autonomy and a degree of "student power" undreamed of even in the insurgent 1960s, Nathan worked up considerable nostalgia for his subject: "Twentieth-century institutions of learning are but pallid simulacra of their lusty forebears," he declared. Despite Woodrow Wilson's professorship and FDR's brain trust, "the Universities of today are but inconspicuous eddies in the vast currents of modern life." [19]

The Mediaeval Universities exhibits a style far less "academic" than the Burr biography; it is not quite the "deadly serious volume" its author described a year later for the readers of *Fantastic Adventures*. Schachner aimed, one reviewer surmised, "to interest that incalculable person, 'the general reader,' in a subject which has hitherto been one of the preserves of scholars who have not condescended to be 'popular.' " [20] It may be true, as Nathan claimed, that a history of the medieval universities would yield "an almost complete history of mediaeval thought and culture," but nominalism and realism are hard subjects to make lively. Schachner was better at depicting the hard-drinking, wenching, blasphemous Goliards. "Gentle reader" was, and is, an elusive target, and Schachner had difficulty reaching the mark.

Nat Schachner, however, benefited from this effort, with his spin-off story "Master Gerald of Cambray." Schachner's writing style was steadily improving, and his description of Paris in 1263, with the aroma of garbage sickeningly mingled with the delectable odor of baking bread, is clamorous and alive. Told from the viewpoint not of Master Gerald but of one of his thirteenth-century students, the story is an honest, if simple, tragedy; the time-traveling professor, although stereotypically timorous, even in a brutal, brawling world cannot resist the teacher's urge to tell people what's what. Defended by his fellows in the "English nation" of the University of Paris when the papal legate demands he be handed over for trial as a heretic (for teaching Copernican astronomy three centuries before Copernicus), Master Gerald tells his friends to "let them have me." The university is too important an intellectual force for the future "to be endangered because of a single man whose tongue was always hastier than his sense. What I spoke was the truth; but I spoke it out of time." And so the shrinking bookworm goes with quiet courage to his death. At the crisis point he has gained insight into his and the world's condition; and that is the difference between true tragedy and a mere downbeat ending.[21]

"Master Gerald of Cambray" appeared in *Unknown*, one of John W. Campbell's many innovations in the pulp science fiction and fantasy field. Shortly after taking over the helm at *Astounding* from Tremaine, Campbell began to recruit and cultivate the new crop of writers who would ignite what SF has ever since called its Golden Age. As he developed these new talents he also continued to buy stories from writers of the previous pulp generation who were able to speak Campbell's language; those who could not rapidly faded away. Jack Williamson, one conspicuous example, successfully adapted to the new order, as witness "Breakdown," "Darker Than You Think," and "With Folded Hands"; but Jack's lifelong friend Edmond Hamilton didn't make the cut (although he continued to publish prolifically elsewhere, out of Campbell's orbit). Nat Schachner's case, it appears, was touch and go.

"City of the Cosmic Rays," in my judgment the most vivid and imaginative of the "Past, Present, and Future" series, appeared in the famous July 1939 issue of *Astounding* (destined to be preserved in hard covers on library shelves forever by the Southern Illinois University Press), which carried Isaac Asimov's first *Astounding* story and also A. E. van Vogt's. One more sequel appeared in December of that year,[22] but some readers were heartily tired of "Past, Present, and Future." A lone teenager wrote to *Astounding*'s "Brass Tacks" letter column urging the editor to publish "a satisfactory concluding episode" to the saga of Kleon, Beltan, and Sam.[23] More typical, however, was the reader in England who said of Schachner: "Give him a rest."

Campbell responded to that overseas critic with an announcement that Schachner was working on "a new series that looks excellent—adventures of a space lawyer!"[24] Two stories in the new series duly appeared in the magazine and were well received.[25] Their plots turn on such questions as what legally happens to a mining claim on a worthless asteroid if it collides with a smaller one that is much more valuable. But they hardly measured up to the other stories published in 1941, arguably *Astounding*'s peak year—the year of "Nightfall" and "Solution Unsatisfactory," of "Universe" and "Adam and No Eve," of "The Mechanical Mice" and "Microcosmic God." Perhaps it was time for pulp author Nat Schachner to take his last curtain call.

One more Nat Schachner story, and a most significant one, appeared toward the end of that year in a magazine not dominated by the Campbell canons: "Eight Who Came Back," in *Fantastic Adventures—Amazing*'s flamboyant consort—for November 1941. A fantasy rather than science fiction, the story uses a favorite Schachner social-critical theme during the ominous years climaxed by World War II: How does one end wars except by making war on the warlike? And isn't that self-defeating? Eight distinguished ghosts, four intellectuals and four soldiers—Socrates, Shakespeare, Voltaire, and Bacon; Napoleon, Caesar, Alexander, and Richard the Lion-Hearted—appear in a pleasant New England college town. Since their ghostly existence depends on people's memories of them, they have decided they must stop humankind from destroying *it*self in order to preserve *them*selves. As Socrates explains: "Brute emotions have taken place of luminous reason. . . . Madmen rule and philosophers languish in concentration camps. It is time to call a halt."

But how? Shall these dead lead the living to Utopia by rational persuasion or by force? They decide to try out their respective solutions on the nearby university. The local school's president, faculty, and student body—together with townspeople, who wouldn't have been there in Schachner's Middle Ages—listen raptly in the college chapel while Socrates debates Napoleon. It is no contest; the philosopher's plea for a world of "tolerance, learning, wisdom, and graciousness" is swept aside by Napoleon's trumpet call for "doers" rather than "theorists" and poets. All the quiet, bookish souls in the audience are seized by war madness, rather in the manner of academic intellectuals during the First World War. "On their uplifted faces and in their furious eyes was stamped indelibly the lust for battle, for blood and carnage and glory"; and the "gentle little professor of aesthetics," the professor of Greek, and the captain of the football team march forth together under Napoleon to conquer.

In the end, the only solution is to exorcise the eight ghosts, leaving humanity to cope with its present problems on its own. The story's hero, after he recovers his senses, defends the crowd for having been carried away by Napoleon's oratory, using a social-deterministic ground of a kind then fashionable: "We weren't free to choose." But Socrates rebukes him: "The soul of man is always free. You yielded to that which best expressed your desires."[26] It was a succinct allegorization of the kind of philosophical-moral concerns that had run through all of Schachner's fiction, even at its pulpiest, of the previous ten years, and it was a fitting close to the "Nat" phase of his career.

Nathan, meanwhile, had found a new literary niche: the historical novel. He went down to New Orleans to soak up the local atmosphere, arriving on the first morning of Mardi Gras to find that, of course, there were no affordable hotel rooms. "But I've come to New Orleans to write a book about your city and I can't pay $10 a day," Schachner objected. Hearing this, three operators promptly "grabbed phones and found the author a good place at reasonable rates." Schachner did not, however, simply hang out in the Vieux Carré, although no doubt he derived from firsthand experience the novel's mouth-watering descriptions of New Orleans food. He traveled also to Howard University, Duke University, and the University of North Carolina and consulted overseers' diaries, unpublished plantation account books, pamphlets, newspapers, and "family papers still in private hands," from which he drew "the germs of many of the incidents in this story."[27] The result was *By the Dim Lamps*, a vivid novel of the Civil War and Reconstruction in Louisiana. Its account of sugar cultivation compares favorably with Ellen Glasgow's tobacco growing in *The Deliverance* (a comment I mean as high praise); its characters are more sharply drawn than in any of Nat's pulp stories; and, alas, it has some of the most egregious racial stereotyping this side of Little Black Sambo.[28] Jonathan Daniels, a southern liberal by the standards of that day, called it "a lively book about a violent time"—not very deep, but "almost all of it would be magnificent in technicolor."[29] And that was the fatal catch; it followed *Gone with the Wind* and inevitably had to be compared with that blockbuster. Schachner's Jessie Tait, a liberated woman who has left her husband back in Yankee Boston (he pays her to stay away), is an interesting personage, but she is no Scarlett O'Hara.

Three more works of historical fiction followed: *The King's Passenger*, set in colonial Virginia at the time of Bacon's Rebellion; *The Sun Shines West*, a novel of "bleeding Kansas" in the 1850s, with a Romeo and Juliet plot involving pro- and antislavery settlers; and *The Wanderer*, a fictionalized life of Dante.[30] The three received mixed reviews, ranging from "historical fiction as Americans have come to love it. Full, salty, vigorous, defiantly true and unadorned," through "an absorbing—if somewhat conventional—historical novel," to a devastating judgment (on the Dante book) that the author "gets everything historically right except his central character." Evidently Nathan Schachner had yet to find his literary metier.[31]

He retained enough kinship with his peers in pulpdom to lecture them, in an article published in *The Writer* just as the war drew to a close, that "pulp writers have a job to do"—namely, to break up the racial and ethnic stereotyping that marred so much of their writing (including some of his own).[32] One can only speculate what might have happened had Schachner decided to take another fling as Nat before settling down as Nathan. Advances in technology—the atom bomb, V-2, and radar—had made the extravagant fiction of yesterday the cold fact of today; science fiction had lost a portion, at least, of its disreputable image. Ray Bradbury branched out from *Weird Tales* and *Planet Stories* to *Harper's* and *Mademoiselle*; episodes of Robert Heinlein's future history began to appear not only in *Astounding* but also in the *Saturday Evening Post*. And as science fiction moved on into the 1950s, it took on a strong tinge of social satire. Writers created worlds as mad as any in Nat Schachner's stories—worlds in which the author of "Mind of the World," "Island of the Individualists," and "City of the Corporate Mind" would have felt right at home.

Nat's early collaborator, Arthur Zagat, did stick with their common pulp milieu. He founded a writers' workshop in New York City to help war veterans break into writing, and at the time of his death in 1949 Zagat was teaching short story writing at NYU.[33] But in 1946 Nathan published a biography of Alexander Hamilton, and the die was cast. Suddenly, after years of operating on the margins of mainstream literature, he was given two full columns of mostly laudatory notices by the *Book Review Digest*. He was warmly welcomed into the Tribe of Historians by the distinguished Jefferson scholar Dumas Malone, strongly seconded by history professors John Krout and Roy F. Nichols.[34] When an author is publicly told, as Schachner was by Gerald Johnson, that he is "not merely good, but very good," that he has produced "the best life of Hamilton that has yet been written," and that "it is going to be a strong contender for the Pulitzer Prize," it is understandable if he decides to push his luck.[35]

After a pause to do a brief history of the American Jewish Committee (*The Price of Liberty* [1948]), Schachner wrote a two-volume biography of Thomas Jefferson, along with Hamilton and Burr, the leading political rivals in the 1790s. The decision was a tactical disaster. Ten years earlier, as one reviewer regretfully observed, Schachner's book would have been considered the most comprehensive and scholarly life of Jefferson yet written.

However, just as the territory of southern-viewpoint Civil War fiction had been preempted by Margaret Mitchell, so the turf of Jefferson studies had been preempted by Dumas Malone.[36] Malone's initial biographical volume *Jefferson the Virginian* came out in the same year with Schachner's *Price of Liberty*; and in 1951, when Schachner published his own two volumes, Malone produced his widely admired *Jefferson and the Rights of Man*. Volume after volume followed, six in all, and at the end of that strenuous performance (1981) Malone *did* win the Pulitzer Prize.

After this eclipse, Nat reappeared for a moment in 1953, combining the "Old Fireball" space lawyer stories from *Astounding* with some new material for a volume from one of the then-flourishing science fiction specialty publishers, Gnome Press. Reviewing *Space Lawyer* for the *New York Herald Tribune*, "H. H. Holmes"—known under another pen name, Anthony Boucher, as the humanely cultivated editor of *The Magazine of Fantasy and Science Fiction*—hailed it as "the year's most amusing sheer space opera" and hoped "that Mr. Schachner may take time off from his well reputed historical biographies to give us more."[37] It was not to be. Nathan's next book, *The Founding Fathers*, narrated the political history not of the 9700s but of the 1790s.

This was, in my judgment, a better work—certainly it was better received—than the Jefferson biography; in a time when American historians under cold war pressures were adopting a stuffy "consensus" interpretation of the American past, Schachner stoutly, and I think rightly, insisted on a dialectic of political conflict, although he saw it more in personal than in class terms. Logically ending in 1801 with Jefferson's lofty inaugural statement, "We are all Republicans, we are all Federalists"—and with a suggestion by Schachner that ex-president John Adams, could he have heard those words as his coach rolled away, might have greeted them "with a sardonic laugh"—the story obviously called for a sequel, and Schachner began to research and write one,[38] but on October 2, 1955, at age sixty, he died of a heart attack. His epitaph might well be the ideal that Emerson had stated long ago in *The American Scholar*: "You must take the whole society to find the whole man. Man is not a farmer or a professor or an engineer, but he is all."

Notes

1. Nathan Schachner, *The Mediaeval Universities* (New York: Frederick A. Stokes, 1938); Nat Schachner, "Master Gerald of Cambray," *Unknown* (June 1940): 125–62.

2. Peter Nicholls, ed., *The Encyclopedia of Science Fiction* (London: Granada, 1979). The Donald Tuck compendium similarly credits Schachner as "noted for brilliant biographies" and further states that he "left science fiction in the early 1940's" (Donald H. Tuck, ed., *Encyclopedia of Science Fiction and Fantasy* [Chicago: Advent, 1978], p. 380). The last statement is almost, but not quite true, for Schachner's novel *Space Lawyer*, published in 1953—after his Jefferson study and prior to *The Founding Fathers*—contained newly written material that had not previously been published in the magazines. In its obituary notice *Newsweek* (October 17, 1955) more roundedly characterized Schachner as a "one-time lawyer turned historian . . . science-fiction writer . . . biographer . . . and a founder of the American Rocket Society."

3. "Meet the Author," *Fantastic Adventures* (September 1939): 91; Stanley J. Junitz, *Twentieth Century Authors*, first supplement (New York: H. W. Wilson, 1955), p. 875.

4. Nat Schachner, "The Return of Circe," *Fantastic Adventures* (August 1941); "The Dragon of Iskander," *Top Notch* (April 1934), reprinted in *Fantastic* (July 1962): 32. Sam Moskowitz, perhaps sensing even then that Schachner's reputation might be going into eclipse, introduced the reprint with a promotional line: "Frequently a writer will play a key role in the revitalization of a literary movement without claiming or receiving credit for his achievement" (p. 19). Sadly, "Dragon"—a routine pulp adventure—hardly qualifies as a literary catalyst.

5. Nat Schachner, "Past, Present, and Future," *Astounding Stories* (September 1937): 60–89. Compare the reaction of the Time Traveller and his friends, early in H. G. Wells's *The Time Machine*, with the Very Young Man's remark that if one only had time travel, "One might get one's Greek from the very lips of Homer and Plato": "The German scholars have improved Greek so much." I am indebted to Eric Rabkin for pointing out this literary echo from a work with which all science fictionists of Schachner's generation were familiar.

6. "Meet the Author." According to the *National Cyclopedia of American Biography* (New York: James T. White, 1961), 43: 277, Schachner practiced law in New York City until 1936. A sketch of Arthur Leo Zagat's life appears in ibid., 37: 344.

7. Nat Schachner, "Ancestral Voices," *Astounding Stories* (December 1933): 70–

81. Having discussed this anti-Nazi theme in 1930s SF elsewhere, I will not rehash that argument here; see "The Phantom Dictator: Science Fiction Discovers Hitler," in *The Creation of Tomorrow: Fifty Years of Magazine Science Fiction* (New York: Columbia University Press, 1977), chap. 5.

8. In case anybody missed the point as to who "Herr Hellwig" really was, the artist who illustrated the story gave him the characteristic cowlick and toothbrush mustache. Albert I. Berger makes this point, and much more, in his impressive—Brian Aldiss calls it magisterial—history of *Astounding* in Marshall Tymn and Mike Ashley, eds., *Science Fiction, Fantasy, and Weird Fiction Magazines* (Westport, Conn.: Greenwood Press, 1985); Aldiss, *Trillion Year Spree* (New York: Avon Books, 1986), p. 464, n. 27.

9. H. G. Wells, *The Shape of Things to Come* (New York: Macmillan, 1933), pp. 169, 174, 176, 191. Although this book was the source for the Alexander Korda film *Things to Come* (1936), starring Raymond Massey and Ralph Richardson, for which Wells himself wrote the script, these are *very* different works; the one should not be considered simply a transcript for the other (movies rarely are).

10. Nat Schachner, "Redmask of the Outlands," *Astounding Stories* (January 1934): 2–34. Mawkish and melodramatic? Yes, of course; but if Hollywood people are looking for a science fiction property less expensive to mount than the Lucas-style space opera and less grimly regressive than the *Road Warrior* series, they could do a lot worse than "Redmask" or "Mind of the World" or the adventures of Kleon, Beltan, and Sam.

11. For Schachner this argument was something of a recantation. Impatient with the drift of the depression, he had dabbled for a time with Technocracy, writing one story in which he forecast a successful overthrow of American gangsters, oil profiteers, and other such troglodytes by a soviet of scientists, managers, and engineers. See Nat Schachner, "Revolt of the Scientists," *Wonder Stories* (April–May–June 1933).

12. Nat Schachner, "Mind of the World," *Astounding Stories* (March 1935): 64–98. The same issue of *Astounding* carried his story "When the Sun Dies" under the pseudonym Chan Corbett (pseudonyms were a frequent ploy in pulp publication to avoid having one writer's name appear twice on the contents page of a magazine that had bought two of his or her stories). The story, in which doomed fortresses end up huddled under masses of glacial ice, each redoubt so isolated from its nearest neighbor that "as far as physical communication was concerned, it might have been established in a valley of the moon," is yet another variant of Schachner's cities-in-the-wilderness theme.

13. Nat Schachner, "Sterile Planet," *Astounding Stories* (July 1937): 52–70; "Past,

Present, and Future," p. 73; "City of the Rocket Horde," *Astounding Stories* (December 1937): 112–35; "Island of the Individualists," *Astounding Science-Fiction* (May 1938): 42–62. Note that between the appearance of the last two stories the magazine changed its name—one of the earliest of John Campbell's editorial reforms.

14. When Isaac Asimov picked this story for a generous-sized anthology of magazine SF from the 1930s, he testified to Schachner's impact on his own work: "When I came to write *The Foundation Trilogy*, there were times when the voice of Schachner sounded in my ear" (Asimov, ed., *Before the Golden Age* [Garden City, N.Y.: Doubleday, 1974], p. 877). Since the Good Doctor continued to add to the Foundation saga up until 1992, one could say that Schachner continues modestly to influence the field. My own short story, "Joram among the Dogs" (*Fantasy and Science Fiction*, August 1988), owes something to Schachner's "Past, Present, and Future" series as well.

15. Reviews ranged from *Commonweal*'s "challenging . . . scintillating in style and scholarly in substance . . . definitely supersedes all earlier studies of the life of Aaron Burr," to the judgment by Henry Steele Commager that Schachner's "book is one long brief for the defense, at times learned and persuasive, at times clever and disingenuous, but mainly passionate and prejudiced." W. F. McCaleb, in the *American Historical Review*, on the other hand, charged the pro-Jefferson, anti-Burr critics with having "striven to hide the story beneath a heap of partisanship and vituperation" fueled by what he termed their slavish adherence to Henry Adams's venerable and massive history of the Jefferson and Madison administrations, which had concluded that Burr's reported treasonable intentions were real. See *Commonweal*, October 1, 1937; *Books*, October 3, 1937; *American Historical Review* (July 1938).

16. Such is the judgment of Morton Borden, who has written and published extensively on the Federalist-Jeffersonian era. Although Borden considers this biography of Burr to have been superseded by more recent studies, his own appraisal of Schachner personally is of "a Renaissance man" with "an encyclopedic knowledge of so many things. . . . I was always most impressed with the man" (Borden, telephone conversation with the author, February 14, 1989).

17. William Rehnquist, "The Impeachment of Justice Chase," lecture before the University of Arizona Law School, February 7, 1989. This citation should *not* be taken as my endorsement of this Chief Justice's legal-political philosophy! Rehnquist's lecture did, however, strike me as a well-founded argument by a person well versed in the history of the Supreme Court. (One takes wisdom wherever one can find it.) Compare Leonard Baker, whose seventy-page discussion of the Burr treason trial begins by declaring that of "the three ex-

planations of Burr: traitor, confidence man, and loser," "history does not reveal which is correct" (Leonard Baker, *John Marshall: A Life in Law* [New York: Macmillan, 1974], p. 451).

18. Nathan Schachner, *Aaron Burr: A Biography* (New York: Frederick A. Stokes, 1937), p. 517. Compare Nat Schachner, "Mind of the World." Schachner's personal judgment—or bias—may be inferred from the listing, among clubs and organizations to which he belonged, of the Aaron Burr Association; see *National Cyclopedia of American Biography*. Gore Vidal, in his fictionalized version (*Burr: A Novel* [1973]), outdid Schachner in Burr affiliation by dedicating the work to his nephews, Ivan, Hugh, and—Burr!

19. Nathan Schachner, *The Mediaeval Universities*, p. 3. Articles by Schachner were also beginning to appear in mainstream magazines; e.g., "The Truth about Aaron Burr," *American Mercury* 45 (October 1938).

20. Review signed by "S. C. C.," *Christian Science Monitor*, October 5, 1938. A canon of the Church of England complained of Schachner's book that although "all that he says is correct," he did not get to the "spiritual realities" enshrined in those universities (Canon Roger Lloyd, in the *Manchester Guardian Weekly*, July 5, 1938).

21. Nat Schachner, "Master Gerald of Cambray," pp. 151, 155. This tale of the modern man displaced in time to a harsh and unfamiliar environment which dooms him has a spirit akin to, and foreshadowing, more sophisticated works like Poul Anderson's "The Man Who Came Early."

22. Nat Schachner, "City of the Cosmic Rays," *Astounding Science-Fiction* (July 1939): 47–66; "City of the Corporate Mind," ibid. (December 1939): 45–70. It may be appropriate that the series ended thus, inconclusively; the antithesis between "selfish, anarchic, ego-tripping individualism and soul-destroying, mind-dissolving collectivism" (as I termed them in *The Creation of Tomorrow*, p. 142) as Schachner set them up may have become logically irresolvable.

23. Paul Carter, letter in "Brass Tacks," *Astounding Science-Fiction* (November 1941): 161. And, no, George, I don't usually list items of this kind on my vita.

24. E. E. Simpson, letter in "Brass Tacks," *Astounding Science-Fiction* (March 1941): 157; Campbell's response at p. 156 (he regularly couched his replies to readers as headnotes to their letters, not postscripts—giving himself the first word). That reader also didn't have much use for E. E. Smith, or even Robert Heinlein, of whom Simpson wrote: "He is an opportunist in his plots, and an opportunist develops into a hack-writer." Regretfully, I find this an all-too-accurate prophecy of what eventually happened to Heinlein.

25. Nat Schachner, "Old Fireball," *Astounding Science-Fiction* (June 1941): 79–105 (handsomely illustrated by Charles Schneeman); "Jurisdiction," ibid. (August 1941): 9–36 (Schachner's last cover story, with a typical sleek Hubert

Rogers painting). In the tabulation of readers' votes, both stories managed second-place finishes in that highly competitive year; one beat out Ross Rock-lynne's rather good SF whodunit "Time Wants a Skeleton," and the other was edged only by the second installment of Heinlein's "Methuselah's Children," which drew a rare statistically perfect 1.000. "The Analytical Laboratory," ibid. (August 1941): 109, (October 1941): 48.

26. Nat Schachner, "Eight Who Came Back," *Fantastic Adventures* (November 1941): 44–72. I infer that the locale is New England from a reference to "the 9:40 [train] from Boston."

27. Nathan Schachner, *By the Dim Lamps* (New York: Frederick A. Stokes, 1941), p. vii. The anecdote about Schachner's arrival in New Orleans is from the *Saturday Review of Literature*, February 22, 1941, p. 18.

28. Schachner assumed, as did almost all white professional historians at that time, the then-conventional interpretation of southern Reconstruction that had been put forth at the turn of the century by William A. Dunning and John W. Burgess. Few such scholars had read, let alone accepted, the monumental revisionist work by W. E. B. Du Bois (*Black Reconstruction*, published in 1935); and those who knew that book usually shied away from its explicitly avowed Marxism. Actually, Schachner made a shrewd choice of story setting; of all the reconstructed states, Louisiana in all probability came closest to the traditional view in its experience of Reconstruction. Even Du Bois conceded that "types like [Henry Clay] Warmoth," who figured prominently in Schachner's novel as a villain, "represented the carpetbagger and scalawag at their worst." However, Du Bois's balancing insight—"the shrewd and venal and dishonest Negro elements were characterized as typical and used as an excuse for cheating and lawlessness by elements in the white population just as dishonest and much more influential"—was not fully incorporated into Schachner's perception of what happened. W. E. B. Du Bois, *Black Reconstruction in America* (1935; New York: Atheneum, 1969), pp. 461, 483.

29. *Saturday Review of Literature*, March 15, 1941. The *New York Times* reviewer praised the book as "an excellent example of how much can be done in fiction with research as the basis," but conceded it was no *Gone with the Wind*.

30. *The King's Passenger* (Philadelphia: J. B. Lippincott, 1942); *The Sun Shines West* (New York: D. Appleton–Century, 1943); *The Wanderer* (New York: D. Appleton–Century, 1944).

31. *Books*, May 24, 1942, reviewing *The King's Passenger*; *Book Week*, November 21, 1943, reviewing *The Sun Shines West*; *Saturday Review of Literature*, November 18, 1944, reviewing *The Wanderer*.

32. Nat Schachner, "Pulp Writers Have a Job to Do," *The Writer* (August 1945):
    243–44. For an example of just such stereotyping in Nat's own work, note
    the drunken halfbreed, Juan, who guides Sam Ward to the ancient Mayan
    temple in the Guatemalan jungle, where treacherous Mayans lock him in to
    join Kleon in suspended animation until the ninety-eighth century. For an
    example from Nathan's work, ponder the mighty, very black Negro named
    Quash in *By the Dim Lamps*, who falls Homerically in battle on the streets
    of New Orleans near the story's end. (Actually, Quash represented a short
    step *away* from the stereotype, since Nat credited him with high, if malign,
    intelligence, which, since he was also depicted as a pure-blooded black, Quash
    could not have derived from some white ancestor. But Quash's native intellect
    is presented as an aspect of his villainous menace.) Fiction writers, both pulp
    and otherwise, had a long way to go to do the job Schachner urged on them
    in 1945.

33. *National Cyclopedia of American Biography*, article on Arthur Leo Zagat.
    Zagat and Schachner had also been active in the War Writers' Board, which in
    the spring of 1945 called a conference of writers, editors, and publishers to ex-
    pose "The Myth That Threatens America"—namely, "that this is overwhelm-
    ingly an Anglo-Saxon, white, native-born Protestant country." See Nathan
    Schachner, *The Price of Liberty* (New York: American Jewish Committee,
    1948), p. 166.

34. Malone's review appeared in the *Saturday Review of Literature*, June 15,
    1946; Nichols's in the *Christian Science Monitor*, June 13, 1946; Krout's in
    the *New York Times*, June 16, 1946. That Schachner lacked a Ph.D. may have
    been less of a barrier than it might seem to the professoriat of a later day;
    Allan Nevins, after all, the most published American professional historian of
    the century, lacked one. Nevins's prize-winning biography of Grover Cleve-
    land appeared in 1932, well before Schachner started writing nonfiction, and
    could have served as a model of what was possible.

35. Gerald Johnson, *New York Herald Tribune Weekly Book Reviews*, June 2,
    1946. My own reading of Schachner's Hamilton study is that it stands up
    rather well; having no controversial thesis to defend, it is more judicious (and
    less long-winded) than the Burr book, and it compares favorably, I believe,
    with John C. Miller's highly regarded *Alexander Hamilton: Portrait in Para-
    dox* (New York: Harper and Brothers, 1959). But a hazard in writing any
    book of this kind is shared with the writers of scientific treatises: one becomes
    displaced by new data. When a team of tireless researchers undertook the
    compilation of a definitive modern edition of the papers of Alexander Hamil-
    ton, they kept turning up previously unknown packets of Hamilton letters and

documents. (Also, much material that Schachner had to dig out from manuscript collections, in the process making some important historiographic contributions of his own, is now conveniently, if expensively, available in print for any other would-be Hamilton biographer.) Harold C. Syrett et al., *The Papers of Alexander Hamilton* (New York: Columbia University Press, 1961–).

36. Douglass Adair, in *New York Herald Tribune Book Reviews*, December 9, 1951. What surprises me in Schachner's Jefferson study is how much the writing quality sags by comparison with the Hamilton and Burr biographies. Logically, Jefferson and Schachner, both "Renaissance men," ought to have been made for each other. As Schachner himself observed in his foreword, Jefferson "dabbled in many sciences, and helped illuminate them all," along with much more to the same effect (Nathan Schachner, *Thomas Jefferson: A Biography* [New York: Appleton-Century-Crofts, 1951], p. vii).

37. "H. H. Holmes," in *New York Herald Tribune Book Reviews*, February 21, 1954. The Holmes nom de plume was used for that writer's East Coast detective fiction reviews and for his own whodunits; on the West Coast he reviewed books and edited *Fantasy and Science Fiction* as Anthony Boucher; in the Berkeley, California, phone book he was William A. P. White.

38. Nathan Schachner, *The Founding Fathers* (New York: G. P. Putnam's Sons, 1954), p. 564. In the 1950s Morton Borden (see n. 16, above) undertook a posthumous revision of the not-quite-completed sequel, but that work was never published.

Chapter 6

The Voice of Cthulhu:
Language Interaction in
Contemporary Horror Fiction

Karen A. Hohne

Horror literature is fundamentally preoccupied with the clash that occurs between ideologies in power (official) and disenfranchised (unofficial) ideologies. More particularly, the unofficial voice that mainstream ideology attempts to drown out in popular culture finds in horror a locus for expression. These unofficial ideologies are concretized as particular languages. In the violent ideological interaction that occurs in horror fiction, unofficial ideologies burst apart the ironclad narrative of officiality, overtaking the characters' or even the narrator's speech. In this way the situation of lived reality, which in fact so deviates from its official version, is depicted in horror literature: literature does not merely reflect reality or offer some slightly edited version of it, but in part discusses reality in a literary tongue, depicting the overthrow of a dominant, prestigious language by subordinate, devalued languages in order to represent official ideology's actual inability to gloss the universe, despite its insistence to the contrary.

It is logical that romanticism provided the genesis of horror; the movement's philosophical assumption that the universe must be extended to include what had previously been excluded (the unofficial) provided a blueprint for horror's ideological interaction. All that was rendered voiceless by neoclassicism speaks in romanticism: the subconscious (the other within), the folk (the other within one's own society), other cultures, and history itself (as a series of voices). Compared with neoclassicism, romanticism is characterized by its ear for other voices.[1] It is not for nothing that romanticism marks the elevation of the novel to the top of the literary pyramid, for the novel celebrates heteroglossia and the interaction of languages. This essay, however, examines not horror *novels*, which as novels would be likely to contain ideological interaction, but horror *stories*, specifically, those of Edgar Allan Poe, H. P. Lovecraft, and Stephen King, which as stories should lack any inherent tendency to heteroglossia. Analysis reveals a chronological increase in the depth and breadth of the ideological clash in horror literature. In Poe's stories this clash is confined for the most part to the content and does not encroach on the form. In Lovecraft's works ideological interaction occurs in the incorporation of various unofficial languages into the speech of the characters and even of the narrator, while King makes use of a large number of unofficial languages spoken by characters and by the narrator. Thus the ferocious battle between the two sets of ideologies gradually overwhelms horror's narrative; in fact, it is appropriate to say that this battle *is* horror's narrative, that it *is* the story being told.

Although other ideologies occur in his references to outré books (in other languages), Poe's use of foreign languages for the epigraphs, and his occasional incorporation of other genres (such as poetry or excerpts from novels), make unofficiality generally appear embodied not in an actual language so much as in the person of the narrator and in his acts. Here are truly unofficial narrators—madmen and murderers ("Tell-Tale Heart," "The Black Cat," "The Imp of the Perverse," "The Cask of Amontillado")— people on the very edge of society (and thus of officiality) who are given the opportunity to tell their stories. Unofficiality is depicted in word and deed in the official realm of literature. It is not gratuitous that the motif of the hidden exposed recurs (the cat and corpse in the basement wall, the mask not a mask, Fortunato's tomb, the heart under the floorboards), for the hidden is unofficiality, which is entombed within the silence officiality imposes upon it: outside, unseen, and unheard until exposed by horror. These madmen narrators often describe themselves as great liars in their everyday lives, that is, as crafty manipulators of languages (as we must be, in order to get around officiality); thus the truth we do hear sounds all the sweeter.

The subject of Poe's stories is another area in which the previously unheard is given voice: for example, the torture of a condemned man (who, further, does not protest his innocence and who must therefore be guilty; "Pit and the Pendulum") and murder committed for the sake of revenge or, better yet, simply because it offends one's own spirit (as in "The Black Cat"). In other, similarly constructed literature such "immorality" is in fact the literary reflection of officiality's real condemnation and criminalization of all that is other to it and which therefore challenges its authority.[2] Here, even a cat has a voice, and it may speak clearly enough to discover the dead in this unofficialized world. Stories like "The Pit and the Pendulum" provide obvious metaphors for the unofficial-official interaction: the condemned man is saved from the most official of all officialities, the Inquisition, by a (totally other) foreign invader. Generally in Poe's stories, however, ideological interaction occurs in the content, the world depicted, and not in the form, the depiction. It is with later writers such as Lovecraft that the clash between official and unofficial begins to spill over from the content to the form and to be crystallized in direct speech.

H. P. Lovecraft, long incorrectly assessed as a bad writer, is a suitable transitional figure between Poe and King. He is often named as an influence by modern horror writers (including King), he himself claimed to have been greatly influenced by Poe, and he was in actuality quite a good craftsman. The fact that his work appeared primarily in pulp magazines is as it should be, since present horror, now dominated by the novel, is generally found in the supermarket, not the library.

Like Poe, Lovecraft not infrequently gave over the task of narration to madmen. In his world, understanding other languages, which permits the completion of a narrative from scattered language fragments, usually leads to madness; conversely, madness increases one's language abilities. But even sane narrators depart from official language in their own peculiar speech (which I have dubbed Old High Literary), report languages other than their own (Scientific, Rural, Eighteenth-Century Conversational, Magical, Cthulhu, Academic, Journalese, etc.), interact with the speakers of these languages, and even learn from them (especially from Cthulhu). In general, in Lovecraft's stories unofficiality is not relegated to the more distant and contained sphere of content; it advances on the reader, expressing itself in direct, indirect, and narrative speech.

A closer examination of the languages constituting these works reveals the following set of basic relationships:[3]

Present—languages in place	Past/future—deposed languages
Scientific	Magical—not narrative
rational	irrational
rulers	ruled (by Cthulhu)
official	unofficial
false knowledge	real knowledge
American	foreign

Old High Literary—city
  rational/irrational
  rulers
  official/unofficial
  more real knowledge
  American

Rural—country
  irrational
  ruled
  unofficial
  most real knowledge
  American

Eighteenth-Century Conversational—
  city/country
  Age of Reason
  rulers
  unofficial now
  more real knowledge
  American/foreign

Cthulhu—alien
  irrational—no narrative
  rulers
  unofficial now
  most real knowledge
  foreign

The most powerful knowledge is provided by unofficial languages—the more unofficial, the better (Rural and Cthulhu). This represents horror's recognition that ideologies other than the dominant have a greater ability to make sense of the world simply because they are in dialogue with that world. Official languages, which guard their power so jealously, are not in dialogue with the world; they are capable only of shouting their power and alleged worth at it.

There exists a basic dichotomy between languages in place, on the one hand, and deposed languages, on the other. Neither category is composed solely of official or unofficial languages, but certainly officiality, especially in its Scientific avatar, dominates the present. Scientific is proved inadequate to the characters' actual experience through its interaction with Rural, as in Lovecraft's "The Colour out of Space," in which speakers of Rural keep alive the narrative truth that is "lost" by Scientific. The secondary narrator, rustic Ammi Pierce, can (with the narrator's help) tell the story of a meteorite from beginning to end, but the scientists who visit the site and take several samples of the object "lose" them—the samples literally disappear, and "in time the professors felt scarcely sure they had indeed seen [it] with waking eyes."[4] They cannot hold onto even the physical matter of unofficiality. When the Rural speakers ask the Scientific speakers for help, indicating the poisoning of their land and animals caused by the meteorite, their stories are disbelieved, and we are told "there was really nothing for serious men to do . . . , for superstitious rustics will say and believe anything."[5] Even at the story's end, the dust the scientists analyze initially gives off strange spectra but later does not—again, the truth of reality passes away in officiality's lethal grip. The language of power must reject anything unacceptable to its own narrative.

What is particularly interesting about Lovecraft's stories is that their narration is not a one-sided affair. The narrator often pieces his story together from salvaged artifacts of other languages—newspaper articles, notes, diaries, wire recordings, records, tapes, letters, even works of art— and sometimes collaborates with native speakers of other languages to make the story (rural folks in "The Colour out of Space" and "The Shadow over Innsmouth," an artist in "The Call of Cthulhu"). This latter sort of story telling is highly cooperative: "Often I had to recall the speaker from ramblings, piece out scientific points which he knew only by a fading parrot memory of professors' talk, or bridge over gaps, where his sense of logic and continuity broke down."[6] Both speakers possess only parts of the story; neither part is sufficient unto itself—each requires interaction with the other to be completed.

The narrator's own language is perhaps the most complex. It makes some bid for power by gesturing to the literary (references to Poe) and by its placement in the text—it is where we expect to meet literary language: the speech of the narrator. Poe's influence on Lovecraft is there (and, note, nowhere else) quite strong—his narrator's syntax strains under the load of prepositional phrases, adjectives in triplets, and double adverbial modifiers. Lovecraft, however, chooses not simply to duplicate but to refract Poe's language, adding archaisms that Poe did not use. What is then freshly produced points to a language obsolete, having lost its power (just as the archaisms, once part of official language, have been stripped of the power of that officiality). Thus an off-center version of a previously official language (a particular literary language) masquerades as official, as literary language. This seems to be an attempt to boost this language from unofficial to official status, a direction echoed in the stories' content and in the other languages, especially Cthulhu—the Old Ones once ruled (were official), now do not (and are totally unofficial and other), but try unceasingly to recapture power by refraction, by entering into dialogue.

Old High Literary is unique because it is a mediating language that can touch all others. Likewise, the combination of the familiar with the alien (archaisms) is reiterated in the direct speech of characters (combining languages). Even in what ought to be so familiar as to be invisible (narrative language), there is otherness. Rural language is historical, is memory. Although officiality permits it no credence, truth does not slip away from Rural. Eighteenth-Century Conversational is, similarly, the memory of the eighteenth century, and like Rural it represents access to other languages, such as Magic or Cthulhu. Scientific is the most powerful language in that it has the right to approve or disapprove the truth of the other languages; it has the right to disregard any other discourse, to have the last word. Cthulhu and Scientific seem unable to directly interact fruitfully; their relationship is much as that which exists between the geological display in "The Call of Cthulhu" and the informative shelf lining (newspaper) it rests upon.[7] Cthulhu must always burst Scientific apart as inadequate, a lie, because Scientific, as official, *pretends to know everything*. Readers will recognize this arrogance, which generally characterizes science when it is depicted in various forms of popular culture.

I have given the name Cthulhu, taken from Lovecraft's corpus, to the language associated with the Old Ones, godlike beings from another dimension. Its human speakers are generally as far from society's official center as the home of the Old Ones is from Earth; they are half-castes, rural "degenerates," mulattoes, and other social transgressors. While speakers (in this case, doers) of unofficiality in Poe break the law written in law books, Lovecraft's unofficial speakers break unwritten laws. They not only perform forbidden acts and speak forbidden words, they are themselves forbidden. Their language, full of brutal consonants, is ugly, but *it works*. No other language in Lovecraft's world is as potentially powerful; when Cthulhu is spoken, it invariably leads to some result (which cannot be said for Scientific, the power language in place).

Cthulhu is so unofficial and therefore so other that it is opaque to us. Such opacity shares nothing with the lumberings of Scientific ("Widmanstatten figures," for example),[8] for that impenetrability may be remedied with the aid of a good dictionary. Cthulhu itself is only the meanest approximation of a far richer communication. Far from signifying an underlying racism (the language of the unofficial other as gibberish), its use in these works implies that a completely other ideology has the capacity for great power; it can reveal secrets about our own world that are not otherwise accessible and can uncover worlds heretofore unknown and unknowable to any other language.

As Lovecraft claimed indebtedness to Poe, King pays tribute to Lovecraft (sometimes quite deliberately, as in "Jerusalem's Lot"). Lovecraft's attention to dialect becomes in King a focusing on idiolect. Like Lovecraft, King usually situates his tales in a relatively confined region of the United States, uses local color, and refers to a locality as if it were shared by the reader.

Nevertheless, the contrast between Lovecraft's prim narrative speech and King's rough-cut narrators, who employ no literary language at all, seems to permit no common ground to exist between them. King's narrators' speech is highly oral (sentences strung together with *and*, for instance) and is full of unofficial slang and obscenities. Yet it bears a direct relationship to Lovecraft's hothouse discourse. Both are unofficial languages elevated to the position normally occupied by literary language, and both therefore make some bid for officiality. Both draw attention to language, and both act as mediators, providing a network for various languages to interact. It is not uncommon for sentences in other languages to impinge on the narrator's speech in Old High Literary (and these fragments are usually more truthful), so in its tendency to lie (put forward false knowledge), Old High Literary preserves some aspect of officiality). In King these other languages may shatter into smaller fragments and salt themselves throughout the characters' speech. But it would be wrong to believe that this narrative is purely slang, lacking even the slightest tinge of elevated (and thus official) language; just as Lovecraft's narrative speech is an off-center version of literary, King's narrative speech is an off-center version of slang, an interpretation that refracts it through a literary lens: "The bulbs couldn't banish the twelve-year darkness; it could only push it back a little and cast a sickly yellow glow over the whole mess."[9] Here, the literary and almost biblical "banish the darkness" seasons the conversational "a little" and "the whole mess."

In our society, orality has never had the power of the written word; it is nearly as unofficial as Cthulhu, which is more often overheard than written and which at least sometimes is the approximation of a telepathic process. King's narrative speech, stretched further into unofficiality than oral tendencies would imply, is marked by the intrusion of thoughts. Rendered in italics, these generally utilize typeface to signify, and they often lack punctuation. It is here that some of the greatest tension between the official and the unofficial is created, for thought may contradict speech and thus take on the role of the unofficial, revealing the narrator's speech as inadequate to the situation: "'As I said, there was a slight problem . . .' *Yes. Horror, lunacy, and death. How's that for a slight problem, kids?*"[10] For a somewhat more subtle usage, where the insistence is on one's own word over the preferred (official) word for an item: The bathroom (*!basement!*) was built like an L.[11] It is as if the fact that spoken speech is being used to narrate officializes it enough to require another sort of "spoken" speech, thought, to deflate it, so that thought is to spoken as spoken is to written. This does not constitute a contradiction, as it seems that unofficiality and officiality are relative terms. So far I have not found evidence to show that one is inherently, structurally different from the other; no one has as yet examined this question.

Unofficiality in King is never as impenetrable as it can be in Lovecraft; there are no languages so other as to refuse to yield to our understanding, and King's characters are almost never of the "forbidden" sort that populate Lovecraft's world. Lovecraft's narrators' speech tends more toward the official, while King's world is generally much more *in* unofficiality than Lovecraft's; popular culture is celebrated and accepted as a vital aspect of the narrative of our lives. It is unlikely that an untranslatable unofficiality exists in a world so unofficial.

King, much more clearly than either Lovecraft or Poe, depicts the official as monstrous, the peddler of dangerously false knowledge, but just as in Lovecraft, officiality, whatever the version, pretends to know everything. Although Scientific exists in King and likewise leads to lethal consequences, official language is offered in more variety. Religiousness, for instance, is revealed as deadly in such figures as Mrs. Carmody of "The Mist" and the murderous children of "Children of the Corn," all of whom speak a version of King James Old Testament, heavy on Revelation.

If one looks at these authors in their chronological order, it is apparent that what increases is unofficiality itself, which moves from the background position of content in Poe to the middle ground with Lovecraft, occupying there the speech of the characters and tainting the narrator's language. It is in King that unofficiality takes over the narrative, dominating the narrator's language and manifesting itself even in his truth-telling thought. In all three, however, unofficiality is characterized by its constant attempts to engage in dialogue, to interact, and is generally associated with real knowledge—the truth of the story itself, of narrativity—while official language means bafflement (false knowledge), the inability to make sense, to make a story that fits the situation, because the ability to listen is lacking. A language combining these two, as does the narrative language of Lovecraft and King, brings to the foreground the very interaction that is so important to horror, that so characterizes it.

Notes

1. Risking perhaps legitimate charges of excessive formalism, one might say that horror actually tells and retells a chapter of literary history—that fractious time when many-voiced romanticism, still unofficial, fought it out with the droning officiality that was monologic neoclassicism.

2. K. A. Hohne, "*Skaz* [dialect story] and Babel's *Konarmija* [Red cavalry]" (Ph.D. diss., Indiana University, 1986). Notice that unofficiality's deviance is characterized in Lovecraft as "unspeakable," calling to mind that which is permitted no voice as well as the forbidden and perverted; that is, to be criminalized is to be voiceless, and vice versa.

3. Examples from H. P. Lovecraft, *The Dunwich Horror and Other Stories* (Sauk City, Wisc.: Arkham House, 1963).

   Scientific: "It had acted quite unbelievably in that well-ordered laboratory; doing nothing at all and showing no occluded gases when heated on charcoal, being wholly negative in the borax bead, and soon proving itself absolutely non-volatile at any producible temperature, including that of the oxy-hydrogen blowpipe" (p. 64).

   Magical embedded in Old High Literary: "Night would soon fall, and it was then that the mountainous blasphemy lumbered up its eldritch course. *Negotium perambulans in tenebris* . . . The old librarian rehearsed the formulae" (p. 192).

   Eighteenth-Century Conversational: "wherein there were a Rattling and Rolling, Growning, Screeching, and Hissing, such as no Things of this Earth cou'd raise up" (p. 162).

   Rural: "*some day yew folks'll hear a child o' Lavinny's a-callin' its father's name on the top o' Sentinel Hill!*" (p. 165).

   Cthulhu: "*Ygnaiih . . . ygnaiih . . . thflthkh'ngha . . . Yog-Sothoth*" (p. 200).

4. Ibid., p. 66.

5. Ibid., p. 69.

6. Ibid., p. 63.

7. Ibid., p. 149. The inadequacy of scientific study is repeated elsewhere, as in "Call of Cthulhu," pp. 139, 146, 150.

8. Ibid., p. 65.

9. Stephen King, *Night Shift* (New York: Signet New American Library, 1978), p. 39.

10. Stephen King, *Skeleton Crew* (New York: Signet New American Library, 1985), p. 242.

11. Ibid., p. 156.

Chapter 7

The Soul of the Plot:
The Aesthetics of Fin de Siècle
Literature of Horror

Susan J. Navarette

> Out of the secret places of a unique temperament he brought forth strange blossoms and fruits hitherto unknown; and for him, the novel impression conveyed, the exquisite effect woven, counted as an end in itself: a perfect end.
> —Walter Pater, "Leonardo da Vinci" (1873)

H. G. Wells referred to the 1890s as "a good and stimulating period for a short story writer"; "short stories," he claimed, "broke out everywhere." [1] The unprecedented growth and popularity of the short story genre in the last decades of the nineteenth century correlates with an increase not merely in the number but also in the literary quality of stories of horror and the supernatural. Unlike the late (and increasingly formulaic) Gothic romances that were their ancestors, late Victorian stories of the supernatural were remarkably diverse and frequently experimental, emerging, as E. F. Bleiler has suggested, in a "shower of different forms, with many different types of association with the supernatural." [2] Their appearance marked the sort of significant development in literary form that Terry Eagleton, quoting Leon Trotsky, saw as having "evolved under the pressure of an inner need, of a collective psychological demand," itself deriving from "significant changes in ideology" within a culture.[3] The gradual impact of contemporary scientific theory—which, in all of its various incarnations, seemed to be characterized by a dysteleological emphasis on fragmentation, variability, and entropy—brought about shifts in social and ideological perspectives within nineteenth-century English culture and society. Distilled, in part, in the alembic of a cultural consciousness thus tempered by an attritive sense of dislocation, futility, and alienation, the emergent literary forms and movements bear the mark of the cultural anguish of which they are the peculiar expression. Two of these—fin de siècle literature of horror and the decadent movement, which took root in England in the last decades of the nineteenth century—share certain striking and mutually revealing similarities.

Although many of those who called themselves decadent differed wildly in their sense of what the term entailed, decadent literature in general was heralded as a genre celebrating the abnormal beauty of disease—what Charles Baudelaire called "la phosphorescence de la pourriture" (the phosphorescence of decay); it was further characterized by a morbid attention to form and a perversity that arose out of the conjunction of ingenious, complicated, and "jeweled" language and the repulsive and sometimes morally repugnant ideas conveyed by that language.[4] (*Jeweled* is, of course, a subjective term; I mean the sort of fevered, hallucinatory prose indulged in by Matthew Phipps Shiel in such works as "Xélucha" [1896], in which he wrote, for example: "Warmed, he did not refuse the revel, the dance, the darkened chamber. It was utterly black, rayless; approached by a secret passage; in shape circular; the air hot, haunted always by odours of balms, bdellium, hints of dulcimer and flute; and radiated round with a hundred thick-strewn ottomans of morocco."[5]) In a letter to the editor of the *Yellow Book*, Max Beerbohm hinted that a dynamic existed in the decadent style between form and content, for he saw decadent literature as characterized by "paradox and *marivaudage,* lassitude, love of horror and all unusual things, a love of argot and archaism and the mysteries of style."[6] In the preface to an edition of Charles Baudelaire's *Les Fleurs du mal* (1857), Théophile Gautier defined the "new" style—he was loath to call it decadent—as one that strives to take "colours from all palettes, [and] notes from all keyboards" in order to convey "in . . . new forms and words that have not yet been heard . . . the subtle confidences of neurosity, . . . the confessions of aging lust turning into depravity, and . . . the odd hallucinations of fixed ideas passing into madness."[7]

In emphasizing the characteristic lassitude, neurosity, depravity, and madness of decadent literature, Gautier's comments, as well as Beerbohm's, underscore the fact that the decadent style was symptomatic of what Arthur Symons, in his essay "The Decadent Movement in Literature" (1893), described as the *"malaise fin de siècle."*[8] Edmond and Jules de Goncourt traced the source of this "modern melancholy"—which they also referred to as *"la névrose"*[9]—to a misplaced faith in the concept of progress: "Do you know," they asked, "if the sadness of the century does not come from overwork, movement, tremendous effort, furious labor, from its cerebral forces strained to the breaking point, from overproduction in every domain?"[10] Other decadents saw it as a function of a growing dissatisfaction among the younger generation, who, impatient with the ossified traditions and attitudes of the past, staged a "revolt," according to Symons, "from the bondage of traditional form, of a form become rigid."[11] It seems clear, however, that this malaise, or cultural anxiety, was produced largely by the ongoing revision of the social and physical sciences; indeed, the very terms and phrases employed to address the issue are consistently physiological or psychological in nature. The Hungarian physician Max Nordau, for example, compared the *"fin de siècle* mood" to "the impotent despair of a sick man, who feels himself dying by inches in the midst of an eternally living nature blooming insolently for ever."[12]

In the concluding chapter of his study of the Italian Renaissance, Walter Pater warned that experience had been "reduced to a group of impressions," themselves "unstable, flickering, inconsistent," and that therefore a "counted number of pulses only is given to us of a variegated, dramatic life."[13] Although the origins of the statement are complex, it seems clear that it functioned as a veiled and anxious response to scientific evidence—to Lord Kelvin's second law of thermodynamics, Balfour Stewart's "elementary treatise" on the conservation of energy, Sir Charles Lyell's theory of uniformitarianism, and, of course, the theory of biological evolution advanced by Charles Darwin and others writing both before and after him—which suggests that all things inherently tend toward a state of dissolution, fragmentation, and entropy.[14] In short, it had begun to appear that man inhabited a world that H. P. Lovecraft later characterized in "The Silver Key" (1939) as a "blind cosmos" grinding "aimlessly on from nothing to something and from something back to nothing again," heedless of the "minds that flicker for a second now and then in the darkness."[15] Pater proposed that the only way to recover what had been lost through what Barton L. St. Armand called the "progressive desacramentalization of the modern world through rationalism, science, and technology" was "[to] burn always with this hard, gemlike flame, to maintain this ecstasy," and to embody this sensual experience in a style that represented "a total gesture of the whole personality"; in essence, to counter, as Clive Scott put it, "the variable transmissions from the world with one's own variability." [16]

In a general sense, then, cultural attitudes and aesthetic trends are precipitated by, or at least correspond to, trends in contemporary science. The decadent movement in literature, for example, could be said to have evolved out of the collective need of those artists who sought to preserve the integrity of their individual "dream of a world"—an artistic vision they sought to endow with an inviolable permanence in a world of relative values. To those more concerned with cultural decadence, the form and style of the typically decadent text testified to the presence of atavistic and retrogressive tendencies within certain individual members of a species and thus represented a manifestation of one of those latent "reactionary curves," which, according to the nineteenth-century Italian criminologist Cesare Lombroso, even the most privileged peoples must inevitably describe.[17] Max Nordau's *Entartung* (*Degeneration*), a translation of which appeared in England in 1895, represents one of the more popular treatments of cultural degeneration, a notion that had been in the air at least since the mid-nineteenth century. In it, Lombroso's student and disciple explores the manner in which the characteristics of retrogressive atavism might reveal themselves in the individual whose pronounced aesthetic sensibility or intellectual capacity—what Lombroso defined simply as genius—could be seen as an indication of "neurotic degeneration." [18] Though one might search in vain for the physiognomic signs of decadence—gigantic stature, submicrocephalism, or a distorted sense of hearing—in Gautier, Baudelaire, Joris-Karl Huysmans, or Oscar Wilde, Nordau nevertheless viewed each of these writers as a *"morbid deviation from the original type,"* a "repulsive *lusus naturæ*" (16–24). He argued that one would find the counterpart to the "asymmetry of face and cranium" characteristic of the "born criminal" element in the abnormal mental physiognomy of these "higher degenerates" or "graphomaniacs." [19] They differ from other men in their atrophied sense of morality, their "unbounded egoism," their "impulsiveness," their "emotionalism" and "pessimism," and their "contempt for the world and men" (18–19). According to Nordau, it was unnecessary to know, for example, that Baudelaire died of general paralysis following a lapse into insanity, for "even if no such horrible end had protected the diagnosis from all attack, there would be no doubt as to its accuracy, seeing that Baudelaire showed all the mental stigmata of degeneration during the whole of his life" (284).

Although individual decadents and aesthetes no doubt took exception to some of the conclusions drawn by physicians such as Nordau and Lombroso, they nevertheless would have agreed with the former that a work of art, whose primary function is the "self-deliverance of the artist," is "psycho-physiologically accurate" to the extent that within it are encoded the psychological and physiological characteristics of its maker (324). In Gautier's description of the "new" style, for example, Nordau found evidence to support his belief that the "decadent language" is in fact an extension of a

mystically degenerate mind, with its shifting nebulous ideas, its fleeting formless shadowy thought, its perversions and aberrations, its tribulations and impulsions. To express this state of mind, a new and unheard-of language must in fact be found, since there cannot be in any customary language designations corresponding to presentations which in reality do not exist. (300)

He argued that a text, like the mind that produced it, displays certain consistent traits by means of which it announces the predisposition of its maker: quoting Lombroso, he alleged that "if they are painters . . . then their predominant attribute will be the colour-sense; they will be decorative. If they are poets, they will be rich in rhyme, brilliant in style, but barren of thought; sometimes they will be 'decadents' " (24). Incriminating as he intended to be, Nordau probably came closer to disclosing the true motivation behind the decadents' devotion to form and technique than did T. S. Eliot when, in an appreciation of Baudelaire, he hazarded the guess that "the care for perfection of form, among some of the romantic poets of the nineteenth century, was an effort to support, or to conceal from view, an inner disorder."[20] As Symons announced in his study of the decadent movement, "Healthy we cannot call it, and healthy it does not wish to be considered."[21]

Acutely conscious of language, the decadent writer, rather than *describing* his emotional state, engendered his prose with his neurosis. Thus the truly decadent story, poem, or text conveys beauty, disease (which is also dis-ease), or tension not in any traditional sense—through characterization or plot—but rather in the very complexity of its form: in the contours, shadows, and rhythms created by language itself. In *The Picture of Dorian Gray* (1891), for example, Basil Hallward acknowledges that his is an age in which men treat art "as if it were meant to be a form of autobiography," a notion Wilde paraphrased in the preface to the work when he wrote that the "highest as the lowest form of criticism is a mode of autobiography."[22] One arrives at meaning, then, in isolated works of fin de siècle literature by reading the encoded signs and "stigmata," as well as the accompanying themes and ideas, just as Lombroso searched for physical traits, and Nordau for psychological ones, in order to "read" the body and thereby predict human behavior.

The idea of decadence, as well as the decadent style, appealed to fin de siècle horror writers because it established a necessary dynamic between external forms and internal (or even cosmic) disorders. Like the Gothic romance itself, which Maurice Levy described as "an expression of the anguish engendered by the historical context," these later stories attempt to delineate and discover the source of the psychological fears and sense of cultural anxiety that impelled their creators to experiment with this "underground" genre.[23] In one sense, many late nineteenth-century stories of horror and the supernatural are "decadent" precisely because they derive their themes and attendant leitmotifs from popular reinterpretations of scientific theories that had served to undermine the High Victorian faith in the inherent stability and continued advancement of man and his society. The fear that such theories engendered in the popular mind was expressed by Thomas Henry Huxley in the Prolegomena he published a year after he delivered his controversial Romanes lecture, "Evolution and Ethics" (1893): "[Man] may develop a worthy civilization, capable of maintaining and constantly improving itself, until the evolution of our globe shall have entered so far upon its downward course that the cosmic process resumes its sway; and, once more, the State of Nature prevails over the surface of our planet."[24] Lovecraft's later assertion that the "most terrible conception of the human brain" must necessarily derive from "a malign and particular suspension or defeat of those fixed laws of Nature which are our only safeguard against the assaults of chaos and the daemons of unplumbed space" surely originated in the surviving vestigial remnants of an anxiety sustained by his Victorian precursors, who feared that their laws governing human behavior and the systems of belief—once considered fixed and stable—would be exploded, just as man's faith in his innate biological superiority, in his anthropocentric worldview, and in the finely balanced (and divinely sanctioned) workings of his universe had been.[25]

The suspension of those "fixed laws of Nature" had its counterpart in the corresponding suspension of the fixed laws of narrative structure, linguistic stability, and authorial credibility. Late nineteenth-century horror stories are to be distinguished from many of their Gothic precursors to the extent that their creators subscribed to Poe's dictum that "terror is not of Germany but of the soul."[26] Under the tutelage of the decadents, the creators of fin de siècle horror became anatomists of the imagination, incorporating a style of writing that, in its pursuit of irregular, beautiful forms and miasmic atmospheres, recommended itself as the medium best capable of embodying internal madness and degeneration. Highly polished and carefully wrought, their surface beauty and seductive charm mask, if only initially, what Gautier enumerated as "the larvae of superstitions, the haggard phantoms of insomnia, nocturnal terrors, . . . obscure phantasies at which the daylight would stand amazed, and all that the soul conceals of the dark, the unformed, and the vaguely horrible, in its deepest and furthest recesses."[27] Furthermore, it could generate within the reader what Victor Hugo designated the *frisson nouveau:* the instinctive, visceral shudder provoked by the presence of something monstrous or uncanny in the very lines and proportions of a text. In this fashion they learned to create what Lovecraft, an admirer and occasionally an imitator of fin de siècle horror writers such as Oscar Wilde, Matthew Phipps Shiel, and Arthur Machen, described as "the actual anatomy of the terrible or the physiology of fear." This physiology was constructed, he wrote, out of "the exact sort of lines and proportions that connect up with the latent instincts or hereditary memories of fright, and the proper colour contrasts and lighting effects to stir the dormant sense of strangeness."[28] In this sense, decadent horror writers saw themselves not as fantasists but as true realists; they were depicting not the vulgar reality that was crudely visible to the unlessoned eye but rather what Symons had identified as "*la vérité vraie,* the very essence of truth—the truth of . . . the visible world to the eyes that see it; and the truth of spiritual things to the spiritual vision."[29]

Oscar Wilde's Basil Hallward is one such realist. In his portrait of Dorian Gray—the "best work of [his] life" (12) as he terms it—Hallward has learned to "recreate life in a way that was hidden from [him] before" (12), for his idealized subject's presence is felt, in that canvas and even more pervasively in others in which he does not figure at all, "in the curves of certain lines, in the loveliness and subtleties of certain colours. That is all" (13). Hallward's masterpiece is one of two poisonous texts in Oscar Wilde's *Picture of Dorian Gray*, both of which exercise a fatal influence over those who come into contact with them. The portrait is also one of a long line of similarly poisonous or fatal "texts," beginning with Cornelius Agrippa's magic book and including such nineteenth- and twentieth-century incarnations as Robert W. Chambers's *The King in Yellow*, Lovecraft's *Necro-nomicon*, and even Kurtz's deceptively dangerous essay written on behalf of the International Society for the Suppression of Savage Customs, all three of which are described as possessing mind-altering qualities. Critical attention has tended to focus on what is actually the less esoteric of the two texts that figure in Wilde's story: the infamous "yellow" book which Lord Wotton sends to Dorian and which is generally taken to be the fount and inspiration of Dorian's excesses. Yet, as Dorian himself insists, it is "the fatal portrait to which all his misery had been due" (138).

Unlike the story's yellow book, which, with its "curious jewelled style" and its "monstrous" metaphors, provides him with a *prescribed* pattern of hedonistic behavior—an inverted status quo, as it were—the portrait merely *hints* at what Dorian himself is capable of doing by revealing in its very lines and contours the monstrous nature of what he has already done. Although pained, initially, to consider the "desecration that was in store for the fair face on the canvas" (93), Dorian is less intrigued by the ever-degenerating image than by his inability to discern the subtle means by which the canvas testifies to his morbid metamorphosis:

Was there some subtle affinity between the chemical atoms, that shaped them-selves into form and colour on the canvas, and the soul that was within him? Could it be that what that soul thought, they realized?—that what it dreamed, they made true? Or was there some other, more terrible reason? He shuddered, and felt afraid, and, going back to the couch, lay there, gazing at the picture in sickened horror. (84)

Wishing to believe that "form and colour tell us of form and colour—that is all," and that "art conceals the artist far more completely than it ever re-veals him" (101), Basil falls victim to the same horrified fascination when, recognizing the brushwork but not the subject of his canvas, he deduces that the "surface seemed to be quite undisturbed, and as he had left it" pre-cisely because "the foulness and horror had come" from within: "Through some strange quickening of inner life the leprosies of sin were slowly eating the thing away" (136).

The picture functions, then, as an idiosyncratic confession of "aging lust turning into depravity," embodying the unique stigmata of Dorian's own spiritual degeneracy. The ostensible subject is Dorian Gray, more particu-larly his face, the wonderful beauty of which Lord Wotton had earlier described as "a form of Genius . . . higher, indeed, than Genius" (22). The portrait is, however, psychophysiologically accurate (to borrow Nordau's term for *any* work of art) in the sense that it embodies not merely or even primarily Dorian's "genius" but Basil's as well. Basil has managed to do what Lord Henry Wotton covertly longs to do: to "project one's soul into some gracious form, and let it tarry there for a moment" (34). Fearing that it is inscribed with the very "secret of [his] own soul" (8)—a secret he at first refuses to bare "to [the] shallow, prying eyes" (13) of the world—Basil decides to exhibit the picture in Paris only after he rids himself of "the intolerable fascination of its presence" and therefore of the persistent belief that "every flake and film of colour seemed to [him] to reveal [his] secret" (100). Thus infused and made animate with the life-force of its maker, the portrait seems to assume an independent existence, or so Dorian begins to suspect when he remarks that there "is something fatal about a portrait. It has a life of its own" (102).

An important prototype of the decadent horror story, *The Picture of Dorian Gray* treats thematically a number of ideas that influenced the stylistic and aesthetic choices made in later, and more sophisticated, works of decadent horror literature. In spite of the fact that it was one of the first stories to broach the subject of cultural decadence and its attendant stylistic analogue, however, Wilde's portrait is not the quintessential decadent horror story that critics have generally taken it to be. It does, of course, possess many of the earmarks of the genre. It gives a "decadent" treatment to a traditional supernatural theme or motif—in this case, the motif of the doppelgänger that arises as the spectral, subconscious other in such early supernatural fiction as Poe's "William Wilson" (1839), but that reemerges as the latent Darwinian type in later works such as Robert Louis Stevenson's *The Strange Case of Dr. Jekyll and Mr. Hyde* (1886). In other respects, however, it is less characteristic of the typical decadent horror story, which often mines scientific theory for its themes and leitmotifs (Wilde hinted only once that Dorian's behavior might have been dictated by something akin to genetic determinism), and which stresses concision (*Dorian Gray* is a novel), a decorated and self-consciously patterned style (Wilde alluded to jeweled language but only occasionally employed it), and, in its later incarnation, narrative fragmentation (in spite of its aphoristic tendencies, Wilde's text is fairly cohesive in a structural sense).

Like *Dorian Gray*, Walter de la Mare's hitherto suppressed horror story "A: B: O.," written around 1895, exemplifies the dynamic that exists between horror and beauty. "A: B: O." owes its themes and leitmotifs to its cultural milieu. More specifically, it reflects its young author's imperfect understanding of but powerful response to nineteenth-century scientific theory, and in this sense is an apt example of what de la Mare, in another context, described (most ironically, as will shortly be clear) as "the still-born, . . . the dejected inmates of the 2d. box," which "simply because they served their temporary purpose, but no other, are saliently characteristic of their day" because they "could have come into being only when and where they did."[30] "A: B: O." concerns two antiquarians, Dugdale and Pelluther, who discover a map that reveals the resting place of "Antiquities" and set about excavating Dugdale's garden, the site of the supposed buried treasure. After a good deal of digging, hauling, and scraping, the two unearth an old metal chest inscribed with a partially effaced cryptogram: "A: B: O." Prying open the lid of the chest, they find a shriveled creature covered with "coarse fawn hair"; its skull and features bear a "hideous and ungodly resemblance to the human face."[31] Although it has been buried for many years, the creature is still alive, its casket having been provided with a metal tube—a ghastly umbilical cord of sorts—which links it with a yew tree overhead. The two men decide to reinter their "treasure," but the creature escapes them and roams at will throughout London. In the end, Pelluther returns to Dugdale's house only to discover that his friend, now hopelessly insane, has taken the place of the homunculus within the chest.

In forcing us to decipher the cryptogram—which is both the partially effaced word that serves as the story's title and the text itself—and thus to determine the exact correlation between "A: B: O." and the homunculus, de la Mare has established a rather uncomfortable kinship between the reader and the story's main characters, who are, after all, pedants, antiquaries, professors, seekers after forbidden knowledge—the protagonists most favored by horror writers. The two men had believed that their map recorded the burial place of antiquities, perhaps "Old Roman, or Druidical" artifacts. Their treasure is, instead, something that is loathsome and inspires loathing—it is an *abo*mination. De la Mare's emphasis of its human characteristics, however, invites further speculation. Does the chest contain some sort of "*abo*riginal" in the sense of "primitive," or, as *The Oxford English Dictionary* has it, "first or earliest so far as history or science gives record?"[32] Remarkably hirsute, with its "coarse fawn hair," "coarse lashes," and "tangled eyebrow," the creature shows an uncanny resemblance to the early progenitors of man, who, according to Darwin in *The Descent of Man* (1871), were "born hairy and remained so during life."[33] Darwin's seminal 1859 publication, as St. Armand reminded us, "had as much impact on horror fiction as it did on the debate between science and religion, since Darwin's theory of evolution allowed for the possibility of new fictional monsters": the newest and, thematically, the most promising monster being, of course, man himself.[34] De la Mare further correlated the A: B: O. with a throwback, or reversion to type, by characterizing its face as being "thrown back a little," a description that suggests not merely the relation of the head to the body but the relation of the creature to man's elusive forebears.

Various clues in the story, however, point to one other interpretation of the inscrutable acronym—one that is related to the notion of an aboriginal. Our suspicions are confirmed when, rather late in the story, the narrator has a kind of ghastly epiphany and stammers suddenly "abortion—A-B-O, abortion; I knew then" (104). (Perhaps we even know the gender of the aborted fetus, which may have been "*a boy*.") The very shape and physical bearing of the creature attest to the idea that it is a rudimentary human being that has, in spite of its apparent frailty, somehow defied premature death.

De la Mare was not the first author to make human embryos and aborted fetuses the centerpiece of his fictive creations. In "The Peach in Brandy," for example, one of the tales collected in Horace Walpole's privately printed *Hieroglyphic Tales* (1785), the archbishop of Tuum stifles a violent coughing fit by gulping down what he takes to be a medicinal fruit—a peach in brandy—without knowing that the "restorative" is in fact one of the twins that the queen-mother just recently aborted and which her conscientious butler caught up in a glass. Not surprisingly, the image of abortion appealed to the decadents, and to Aubrey Beardsley in particular, whose illustrations of this period (many of which de la Mare would surely have known) are rife with what the artist himself termed embryos who had "survived the abortion."[35] Embryonic creatures creep into his illustrations for *Lucian's True History* (1894), and a decadent Madonna bestows a lazy smile on a human fetus in a drawing called "Incipit Vita Nova" (c. 1893). Human embryos emerge in some of Beardsley's illustrations for *Salome* (1894) and various vignettes from *Bon Mots* (1893), while his original "Design" for Saint Paul's depicts an embryo under glass, a subject of study for the genteel young woman seated beside it. Also apt is Beardsley's "Vignette of Lamb and Jerrold," whose fetus, in spite of the fact that he sports gentleman's garb, serves as an example of unaccommodated man.

Malcolm Easton has speculated that Beardsley may have taken as his model the eight-week-old embryo depicted in volume 3 of Wilhelm His's *Anatomie menschlicher Embyonen* (1885) and later in *Gray's Anatomy* (17th ed.), since a copy of either or both medical works would very likely have had a place in his grandfather's library.[36] De la Mare's homunculus seems to owe its inception to the new biology as well. Arrested in the course of development, the A: B: O.'s shape and physical bearing attest to a theory advanced by the German zoologist Ernst Heinrich Haeckel in his *History of Creation* (1867). Haeckel's theory that ontogeny recapitulates phylogeny—which was derived from the theory of evolution and was very much in the air at the turn of the century—states that the developmental stages of an organism recapitulate, or repeat, the evolutionary history of its species. If we are uncomfortable with the idea that the creature, as aboriginal, *resembles* man in his earliest incarnation, we are shocked to realize that, with its coarse fawn hair, it *is* a human being which, having been caught off guard, so to speak, in the middle of its period of gestation, discloses its inherent bestiality. Similarly monstrous progeny make their appearance in works such as Arthur Machen's "The Three Imposters" (1895), in which the reader encounters Jervase Cradock, out of whose body a "slimy, wavering tentacle" extends; or H. G. Wells's *Island of Dr. Moreau* (1896), with its Beast Folk; or H. P. Lovecraft's "The Dunwich Horror" (1929), whose Wilbur Whateley is "partly human . . . with very manlike hands and head," but whose "torso and lower parts of the body were teratologically fabulous."[37]

Confusion, indefinition, and destabilization are integral both to phylogenetics (the idea on which de la Mare's story is premised) and to evolutionary biology in general—popular treatments, or even distortions, of which are present to a greater or lesser degree in many late nineteenth-century horror stories. Their subjects are *unheimlich* to the extent that necessary dichotomies are destabilized and polarities are conflated. In *The Powers of Horror*, Julia Kristeva defined this kind of horror—which she called abjection—not as that which embodies a "lack of cleanliness or health" but as that which "disturbs identity, system, order. What does not respect borders, positions, rules. The in-between, the ambiguous, the composite."[38] Kristeva has defined her study as "an essay on abjection"; curiously, *The Oxford English Dictionary* reminds us that *abjection* refers both to the thing degraded and to the feeling of degradation that it engenders. Pelluther and Dugdale are not merely repulsed by what they find, they are infected with the creature's abjection, for their exposure to the A: B: O. triggers manifestations of their own latent animalism. Aware that he is wrestling with "a dim skulking horror of soul and an inhuman depravity," Pelluther realizes that all of his senses are dead except for that of hearing, of which he notes that he felt his "ears move and twitch, with the help of some ancient muscle . . . long disused by humanity" (99–100). Darwin speculated that our anthropoid ancestors were not merely covered with hair but that their "ears were probably pointed, and capable of movement."[39] Much later, having returned to Dugdale's house to help rebury the A: B: O., Pelluther finds that his friend has substituted himself for the homunculus. Although he is neither misshapen nor hairy, Dugdale has by the story's end reverted (psychologically at least) to type. In his altered mental capacities, this cultured man of letters—Pelluther describes him as a "benevolent kindly gentleman . . . fine in intellect . . . eccentric—not mad" (108)—seems to lend credence to Lombroso's theory that genius is merely a form of neurotic degeneration, and that we are just as likely to find that a recurrence of atavism, rather than a "continuous rise to immeasurable heights of civilization," represents the future condition of any highly developed culture.[40]

The portrayal of Dugdale's descent into madness provides us with the second, and the more shocking, of the two climaxes in the story. Huddled in the casket and clutching a Bible to his side, he asks,

What is life, Pelluther? A vain longing for death. What is beauty? A question of degree. And sin is in the air,—child of diseases and death and springing-up and hatred of life. Fawn hair has beauty and as for bones; surely less for the worms. Worms! through lead? Pelluther, my dear old Pell. Through lead?

. . . You see, it is when a deep abstract belief rots into loathing, when hope is eaten away by horrors of sleep and a mad longing for sleep—Mad! Yet fawn hair is not without beauty; provided, Pelluther, provided—through lead? (107–8)

Dugdale's insanity is inscribed in the prose of his final speech. His rantings—enigmatic and prophetic, yet susceptible of reconstruction—reveal that he has undergone a kind of inverted conversion experience, an instance of spiritual degeneration. In his analysis of a type designated "the sick soul" in *The Varieties of Religious Experience* (1902), William James described both "the phenomenon of conversion or religious regeneration" and its opposite, the overwhelming burden of knowledge "of the consciousness of evil."[41] The healthy-minded person, according to James, enjoys the former state, and in his eyes a "new heaven seems to shine upon a new earth." To the individual suddenly arrested by an irremediable sense of the absolute meaninglessness and absurdity of life, however, the face of nature is transfigured "in the reverse direction": "The world now looks remote, strange, sinister, uncanny. Its color is gone, its breath is cold, there is no speculation in the eyes it glares with. . . . 'I weep false tears, I have unreal hands:

the things I see are not real things.' Such are expressions that naturally rise to the lips of melancholy subjects describing their changed state."[42] Dugdale is one such melancholy subject whose dramatically altered state is the result of an inverted conversion experience, an instance of religious *degeneration*.

Having penetrated the veil of the invisible world, Dugdale acquires the spiritual insight—or, rather, the alternate state of consciousness—which the decadents, according to Symons, so earnestly sought. The *vérité vraie* Dugdale stumbles across, however, transforms him into a raving lunatic and strips him of the abilities the Victorians valued so highly: the ability to be rational, to maintain one's wits in the face of unfathomable darkness (and, implicitly, to deny that such darkness exists), and to make sense of what was, one had finally to admit, utterly incomprehensible. As David Punter, commenting on a related horror story, argued, "the visitation which liberates the human being from the repression of false assumptions also destroys the barriers which retain human individuation: the liberation of desire returns man to his primal association with the beast and destroys his soul."[43] Even as his madness impends, Dugdale knows that his systems and codes have crumbled and that he is lost: "Science," he says, "is slunk away shamefaced; religion is a withered flower. Oh, my friend, what shall I say! How shall I regain myself?" (107).

Arthur Machen was another author who believed that "everything visible was . . . but the veil of a quickening and adorable secret."[44] "The Great God Pan" (1890), for example, portrays characters who penetrate the veil of the visible world and acquire insight into a world that, though "more splendid and more awful than we used to dream,"[45] affords them a final (and destructive) glimpse not of divine grace and salvation but of horror and damnation. "The Great God Pan" tells the story of Helen Vaughan, the daughter of a latter-day Mary, a woman who had been the subject of a surgical procedure that leveled the solid wall of intervening "sense" and allowed her to see the great god Pan. Before she dies, Mary, whose moment of ecstasy in the presence of Pan gives way to lunacy, bears a daughter sired by the goat god; Helen is therefore half human and half beast. Machen's description of Helen's genesis, and particularly of her death throes, in which she undergoes a kind of accelerated reverse phylogeny—her form wavering from sex to sex, descending to the bestial and then reverting to protoplasm—attests to the fact that, like de la Mare, Machen's notion of cultural decadence was shaped in part by his awareness of contemporary emphases in evolutionary biology, which in this story are sensationalized.[46]

Machen surpassed Wilde and de la Mare in his effort to coordinate style and theme, form and idea, and thereby established a dynamic between decadent style and the theme of decay. Like Helen Vaughan's body, the narrative structure of "The Great God Pan" is destabilized and degenerative; Machen's is an "abject" text. The story consists of eight apparently randomly ordered episodes—only much later does it become clear that they are in fact linked. Perhaps more unsettling than the erratic manner in which the story progresses, however, are the lacunae that disrupt the narrative, for "The Great God Pan" is rife with ellipses and omissions, and nowhere is this more striking than in the record of Helen Vaughan's death, which is textually corrupt, incomprehensible in those passages in which the attending physician's terror precludes him from writing legibly or from describing the indescribable. Decadence manifests itself in "The Great God Pan," then, to the extent that the integrity of the narrative structure dissolves before the reader's eyes. The breaks and disruptions in the plot are stylistic signposts of internal, linguistic decay, precisely analogous to the cultural and biological dissolution it describes.

In employing the decadent style in this fashion, Machen implicates his readers in the evolving horror of the text by forcing them to become coconspirators in its creation. His stylistic strategies are similar to those of Henry James, who, explaining the method behind the madness in *The Turn of the Screw* (1898), speculated that "so long as the events are veiled . . . the imagination will run riot and depict all sorts of horrors, but as soon as the veil is lifted, all mystery disappears."[47] Wilde echoed this very idea in the preface to *Dorian Gray,* in which he pointed out that "it is the spectator, and not life, that art really mirrors" (3). In "The Great God Pan," we are forced to fill in the lacunae with material drawn from our own reserves of anxiety and thus cross the line that safely demarcates the fictional world from our own. We are trapped in a nightmare realm which we have unwittingly helped to create, and we encounter there our subconscious, absent other, the existence of whose "hereditary instinct," as Lovecraft called it—the "actual physiological fixation of the old instincts in our nervous tissue"— we tend to deny.[48]

Decadent style manifests itself in a very different but no less effective manner in the supernatural stories of the now largely forgotten Matthew Phipps Shiel. Bleiler detected in Shiel's stories the "conventions of the cultural episode"—the invocation of the decorated style and an obsession with artifice and the "closely hewn metaphysics of horror."[49] In a story such as "Xélucha," for example, Shiel's theme is what Poe referred to in "The Philosophy of Composition" as "the *most* melancholy" and "the most poetical topic in the world": "the death of . . . a beautiful woman."[50] In fact, Shiel's story is a decadent reworking of Poe's already decadent "Ligeia" (1838), recounting the post-mortem experiences of the eponymous Xélucha. (Poe, of course, exerted a considerable influence on decadents and aesthetes as well as on fin de siècle writers, a fact Nordau claimed was only to be expected given that Poe was "gifted but mentally-deranged" [286].) Named after Prosper Merimée, the nineteenth-century French man of letters called by Symons a "cultivated sensualist," the narrator of Shiel's tale happens upon a packet of forgotten letters written by his friend Cosmo, whom he remembers as "the very tsar and maharajah of the Sybarites."[51] Shortly before his death (which occurred in a "balneum of malachite" with "water as a coverlet" [6]—in his bath, that is), Cosmo had written to Merimée praising the seductive charms of Xélucha, whom he saw as the embodiment of the Eternal Feminine but whom we recognize as the typical fin de siècle femme fatale, the Whore of Babylon, the destroying bitch-goddess much beloved of the decadents.

Having rekindled his memories of his dead acquaintances, Merimée sets out on one of his habitual midnight rambles through London, here as in most other decadent horror stories portrayed as a necropolis, a city of dreadful night. In the course of his wanderings he meets a gorgeous woman who reminds him of "Parvati, mound-hipped love-goddess of the luscious fancy of the Brahmin" (7). Gradually, however, we become aware that she is Xélucha, returned from the dead in order to destroy Merimée, whom she had once described to Cosmo as a destroyer of women. He follows her to an abandoned house, and she lures him into a room that impresses him with its "gorgeousness not less than Assyrian." Merimée tells us that "an ivory couch at the far end [of the chamber] was made sun-like by a head-piece of chalcedony forming a sea for the sport of emerald ichthyosauri. Copper hangings, panelled with mirrors in iasperated crystal, corresponded with a dome of flame and copper" (9–10). Incongruous pieces of furniture—a tin candlestick holder containing an old soiled curve of tallow, and a grimy chair, "mean, all wood," with one leg "shorter than its fellows"—suggest to the reader, though not to Merimée, that he is the victim of an illusion. Intent on driving him mad, Xélucha, still unrecognized by Merimée, discourses on metaphysical horrors, at length revealing that the portion of the buried body first sought by the Conquerer Worm is not the eyes, as he has foolishly guessed, but the uvula, "the soft drop of mucous flesh . . . suspended from the palate above the glottis. They eat through the face-cloth and cheek, or crawl by the lips through the broken tooth, filling the mouth. They make straight for it. It is the *deliciæ* of the vault" (14).[52] Sickened yet enthralled at her horror of interest, attracted by her scent of spice and orange-flowers yet repelled by an underlying odor of "mortality over-ready for the tomb," he recognizes her at last as the dead Xélucha and rushes, in a necrophilic rage, to embrace her, but she disappears in "a belch of pestilent corruption" that "[puffs] poisonous upon the putrid air" (17), leaving him a mere deranged shadow of his former elegant self.

The lacquered language—the sort that Bleiler referred to as "elaborate word lapidarism"—of the vignette serves to evoke a feverish atmosphere, which in turn allows Shiel to suggest that the narrator's experiences take place in a world at once actual and spectral.[53] Such an atmosphere is essential if the reader is to be transported, gradually, from a comfortable and familiar environment to an alien and threatening one in which the (frequently although covertly phallic) "ominous thing," as M. R. James put it, will be allowed to emerge naturally, putting "out its head, unobtrusively at first, and then more insistently, until it holds the stage."[54] This stylistic ormolu also functions, however, as an analogue to the deadly Xélucha herself, for both retain a deliberately abnormal beauty which is, to borrow a phrase from Gautier's definition of the decadent style, "gamy and marbled with corruption."[55] Words, then, carefully chosen and artfully arranged, cast a kind of numinous glow—Baudelaire's "phosphorescence of decay"—on abstract images of corruption; to Dorian Gray's mind, they "give a plastic form to formless things" (20). The lush prose provokes anxiety at the same time that it seduces the reader, who becomes, under its influence, receptive to and even excited by ideas that might otherwise seem abhorrent. In other words, Merimée's experience with Xélucha is paradigmatic of the reader's covertly lecherous experience with the typically decadent horror story, which links provocative sexuality with death—a blending of eros and thanatos—and portrays protagonists whose lusts are not cooled but inflamed in the chill of the grave.

"The Great God Pan" and "Xélucha" are examples of works that, as John R. Reed observed of decadent literature in general, "purposely [violate] expectations while creating a new structure to replace the apparently implied structure assumed by the audience."[56] These stories embody a textual anarchy precisely analogous to the "ego-maniacally" individualistic behavior typical of the decadent artist. In asserting the primacy of his sensations (as Pater had urged him to do) and in following his instincts, the decadent made the "unconscious life the master of consciousness" and allowed the gratification of any particular organ to take "pernicious, and even fatal" precedence over that of the "total organism"; in this fashion, according to Nordau, he threatened the welfare of his entire society (312). As this happens on a microcosmic level within the body, so too does it manifest itself in the rebellious attitudes and behavior patterns of artists themselves, and thus, necessarily, in their texts, which preserve an aesthetic individualism that privileges the individual parts at the expense of the integrity of the whole. Nordau quoted the nineteenth-century French essayist and critic Paul Bourget, who assimilated society to an organism:

The individual is the social cell. In order that the whole organism should function with energy, it is necessary that the component organisms should function with energy, but with a subordinate energy. . . . If the energy of the cells becomes independent, the organisms composing the total organism cease likewise to subordinate their energy to the total energy, and the anarchy which takes place constitutes the decadence of the whole. (301)

Bourget subsequently established the link between scientific and stylistic phenomena when he defined the decadent style—a necessary extension of the highly individualistic decadent artist—as being characterized by insubordination. According to Bourget, in the typically decadent text "the unity of the book is decomposed to give place to the independence of the page," and "the page is decomposed to give place to the independence of the word."[57] We can compare his definition with that of Havelock Ellis, who argued that, technically, "a decadent style is only such in relation to a classic style." The latter "is beautiful because the parts are subordinate to the whole," while the former "is beautiful because the whole is subordinate to the parts."[58] Bourget's definition in particular, however, testifies to the fact that works of art and literature came increasingly to be treated in cultural and scientific circles as dying organisms subject to laws, to influences—social, cultural, political—and even to infirmities analogous to those of their makers, from whom they may be said to have inherited their distinctive features (as earlier, for example, there had been bodies, political and legal).

In describing it as "irreparably damaged in its organism, weakened by the age of ideas, exhausted by the excesses of syntax, and sensitive only to those curiosities that render the sick feverish," Joris-Karl Huysmans implicitly correlated the "decadence of a literature" with a terminally ill patient; in both, the outward form testifies to the presence of a ravaging inward malady.[59] In other words, in those late nineteenth-century works of literature and art that employ a self-consciously decadent style, it "is simply expression," as Oscar Wilde's Lord Henry Wotton has it, "that gives reality to things": "Words! Mere words!" thinks Dorian as he succumbs to his friend's influence. "Was there anything so real as words?" (94). The works discussed briefly in this essay do not function primarily as sensationalized accounts of spiritualist phenomena; nor are they merely sordid tales of crime and corruption, although their "motley drama" exposes us to what Poe described in "The Conqueror Worm" as "much of Madness, and more of Sin, / And Horror the soul of the plot." Instead, they reveal that fin de siècle horror writers appropriated the decadent style because it facilitated the creation not only of fictional matrices substantial enough to contain the corrosive and degenerative anxieties with which they were endowed, but also of a de-composing text. The cultural decadence that provided them with their subject—ostensible or covert—called for a correspond-ingly subtle linguistic accompaniment which only the decadent style, with its obsessive and sometimes monstrous metaphors, elaborate paraphrases, and often complicated syntax, could provide. Speculating on the origins of the subtle charms of the Mona Lisa, Pater noted that her physical beauty owed its haunting quality to her soul, which had endowed her appearance "with all its maladies." It is, then, her enigmatic spirit, of which her beauty serves merely as a visible sign and outward prefigurement, which has been "wrought out from within upon the flesh, the deposit, little cell by little cell, of strange thoughts and fantastic reveries and exquisite passions."[60] According to this anatomy, the portrait of the Mona Lisa serves as an ana-logue to that of Dorian Gray, for in both a subtle affinity exists between the soul of the subject and the soul of the plot. In the typical decadent horror story, the horror embodied in the soul of the plot is wrought from within, little word by little word, with sentences for symptoms and images for maladies.[61]

Notes

1. H. G. Wells, quoted in *The Eighteen Nineties*, by Holbrook Jackson (London: Jonathan Cape, 1927), p. 228.

2. E. F. Bleiler, ed., *A Treasury of Victorian Ghost Stories* (New York: Scribner, 1983), p. 5.

3. Terry Eagleton, *Marxism and Literary Criticism* (Berkeley: University of California Press, 1976), pp. 24–25.

4. Charles Baudelaire, quoted in "A Note on Paul Bourget," in *Views and Reviews: A Selection of Uncollected Articles 1884–1932*, by Havelock Ellis, 1st and 2d series (Boston: Houghton Mifflin, 1932), pp. 52–53.

5. Matthew Phipps Shiel, "Xélucha," in *Shapes in the Fire*, ed. Ian Fletcher and John Stokes (1896; New York and London: Garland, 1977), p. 4. (All subsequent references to "Xélucha" correspond to this edition and are cited parenthetically.) The effect that prose such as Shiel's produces in the typical decadent horror story is explored in greater detail in later sections of this essay.

6. Max Beerbohm, "A Letter to the Editor," *The Yellow Book* 2 (July 1894): 284.

7. Théophile Gautier, "Une Notice," in *Les Fleurs du mal*, by Charles Baudelaire (1857; Paris: Ancienne Maison Michel Levy Frères, 1890), pp. 17–18.

8. Arthur Symons, "The Decadent Movement in Literature," *Harper's New Monthly Magazine* 87 (November 1893): 859.

9. Ibid., p. 859.

10. Edmond and Jules de Goncourt, quoted in Matei Calinescu, *Five Faces of Modernity* (Durham, N.C.: Duke University Press, 1987), p. 168.

11. Symons, p. 859.

12. Max Nordau, *Degeneration* (New York: D. Appleton, 1895), p. 3. All subsequent references to *Degeneration* correspond to this edition and are cited parenthetically.

13. Walter Pater, *The Renaissance*, in *Walter Pater: Three Major Texts*, ed. William E. Buckler (New York and London: New York University Press, 1906), p. 219.

14. Ironically, these same concepts, understandably threatening to the popular mind, refer to processes that, however indifferent to human aspirations and concerns, operate according to fairly stable and consistent laws or patterns. The dynamic behind natural selection, for example, involves an inherent degree of chance—random variability—which tends arbitrarily, so it seems, either to sustain a species or to effect its demise. Thus, although Darwin articulated some fourteen "laws" of variability, to the popular imagination at that time, natural selection appeared to function according to principles of chance, waste, and pain—principles entirely antithetical to those inherent in a cosmic order established by a beneficent intelligence. For a useful discussion of the manner in which H. G. Wells addressed this specific concern in his early scientific romances, see Bernard Bergonzi, *The Early H. G. Wells* (Manchester,

England: University Press, 1961), and Frank McConnell, *The Science Fiction of H. G. Wells* (New York: Oxford University Press, 1981).

15. H. P. Lovecraft, "The Silver Key," in *The Best of H. P. Lovecraft* (1963; New York: Ballantine Books, 1982), p. 59.

16. Barton Levi St. Armand, *The Roots of Horror in the Fiction of H. P. Lovecraft* (Elizabethtown, N.Y.: Dragon, 1977), p. 9; Pater, p. 219; Clive Scott, "Symbolism, Decadence and Impressionism," in *Modernism, 1890–1930*, ed. Malcolm Bradbury and James McFarlane (1974; Sussex: Humanities, 1978), p. 226.

17. Cesare Lombroso, "Atavism and Evolution," *Contemporary Review* 68 (July 1895): 42.

18. Ibid., p. 46.

19. The term *graphomania* did not originate with Lombroso, but derives from the term *graphology,* which was coined in the early nineteenth century by Abbé Jean-Hippolyte Michon to refer to the systematic study and interpretation of handwriting, described by some psychologists as "the oldest projective method, since the Chinese used it for character study in the 11th century" (*Longman Dictionary of Psychology*, ed. Robert M. Goldenson [New York and London: Longman, 1984], p. 324). Graphomania is a pathological condition in which the sufferer is possessed of "an obsessive desire to write, typically resulting in uncriticized, repetitive, and irrationally valued compositions" (*Dictionary of Psychology*, ed. Howard C. Warren [Boston, Mass.: Riverside, 1934], p. 117). In recontextualizing Lombroso in this fashion, Nordau chose not to differentiate between certain forms of artistic and literary expression, as well as the literary genres with which they are affiliated, and pathological impulses.

20. T. S. Eliot, "Baudelaire," in *Selected Essays* (1932; New York: Harcourt, Brace, 1950), p. 375.

21. Symons, p. 859.

22. Oscar Wilde, *The Picture of Dorian Gray and Other Writings by Oscar Wilde,* ed. Richard Ellmann (New York: Bantam Books, 1982), pp. 13, 3. All subsequent references to *Dorian Gray* correspond to this edition and are cited parenthetically.

23. Maurice Lévy, *Le Roman Gothique Anglais 1764–1824* (Toulouse: Association des publications de la faculté des lettres et sciences humaines de Toulouse, 1968), p. 602.

24. James Paradis, *Evolution and Ethics: Thomas Henry Huxley's "Evolution and Ethics," with New Essays on Its Victorian and Sociobiological Context* (Princeton, N.J.: Princeton University Press), p. 103.

25. H. P. Lovecraft, *Supernatural Horror in Literature* (New York: Dover, 1973), p. 15. Although this anxiety was felt more intensely during the Victorian period, it had manifested itself earlier in Western culture. For example, Alexander Pope anticipates Lovecraft's dark vision in the final apocalyptic lines of *The Dunciad Variorum* (1743):

> 'Signs following signs lead on the Mighty Year;
> See! the dull stars roll round and re-appear.
> She comes! the Cloud-compelling Pow'r, behold!
> With Night Primaeval, and with Chaos old.
> Lo! the great Anarch's ancient reign restor'd,
> Light dies before her uncreating word:
> As one by one, at dread Medaea's strain,
> The sick'ning Stars fade off th'aethereal plain;
> As Argus' eyes, by Hermes' wand opprest,
> Clos'd one by one to everlasting rest:
> Thus at her felt approach, and secret might,
> Art after Art goes out, and all is Night.
> See sculking Truth in her old cavern lye,
> Secur'd by mountains of heap'd casuistry:
> Philosophy, that touch'd the Heavens before,
> Shrinks to her hidden cause, and is no more:
> See Physic beg the Stagyrite's defence!
> See Metaphysic call for aid on Sence!
> See Mystery to Mathematicks fly!
> In vain! they gaze, turn giddy, rave, and die.
> Thy hand great Dulness! lets the curtain fall,
> And universal Darkness covers all.'

26. Edgar Allan Poe, Preface to *Tales of the Grotesque and Arabesque*, in *The Collected Works of Edgar Allan Poe*, 2 vols., ed. Thomas Ollive Mabbott (Cambridge, Mass.: Harvard University Press, 1978), 2:473.

27. Gautier, pp. 17–18. Such works as Henri Fuseli's *Nightmare* (1781) and Francisco Goya's "The Sleep of Reason Brings Forth Monsters" (1793), which served as the frontispiece for his *Caprichos*, provide apt visual analogues to Gautier's definition. All three works emphasize the appropriate nocturnal setting (a metaphor, in each of the pieces, for the unconscious) which, in being shunned by conscious, "daylight" thought, allows for the germination of the soul's delitescent maladies, which emerge as "larvae," "haggard phantoms," and "obscure phantasies."

28. H. P. Lovecraft, "Pickman's Model," in *Best of H. P. Lovecraft*, p. 43.

29. Symons, p. 859.

30. Walter de la Mare, *The Eighteen-Eighties* (Cambridge: Cambridge University Press, 1930), p. xvii. The publication history of "A: B: O." remains something of a mystery. Sometime around 1950, Edward Wagenknecht proposed that de la Mare consider reprinting the *Cornhill Magazine* stories with which, according to Wagenknecht, "his career as fictionist may be said properly to have begun." De la Mare's initial reaction to the suggestion "was that he could not possibly sanction such ghoulish proceedings under any circumstances" (*Eight Tales*, ed. Edward Wagenknecht [Sauk City, Wis.: Arkham, 1971], p. ix). In his introduction to *Eight Tales*, Wagenknecht cites the *Cornhill Magazine* as the source of the story but does not give a date of publication, as he does with the seven other tales included in the collection. "A: B: O." was not, in fact, published in the *Cornhill Magazine*, however, nor have my investigations revealed that it was first published in the other periodicals which were the young de la Mare's favorite repositories for his early stories. In a telephone conversation Wagenknecht mentioned to me that de la Mare had somehow provided him either with information concerning the location of the story or with an actual manuscript; which it was, he could not remember. It remains to be determined, therefore, whether "A: B: O." was republished in 1971 or in fact published for the first time in *Eight Tales* (disinterred, as it were, by its author). The discussion of de la Mare's "A: B: O." included herein represents an abridged version of a larger project now in progress.

31. Walter de la Mare, "A: B: O.," in *Eight Tales*, p. 97. All subsequent references to "A: B: O." correspond to this edition and are cited parenthetically.

32. *The Oxford English Dictionary*, 2d ed., 20 vols., ed. J. A. Simpson and E. S. C. Weiner (Oxford: Clarendon; New York: Oxford University Press, 1989), 1:35. Hereinafter referred to as the *OED*.

33. Charles Darwin, *The Origin of Species and The Descent of Man* (1859; New York: Modern Library, 1936), p. 903.

34. St. Armand, p. vi.

35. Aubrey Beardsley, "To Leonard Smithers," letters 17 and 42, in *Letters from Aubrey Beardsley to Leonard Smithers*, ed. R. A. Walker (London: The First Edition Club, 1937).

36. Malcolm Easton, *Aubrey and the Dying Lady* (Boston, Mass.: Godine, 1972), pp. 178–81.

37. Arthur Machen, "The Three Impostors," in *The House of Souls* (1906; London: Grant Richards, 1923), p. 393; Lovecraft, "The Dunwich Horror," in *Best of H. P. Lovecraft*, p. 114.

38. Julia Kristeva, *The Powers of Horror: An Essay on Abjection* (New York: Columbia University Press, 1982), p. 4.

39. Darwin, p. 524.

40. Lombroso, p. 42.

41. William James, *The Varieties of Religious Experience* (London: Longman, 1902), pp. 151–52.

42. Ibid.

43. David Punter, *The Literature of Terror* (London and New York: Longman, 1980), p. 264.

44. Arthur Machen, "A Secret Language," in *The Glorious Mystery* (Chicago: Covici-McGee, 1924), p. 74.

45. Machen, "The Three Impostors," p. 436.

46. *Protoplasm* is defined in the *OED* as a "viscid, semifluid, semitransparent, colourless or whitish substance . . . manifesting what are known as vital properties" and constituting what Thomas Henry Huxley referred to as the " 'physical basis of life' in all plants and animals, and forming the essential substance of the cells" (*OED* 2:2337). It is worth noting that this specific theme is still very much with us today. In the novel *Altered States* (1978), for example, Edward Jessup (played by William Hurt in the 1980 film version of the same title) portrays a scientist who regresses, stage by stage, all the way back to the original primal cell from which all life on Earth was derived. At various intermediate stages of his experiment, the scientist discovers "signs" of his evolutionary retrogression, as, for example, when he emerges from his sensory deprivation tank looking like "a small, not very formidable furred creature with the brain capacity of a gorilla" and finds himself "impelled by the most primal instincts, to live through the night, to find food, water, to avoid predators, to survive" (Paddy Chayefsky, *Altered States* [New York: Harper, 1978], pp. 121, 120).

47. Henry James, quoted in Leon Edel, *The Stuff of Sleep and Dreams: Experiments in Literary Psychology* (New York: Harper, 1982), p. 307.

48. Lovecraft, *Supernatural Horror*, p. 14. This pervasive feature of fin de siècle horror stories—namely, the persistence of narrative gaps, ellipses, and silences that require the reader to draw on his own reserve of anxiety in order to fix suppressed meanings—did not disappear with the movement itself. In some twentieth-century works, in fact, the debt is quite direct. For example, the idea behind "Room 101" in *1984* (1949) possibly derives from the treatments of horror and positive evil that George Orwell encountered in the writings of Henry James, Algernon Blackwood, Arthur Machen, and Matthew Phipps Shiel, all of whom recognized that explicitness is fatal to the portrayal of the

genuinely terrifying. In a meditation, of sorts, on his treatment of "portentous evil" in *The Turn of the Screw*, Henry James asked, "how was I to save that, as an intention on the part of my demon-spirits, from the drop, the comparative vulgarity, inevitably attending, throughout the whole range of possible brief illustration, the offered example, the imputed vice, the cited act, the limited deplorable presentable instance?"

> One had seen, in fiction, some grand form of wrong-doing, or better still of wrong-being, imputed, seen it promised and announced as by the hot-breath of the Pit—and then, all lamentably, shrink to the compass of some particular brutality, some particular immorality, some particular infamy portrayed: with the result, alas, of the demonstration's falling sadly short. If *my* bad things, for "The Turn of the Screw," I felt, should succumb to this danger, if they shouldn't seem sufficiently bad, there would be nothing for me but to hang my artistic head lower than I had ever known occasion to do.
>
> . . . What, in the last analysis, had I to give the sense of? . . . What would *be* then, on reflexion, this utmost conceivability?—a question to which the answer all admirably came. . . . Only make the reader's general vision of evil intense enough, I said to myself—and that already is a charming job—and his own experience, his own imagination, his own sympathy . . . and horror . . . will supply him quite sufficiently with all the particulars. (Henry James, "Preface to *The Aspern Papers*," in *The Art of the Novel*, introduction by R. P. Blackmur [New York: Scribner, 1934], p. 176)

Orwell's "Room 101" is, of course, a specific place, and the mode of torture with which Winston Smith is threatened is a "particular infamy" to which different readers (depending on the degree of their aversion to rats) will assign different degrees of "brutality." What makes this scene so unsettling is the informing idea behind Room 101; viz., that somewhere there exists a room (or a text) in which the reader confronts his or her own deepest and most abject fears—what Smith's tormentor describes as "the worst thing in the world . . . [which] varies from individual to individual" (George Orwell, *1984* [Oxford: Clarendon, 1984], p. 403), and what Shiel referred to as "those 'faint manifestations of the Unknowable'" which lurk "in our hearts and in our pantings" (M. P. Shiel, "On Panic," in *Science, Life and Literature* [London: Williams and Norgate, 1950], p. 196). The horror in *1984* is not of the thought police but of the soul.

49. E. F. Bleiler, *A Guide to Supernatural Fiction* (Kent, Ohio: Kent State University Press, 1983), p. 454.

50. Edgar Allan Poe, "The Philosophy of Composition," in *Essays and Reviews* (New York: Library of America, 1984), pp. 18–19.

51. Arthur Symons, *The Symbolist Movement in Literature* (1899; New York: Dutton, 1958), p. 120; Shiel, "Xélucha," pp. 3–4.

52. Once again, one sees "Xélucha" as a possible source for one of the more horrific scenes—and images—in Orwell's futuristic nightmare, *1984*. More specifically, the intense delight Xélucha takes in heightening the narrator's morbid fascination as she dwells on the gustatory predilections of the worm is analogous to the gusto with which Orwell's O'Brien informs Winston Smith of the feeding habits of the rats encaged within an iron mask with which the latter will shortly be fitted. "I have pressed the first lever," said O'Brien. "You understand the construction of this cage. The mask will fit over your head, leaving no exit. When I press this other lever, the door of the cage will slide up. These starving brutes will shoot out of it like bullets. Have you ever seen a rat leap through the air? They will leap onto your face and bore straight through it. Sometimes they will attack the eyes first. Sometimes they burrow through the cheeks and devour the tongue" (Orwell, *1984*, pp. 405–6). While no direct evidence establishes the nature and extent of Orwell's familiarity with Shiel's work, a letter Orwell wrote in January 1931 to Max Plowman (who had apparently solicited a list of authors whose work Orwell would be willing to review) describes "anything *by* M. P. Shiel" (Orwell's emphasis) as, in his words, "the kind of thing I like reviewing" (George Orwell to Max Plowman, January 12, 1931, in *The Collected Essays, Journalism and Letters of George Orwell*, 4 vols., ed. Sonia Orwell and Ian Angus [New York: Harcourt, 1968] 1:33). For a fuller discussion of the relationship between Orwell and Shiel, see David Cody, "The Worst Thing in the World: M. P. Shiel and Orwell's *Nineteen Eighty-Four*" (Unpublished manuscript).

53. Bleiler, *Guide*, p. 454.

54. E. F. Bleiler, ed., *Supernatural Fiction Writers*, 2 vols. (New York: Scribner, 1982), 1:433.

55. Gautier, pp. 17–18.

56. John R. Reed, *Decadent Style* (Athens: Ohio University Press, 1985), p. 9.

57. Paul Bourget, quoted in "A Note on Paul Bourget," *Views and Reviews*, p. 52.

58. Havelock Ellis, "Huysmans," in *Affirmations* (Boston: Houghton Mifflin, 1922), p. 175.

59. Joris-Karl Huysmans, quoted in Calinescu, p. 173.

60. Walter Pater, "Leonardo da Vinci," in *The Renaissance*, p. 150.

61. My thanks to Professor David Cody, who, with care, interest, and encouragement, read this essay at each of the *many* stages of its evolution.

Part 3

THE RHETORIC OF STYLE:

FIGURES AND EFFECTS

Chapter 8

Persuasive Worlds and the Rhetorics of Art and Science in Science Fiction

Jefferson Peters

Science fiction writers, like other writers, use a variety of techniques to persuade us that their narrative worlds are true to the human condition. This essay discusses how the rhetorics of art and science authorize fictional worlds. *Rhetoric* refers here to the persuasive use of language. The rhetoric of science as it appears in science fiction has already received appropriate attention. Mark Rose argues that science fiction "invok[es] the scientific ethos to assert the possibility of the fictional worlds it describes."[1] Eric Rabkin believes that "the rhetoric of science has come to dominate fiction as the source for authority."[2] The rhetoric of art and its ethos, however, also play important roles in authorizing fictional worlds. To illustrate my arguments, I analyze Samuel R. Delany's short story "Corona,"[3] a representative fiction useful because it vividly employs both rhetorics and fundamentally concerns them.

Delany authorizes his fictional world by using the rhetorics of art and science to express and evoke emotional and intellectual responses. Two passages from "Corona" exemplify the rhetorics particularly well. In the first passage, from early in the story, Delany presents an artistic view of the music of rock star Bryan Faust, idol of the galaxy. Delany's narrator describes Faust's songs from the point of view of Buddy, a white, slow-witted worker at Kennedy spacehangar: "They shouted and whispered and growled from the wall speaker in the spacehangar . . . the cross-rhythms, sudden silences, and moments of pure voice were picked up by jangling organ, whining oboe, bass, and cymbals. . . . The sounds jammed into his ears, pried around his mind, loosening things" (66–67). Here Delany uses several techniques of the rhetoric of art. First, he personifies Faust's music as a shouting, growling animal. The rhetoric of art quickens the inanimate mechanical world of the rhetoric of science. Second, Delany focuses on the emotional effects of the songs, on how they reach inside Buddy and touch his feelings. Third, Delany employs expressive patterns of beats: "They *shout*ed and *whisp*ered and *growled*." The rhythm of the sentences echoes the rhythm of the songs. Fourth, Delany's words carry affective and qualitative associations rather than technical and quantitative information. "Moments of pure voice" describes times when Faust sings unaccompanied by instruments. Because the narrator calls these moments "pure" rather than using the formal term, a cappella, Faust's voice appears beneficial and good, untouched by evil. Finally, Delany inserts a technical term, *cross-rhythms*, into his artistic rhetoric, which reveals that he knows enough of the scientific side of music to *choose* to avoid it here. Delany then colors the "cross-rhythms" with art by animating the instruments that "pick" them "up." All these techniques help us experience the music aesthetically, sensuously, and emotionally. We feel the raw emotion of the songs as they shout and growl, feel the sounds as they ram into Buddy's mind and pry up his petrified feelings, and thus *feel* the fictional truth that the music moves Delany's characters.

Later in the story, Delany presents a scientific view of Faust's music when Lee, a brilliant nine-year-old black girl, describes "Corona," one of Faust's most popular songs, to her doctor.

The rhythm is very interesting. Five against seven when it's there. But a lot of the beats are left out, so you have to listen hard to get it. . . . There are three melodic motifs. . . . They appear in descending order of rhythmic intensity. There are more silences in the last melodic line. His music is composed of silence as much as sound. (71–72)

While in the first passage Delany uses the rhetoric of art to present the qualitative effects of the music's form and content, here, through Lee, he employs several techniques of the rhetoric of science to describe only the form of Faust's "Corona." First, Lee appeals to her doctor's intellect rather than to his emotions. Instead of expressing, as she later does to Buddy, that

"Corona" is "beautiful . . . so . . . *alive!*" (81), she explains, "The rhythm is very interesting." Lee's passionless speech is objective, and the auditor for the music she implies—"you have to listen hard to get it"—remains objective as well. You'd be listening "hard" for the same technical aspects available to any careful, informed person—not for how it makes you feel. Second, technical terms like *rhythm, beats,* and *melodic line* dominate Lee's description, and instead of personifying them, she leaves them inanimate. Third, Lee conveys quantities, such as "five against seven," rather than qualities. Finally, Lee's sentences display no expressive rhythms, share the same structure, and possess mostly static forms of *to be*. Through these techniques Delany presents the song primarily as a work of science, appealing to our intellects rather than to our emotions to make us *know* the fictional truth that "Corona" possesses an interesting form.

The central theme of "Corona" is that art, not science, may help a person bear life's pain. Early in the story, Buddy is hospitalized after accidentally grinding solvent, steel flakes, and oil into his eye. Lee has been committed to the same hospital because her telepathic sensitivity to people's pain renders her suicidal. Lee's doctor fails to help either patient heal emotionally because he is too scientifically oriented. But when Lee feels Buddy's pain and fear and hears "Corona" playing in his mind, she escapes from her hospital room, finds Buddy, and comforts him. The pair then build a friendship despite their differences in age, race, and intelligence. At the end of the story, Buddy repays Lee's kindness by attending Faust's farewell concert, which enables the girl to experience "Corona" telepathically through her friend's perceptions and so to bear her pain.

Delany employs the rhetorics both to authorize Faust's music and to reinforce his story's theme. Faust's "Corona" names and unifies Delany's story, and, however the rhetorics authorize the important aspects of a fiction—whether characters, settings, plot events, or phenomena such as songs and telepathy—shapes its world and themes. Because in Delany's fictional world art enables people to live with pain, he quickens the songs and our response to them with the rhetoric of art. Because science fails to help people bear misery, Delany has Lee sterilize "Corona" and our response to it with the rhetoric of science.

Although Delany undercuts the rhetoric and ethos of science in "Corona," he still uses them to authorize his text. The rhetorics may both legitimize the aspects of a narrative world and convince us of the relative values of those aspects and of the rhetorics that present them. For example, partly because we believe that "Corona" possesses "five beats against seven," we know that it exists in the fictional world, but we realize that the emotions the song evokes are more valuable than its technical features.

The complementary rhetorics of art and science, then, establish in texts the authorities of their artistic and scientific ethoi. The rhetoric of art, liberated from a modern scientific orientation, is more overtly qualitative, emotive, subjective, and fantastic. The rhetoric of science, reflecting a modern scientific orientation, is more obviously quantitative, intellectual, objective, and realistic. Artistic rhetoric alludes to fictional or real art and artists, scientific rhetoric to science and scientists. The rhetoric of art may call attention to its fictional existence, whereas the rhetoric of science usually does not. The rhetoric of art employs subjective active voice and artistic terms, while scientific rhetoric uses objective passive voice and Latinate scientific jargon. Artistic rhetoric presents phenomena as works of art, as in Clifford D. Simak's "Desertion" when Kent Fowler, freshly transformed into a Loper, runs toward one of Jupiter's ammonia falls: "The music deepened and filled the universe with a spray of magic sound. And he knew that the music came from the tumbling waterfall that feathered down the face of the shining cliff."[4] Scientific rhetoric presents phenomena as works of science, as in Robert L. Forward's *Dragon's Egg:* the neutron star's inhabitants "are flat, amoeba-type creatures about 2.5 mm in radius (0.5 cm in diameter), and 0.5 mm high, with a density of 7 million g/cc."[5]

Different kinds of rhetorics do grow from different artistic and scientific ethoi and establish different effects, authorities, and narrative worlds. The two following excerpts, for example, are artistic in different ways. The first, from Nathaniel Hawthorne's "The Artist of the Beautiful," uses personification and indirection to appeal to our thoughtful aesthetic and moral senses when Owen Warland's creation alights on Danforth's sagacious baby: "As if the butterfly, like the artist, were conscious of something not entirely congenial in the child's nature, it alternately sparkled and grew dim."[6] The second excerpt, from E. T. A. Hoffmann's "The Sandman," employs sensual and effective language to appeal physically to our emotions when Nathanael is enchanted by Dr. Spalanzani's automaton: "He felt as if he were suddenly embraced by burning arms. No longer able to contain himself, rapture and pain mingling within him, he cried: 'Olympia!' "[7]

The next two excerpts are scientific in different ways. In the first, to convince us that the Lunarians have only a *"one chance in seven of winning"* their revolution, Robert A. Heinlein has the supercomputer of *The Moon Is a Harsh Mistress* use a probabilistic rhetoric: "This is an indeterminate problem. How shall I solve It? Pessimistically? Or optimistically? Or a range of probabilities expressed as a curve, or several curves?"[8] The second, from Tom Godwin's "The Cold Equations," features a deterministic rhetoric to persuade us that stowaway Marilyn Lee Cross must die to allow the Emergency Dispatch Ship to complete its mission: "*h amount of fuel will power an EDS with a mass of m safely to its destination; . . . h amount of fuel will not power an EDS with a mass of m plus x safely to its destination.*"[9] A thorough examination of all such varieties lies beyond the scope of this paper, so my references to "the rhetoric of science," for example, assume that such a rhetoric belongs to a larger scientific family.

Although the present study focuses on verbal uses of the rhetorics of art and science, it is useful to note that they may appear visually as well. One visual use of the rhetoric of art lives in Gahan Wilson's story " ⬤ ,"[10] in which a mysterious black spot appears simultaneously on the pages of our book *and* on Reginald Archer's "dazzlingly white" tablecloth and proceeds to grow, consuming space on our page as it eats Reginald's butler, disrupting our neatly arranged printed words as it destroys Reginald's precisely organized life. Visual examples of the rhetoric of science occur in *The Legacy of Heorot*,[11] by Larry Niven, Jerry Pournelle, and Steven Barnes. Here the colonists of Tau Ceti Four organize their new world with "planetary survey maps" of *spotless* mechanical detail.

Two major factors that complicate rhetorical analysis are, first, the interdependence of rhetoric with context, and, second, the rarity of pure examples of either rhetoric. Among other things, plot, character, rhetoric, and even previously established, continually evolving context interdependently create context. Context and rhetoric work together to establish authority and generate theme. Delany uses context to reinforce his story's theme that science alone cannot deal with emotions. Because of the affective context with which Delany has surrounded Faust's music, Lee's use of the rhetoric of science to describe "Corona" and to hide her feelings about the music actually moves us. We sense the feelings that Lee hides, and so her repression of them affects us all the more. Also, because we have just seen the music bursting with personification, when Lee describes it technically, rendering the animate music inanimate—the live animal dead—we feel an emotional void. The scientific rhetoric *indirectly* expresses and evokes emotions, requiring an affective context to do so.

Thus Delany colors science with emotion, without at this point having to use the rhetoric of art. This device is available to all authors. In Eugene Zamiatin's *We*, for example, D-503's first thirty-nine records are often subjective, emotional, and artistic, like the opening of the thirteenth: "I awoke at dawn. The rose-colored firmament looked into my eyes. Everything was beautiful, round." [12] The scientific rhetoric of his last entry, written after he has had his fancy medically removed, devastates us: "Daylight. It is clear. The barometer—760 mm" (217). Zamiatin affects us so without using artistic rhetoric, which D-503 can no longer employ.

Context helps determine whether characters' emotional and intellectual responses to their experiences as conveyed by rhetoric are *congruent* or *incongruent* with our responses to these phenomena as evoked by rhetoric. When the context reveals that a rhetoric or phenomenon is appropriate and positive, our response is more congruent with the character's. So the narrator of "Corona" 's artistic description of the effects of Faust's music on Buddy moves us similarly. At other times, when the context reveals that a rhetoric or phenomenon is inappropriate and negative, our response is more incongruent with the character's. So Lee's unemotional scientific speech distances us.

Congruency reveals our acceptance of the rhetoric, ethos, and content of a fictional moment. Whether our responses are congruent or incongruent with those of the characters controls our understanding of the themes of a fiction. We see this in "Corona" and in two stories that, unlike Delany's, use the rhetorics to condemn artistic ethoi: Robert Heinlein's "The Roads Must Roll" and Jack Vance's *The Last Castle*. In the Heinlein work, when Chief Engineer Gaines, his "intelligent mind clicking along" like an "electromechanical integrator," views "large numbers" of "personnel" as "machines, or figures" to "be measured, examined, classified," [13] he learns why some of his Transport Cadets have mutinied and jeopardized America's vital system of rolling roads. The desperate situation that demands rational thinking, the useful scientific rhetoric that describes the solution to the crisis, and the exaggerated artistic rhetoric that elsewhere describes several repulsively emotional mutineers all reveal that we are to applaud Gaines's cool intellect and to understand, as he does, the efficacy of a mechanical organization of people led by rational men.

Authors may use incongruency to criticize the rhetoric, ethos, and content of a fictional moment, as in *The Last Castle*. Here, instead of working to avoid slaughter at the hands of their rebellious Meks, the foppish aesthetes of Castle Hagedorn recline entranced by the stylized dances of their "Phanes," gauzy "sylphs" who perform by "bending, twisting, swaying to plangent chords of the lute, fluttering their fingers as if feeling for raindrops."[14] The desperate situation that requires immediate action, the exaggerated artistic rhetoric that mocks the Phanes, and the useful scientific rhetoric that elsewhere analyzes the Meks are all to distance us and make us condemn an art-based detachment from reality. Although we may refuse to view people as numbers, or we may prefer art to reality, to understand these fictions correctly we must recognize that Heinlein's story wants us to embrace such a vision and that Vance's wants us to scorn such a preference.

Examples of pure artistic or 100 percent scientific rhetoric are rare and temporary, though. J. D. Bernal asserts that "neither in science nor in art is one to be found without the other."[15] This is especially true of the rhetorics in fiction, for if a writer were successful in excluding the rhetoric of art or science from a text, we either would not feel the truth of what we read or would not know it. In a fantasy awash with a purple-hued rhetoric of art such as H. P. Lovecraft's *The Dream-Quest of Unknown Kadath*, when Randolph Carter, explorer of dreamland, leads his nightmare army of glibbering ghouls and noxious night-gaunts toward the Cold Waste, he empirically proves that an eldritch, nameless, frightful, following *thing* is no "hippocephalic bird."[16] In Larry Niven's hard science fiction story "Neutron Star," when Beowulf Shaeffer, explorer of outer space, empirically struggles to understand the gravitational force of BVS-1, he describes the surrounding stars as "glar[ing] with an angry, painful light."[17]

In fact, the rhetorics may appear together in any given story, passage, sentence, or word. This may result from the volatile nature of language, which allows the connotations of many words to shift back and forth from more artistic to more scientific meanings. Even in a scientific work like the *Principia*,[18] Newton verbalizes the universal law of gravitation using a metaphoric verb, *attract*, which animates "two attracting bodies." Therefore, when the rhetorics meld in a fiction, we examine their interactions and relative effects. Of course, any example of rhetoric may approach art or science more closely than any other, and the rhetorics often appear separate, as in the two passages from "Corona."

Although the rhetorics separately authorize the two passages from "Corona," elsewhere in the story they meld, for Delany's thoughts on art and science are more complex than simply art is good, science bad. Rather, art and science are positive when they unite as complementary opposites, with art in control. Faust communicates his art with scientific devices like "Scopitones." Without their unique forms his songs would lose their emotional power. To live, Lee needs art partly because of its technical form, its cage for pain. As she says to Buddy, Faust's music presents "pain contained, ordered, given form and meaning" (81). We first meet Lee after she has been listening to "Corona" *and* trying to integrate the area within a curve. *Corona* as an astronomical term denotes a white or colored ring encircling a luminous celestial body, but it also refers to a crown, a work of art crafted for kings, and to a halo, a circle of light possessed by saints. Here it also names two works of art: Faust's song and Delany's story.

Throughout Delany's narrative, art assimilates science, especially at the conclusion, when Lee experiences Faust's performance of "Corona" through Buddy's mind.

Bryan Faust walked across the platform to the microphones. Comets soared over his shoulders and disappeared under his arms. Suns novaed on his chest. Meteors flashed around his elbows. Shirts of polarized cloth with incandescent, shifting designs were now being called Fausts. Others flashed in the crowd. He pushed back his hair, grinned, and behind the police-block hundreds of children screamed. He laughed into the microphone; they quieted. Behind him a bank of electronic instruments glittered. The controls were in the many jeweled rings hanging bright and heavy on his fingers. He raised his hands, flicked his thumbs across the gems, and the instruments, programmed to respond, began the cascading introduction to *Corona* [sic]. Bryan Faust sang. Across Kennedy, thousands—Buddy among them—heard.

And on her cot, Lee listened. "Thank you, Buddy," she whispered. "Thank you." And felt a little less like dying. (86)

Here the artistic rhetoric transforms the scientific into art and so establishes a new authority based on this meld. Comets, suns, and meteors may refer to inanimate astronomical phenomena. But the narrator transcends this scientific information: Faust is a rock *star*, a heavenly body at the center of a beautiful and volatile universe attracting comets and meteors to soar and flash about his body and causing suns to nova on his heart. The comets soar, rising to more exalted states. All four verbs—*soar, disappear, nova,* and *flash*—animate their astronomical subjects, who have come to worship Faust like the human audience. Immediately, however, the narrator scientifically explains the behavior of the celestial bodies: they are polarized, flashing shirts, products of electronics and magnetics. The rhetoric of science appears ascendant until we read that the polarized shirts bear "shifting designs," unstable but organized works of art.

The concluding passage continues to shift back and forth between the two rhetorics, until Faust begins "the cascading introduction to *Corona*," and an artistic emphasis closes the story. Through synesthesia we hear *and* see music, which we normally perceive only aurally. The watery sounds tumble down a cliff, carrying our hearing and vision with them. The alliterating hard *c* sounds—"*cascading introduction to Corona*"—function onomatopoeically: the hard *c*'s crash down one after the other, as the sounds of the song are falling. And the last sentence of "Corona" describes how Lee "*felt* a little less like dying."

When Buddy tries to approach Faust's stage for Lee, the narrator describes Buddy's tattoo for the first time: "*To Mars I Would Go for Dolores-jo*, inscribed on Saturn's rings" (84). The tattoo does more than emphasize Buddy's ignorance of astronomy; it cages pain: Dolores-jo, whose name connotes "dolorous," is a long-lost girlfriend. As Buddy would go to Mars for Dolores-jo, so he approaches Faust for Lee. For his audience, Faust is a figure of romance and science. In the tattoo the rhetoric of art assimilates science by romanticizing an inanimate planet and by misusing the facts of astronomy to crown Mars with the rings of Saturn. The tattoo, like the shirts called Fausts, the song "Corona," and the story "Corona," is a romance of astronomy, a *science fiction*. The tattooer, Faust, and Delany order pain with their art; and like all science fiction artists, they romanticize science and authorize their art by melding the rhetorics of art and science.

From Francis Bacon's *Novum Organum* (1620) on, many people have separated art and science into two truths, the goals of two cultures. Possibly, however, each is necessary for a full appreciation and expression of the other. Dan Dreiberg, aka the "Nite Owl," passionate ornithologist and sensitive superhero of Alan Moore's *Watchmen*, certainly believes so. In his article on owls, "Blood on the Shoulder of Pallas," Dreiberg argues that unless scientific facts

can be imbued with the flash of poetic insight then they remain dull gems; semi-precious stones scarcely worth collecting. A scientific understanding of the beautifully synchronized and articulated motion of an owl's individual feathers during flight does not impede a poetic appreciation of the same phenomenon. Rather, the two enhance each other, a more lyrical eye lending the cold data a romance from which it has long been divorced.[19]

Dreiberg, our imaginary authority, describes a complete and rich way of perceiving the world. As art and science unite in his article, so they mix somehow in the rhetorical fabrics of all fictions. And when fictions bear the truth of the human condition, and writers use both rhetorics to authorize their worlds, art and science together affirm one truth.

Notes

1. Mark Rose, *Alien Encounters* (Cambridge, Mass.: Harvard University Press, 1981), p. 20.

2. Eric S. Rabkin, "The Rhetoric of Science in Fiction," in *Critical Encounters II*, ed. Tom Staicar (New York: Frederick Ungar, 1982), p. 42.

3. Samuel R. Delany, "Corona" (1967), in *Distant Stars* (New York: Bantam Books, 1981). All future references are to this edition and are cited by page number within the text.

4. Clifford D. Simak, "Desertion," in *City* (New York: Ace Books, 1952), p. 114.

5. Robert L. Forward, *Dragon's Egg* (New York: Ballantine Books, 1980), p. 292.

6. Nathaniel Hawthorne, "The Artist of the Beautiful," in *Future Perfect*, rev. ed., ed. H. Bruce Franklin (New York: Oxford University Press, 1978), p. 63.

7. E. T. A. Hoffmann, "The Sandman," in *Tales of E. T. A. Hoffmann*, ed. and trans. Leonard J. Kent and Elizabeth C. Knight (Chicago: University of Chicago Press, 1969), p. 114.

8. Robert A. Heinlein, *The Moon Is a Harsh Mistress* (New York: Ace Books, 1987), p. 75.

9. Tom Godwin, "The Cold Equations," in *Science Fiction Hall of Fame*, ed. Robert Silverberg (New York: Avon Books, 1971), p. 556.

10. Gahan Wilson, " '   ,' " in *Again, Dangerous Visions*, ed. Harlan Ellison. Science Fiction Book Club Edition (New York: Doubleday, 1972).

11. Larry Niven, Jerry Pournelle, and Steven Barnes, *The Legacy of Heorot* (New York: Simon and Schuster, 1987).

12. Eugene Zamiatin, *We*, trans. Gregory Zilboorg (New York: E. P. Dutton, 1924), p. 67. All future references are to this edition and are cited by page number in the text.

13. Robert Heinlein, "The Roads Must Roll," in *Science Fiction Hall of Fame*, ed. Robert Silverberg (New York: Avon Books, 1971), pp. 91, 109.

14. Jack Vance, *The Last Castle*, in *The Hugo Winners*, vols. 1 and 2, ed. Isaac Asimov. Science Fiction Book Club Edition (New York: Doubleday, 1971), p. 522.

15. J. D. Bernal, *Science in History*, 3d ed. (London: C. A. Watts, 1965), p. 16.

16. H. P. Lovecraft, *The Dream-Quest of Unknown Kadath* (New York: Ballantine Books, 1970), p. 121.

17. Larry Niven, "Neutron Star," in *The Hugo Winners*, vols. 1 and 2, ed. Isaac Asimov. Science Fiction Book Club Edition (New York: Doubleday, 1971), p. 557.

18. Isaac Newton, *Mathematical Principles of Natural Philosophy*, 3d ed., trans. Andrew Motte; trans. rev. Florian Cajori (Berkeley: University of California Press, 1934).

19. Alan Moore, *Watchmen* (New York: D. C. Comics, 1986–87), chap. 7.

Chapter 9

Just How Frumious Is a Bandersnatch?
The Exotic and the Ambiguous
in Imaginative Literature

Joseph D. Miller

The appropriate point for the initiation of an essay on the use of exotic and ambiguous description in fantastic literature must be, almost by definition, Lewis Carroll's "Jabberwocky":

> 'Twas brillig, and the slithy toves
> Did gyre and gimble in the wabe:
> All mimsy were the borogoves,
> And the mome raths outgrabe.

> "Beware the Jabberwock, my son!
> The jaws that bite, the claws that catch!
> Beware the Jubjub bird, and shun
> The frumious Bandersnatch!"

> He took his vorpal sword in hand:
> Long time the manxome for he sought—
> So rested he by the Tumtum tree,
> And stood awhile in thought.

And, as in uffish though he stood,
The Jabberwock, with eyes of flame,
Came whiffling through the tulgey wood,
And burbled as it came!

One, two! One, two! And through and through
The vorpal blade went snicker-snack!
He left it dead, and with its head
He went galumphing back.
"And hast thou slain the Jabberwock?

Come to my arms, my beamish boy!
O frabjous day! Callooh! Callay!"
He chortled in his joy.

'Twas brillig, and the slithy toves
Did gyre and gimble in the wabe:
All mimsy were the borogoves,
And the mome raths outgrabe.[1]

Now let us turn our attention to something a bit different. This is my own pastiche of the Carroll poem; I call it "Uzi Jockey":

'Twas autumn and the fallen leaves
Did gyre and gambol in the wind:
All yellowed was the grassy weave,
The snows would soon begin.

"Beware the Kodiak, my son!
The jaws that bite, the claws that rake!
Beware the mountain lion and shun
The underfoot rattlesnake!"

He took his Uzi's grip in hand:
Long time the fearsome foe he sought—
So rested he by the pinewood tree,
And stood awhile in thought.

And, as in frozen thought he stood,
The Kodiak, with claws like steel,
Came snuffling through the barren wood,
And thought "I sense a meal!"

The bullets flew and sportsman true
The leaden spray was right on track!
He left it dead, and with its head
He went full gallop back.

"And hast thou slain the Kodiak?
Come to my arms, my sporting boy!
O glorious day! Hoo ray! Hoo ray!"
He chuckled in his joy.

'Twas autumn and the fallen leaves
Did gyre and gambol in the wind:
All yellowed was the grassy weave,
The snows would soon begin.

With the exception of some scattershot aimed vaguely in the direction of the National Rifle Association, the former and latter poems differ in one respect. In my pastiche, all neologisms have been replaced with English terms that are at least tonally plausible in terms of the original. There is no doubt that the original is far superior to the "deconstructed" version.

But why should a variety of nonsense terms contribute so much more than their pedestrian equivalents? This question exemplifies the central issue of this essay; that is, what is the role of ambiguous description in fantastic literature? By "ambiguous," I particularly refer to the obscure, the indistinct, the uncertain.

The Carroll poem is an excellent jumping-off point. Science fiction authors seem to be particularly fascinated by "Jabberwocky." In 1943 Henry Kuttner suggested in his story "Mimsy Were the Borogoves" that the poem is actually an accurate description of events transpiring in the far future.[2] Bandersnatchi are favored members of Larry Niven's "Known Space" bestiary.[3] And Roger Zelazny has recently added the Bandersnatch and the Jabberwock to his cast of characters in the "Son of Amber" series.[4] I argue here that this infatuation with "Jabberwocky" is of diagnostic significance in an analysis of style in science fiction.

I think it is possible to argue the goals of science fiction right up to the final heat death of the universe (and in previous Eaton Conferences in Riverside that has seemed to be an imminent possibility!). However, I suspect everyone can agree that a major, if not the major, goal is attainment of an emotional apprehension of subjects lying beyond our current comprehension. Good science fiction extrapolates from the known to the unknown, but it cannot provide a detailed "map of Hell."[5] Too detailed a map would make Hell simply another suburb. This argument leads to the contention that truly evocative style in imaginative literature must incorporate elements of the ambiguous and the obscure. I do not, however, hypothesize that science fiction and fantasy differ qualitatively from other genres in this regard, but rather that the imaginative literature differs, by necessity, in sheer quantity of descriptive obfuscation. In fact, the depiction of exotic cultures in mainstream literature often utilizes these same techniques to convey a feeling of the outre (e.g., *Shogun* or *Gorky Park*).[6]

In this essay I compare successful applications of this surrealistic style with representative failures in the attempt to convey a sense of the fantastic. I suggest that the failures often result from an overly literalist, nuts-and-bolts descriptive approach. I do have an ulterior motive here; an analysis of style requires adequate sampling of text. Thus it is a necessary pleasure to present some of my personal favorites, including some of the greatest evocative successes and some of the most dismal failures in the imaginative literature.

A good place to begin the analysis is a scene from the progenitor of the cyberpunk subgenre, K. W. Jeter's *Dr. Adder*:

"Just a minute," said Limmit, rising and heading for the door opening onto the bathroom. "Funny—all that time in the sewers, and I could hardly take a crap to save my life the whole time." He pushed the door open. Great splotches of drying blood splashed in static patterns across the floor and walls; small spots like red stars spattered across the ceiling. A corpse, twisted and unrecognizable, stiffening in the contortions of violent death, lay half out of the bathtub and across the tiny room, one hand cradled in the curved trap of the sink's drainpipe, his head, or what remained of it, partially submerged in the toilet bowl. The still water had turned into translucent rose. . . . Limmit reached in and pulled the shattered head out of the bowl, dripping. Little clumps of brain tissue, like soft pink cauliflower, and one perfect staring eye floated in the red water. Ah, fuck it, he thought, and squatted on the toilet seat after dropping his pants down to his knees. Living in L.A. sure makes you callous.[7]

A more graphic evocation than this is hard to imagine. But I maintain that this is not evocation of the fantastic or the mysterious; this is evocation of horror. The directors of the grade B science fiction movies of the 1950s were well aware of the distinction I am trying to draw. The creature is almost never revealed until the last reel (although this is also partially attributable to the poverty of special effects in these films; consider James Arness as Giant Carrot in the original version of *The Thing*).[8] This use of the *presque vu* allows the maximization of mystery and suspense. But John Carpenter's version of *The Thing*[9] leaves almost nothing to the imagination and rightly suffers in comparison with the original film, and certainly with John Campbell's story "Who Goes There?"[10] the inspiration for both films. Similarly, movies such as *Aliens* and *The Fly*[11] are certainly powerful and disturbing, but chronic visual overstatement only habituates the viewer to what should be truly alien.

Here is another example of overstatement, from David Gerrold's *A Matter for Men*:

Feeding! It was rending the child limb from limb! Its gaping mouth was frozen in the act of slashing and tearing at his struggling body. The Chtorran's arms were long and double-jointed. Bristly black and insectlike, they held the boy in a metal grip and pushed him toward the hideous gnashing hole. The camera caught the spurt of blood from his chest frozen in midair like a crimson splash. I barely managed to gasp, "They eat their—their prey alive?" Dr. Obama nodded. "Now I want you to imagine that's your mother. Or your sister. Or your niece."[12]

Although I rather enjoy an occasional contest between flamethrowers and giant centipedes, I doubt that this descriptive style is likely to generate even a hint of the intrinsic strangeness that must occur at first contact with aliens. A passage describing the Old Ones from the *Necronomicon* of the mad Arab, Abdul Alhazred, does a much better job:

By Their smell can men sometimes know Them near, but of Their semblance can no man know, saving only in the features of those They have begotten on mankind; and of those are there many sorts, differing in likeness from man's truest eidolon to that shape without sight or substance which is Them. They walk unseen and foul in lonely places where the Words have been spoken and the Rites howled through at their Seasons. The wind gibbers with Their voices, and the earth mutters with Their consciousness. . . . Great Cthulhu is Their cousin, yet can he spy Them only dimly. Il Shub-Niggurath! As a foulness shall ye know Them. Their hand is at your throats, yet ye see Them not; and Their habitation is even one with your guarded threshold. Yog-Sothoth is the key to the gate, whereby the spheres meet.[13]

Lovecraft was the master of tone. Exotic nomenclature and a baroque style allow us to "see through the glass darkly," and what we see is far more alien than giant centipedes. Another master of this style was William Hope Hodgson, as is evident in a passage from *The House on the Borderland*:

An idea came swiftly, and I turned, and glanced rapidly upwards, searching the gloomy crags, away to my left. Something loomed out under a great peak, a shape of greyness. I wondered I had not seen it earlier, and then remembered I had not yet viewed that portion. I saw it more plainly now. It was, as I have said, grey. It had a tremendous head; but no eyes. That part of its face was blank.

Now I saw that there were other things up among the mountains. Further off, reclining on a lofty ledge, I made out a livid mass, irregular and ghoulish. It seemed without form, save for an unclean, half-animal face, that looked out, vilely, from somewhere about its middle. And then, I saw others—there were hundreds of them. They seemed to grow out of the shadows. Several, I recognized, almost immediately, as mythological deities; others were strange to me, utterly strange, beyond the power of a human mind to conceive.

On each side, I looked, and saw more, continually. The mountains were full of strange things—Beast gods, and Horrors, so atrocious and bestial that possibility and decency deny any further attempt to describe them. And I—I was filled with a terrible sense of overwhelming horror and fear and repugnance; yet, spite of these, I wondered exceedingly. Was there then, after all, something in the old heathen worship, something more than the mere deifying of men, animals and elements? The thought gripped me—was there? [14]

Baroque? Rococo? Undoubtedly. But still, it is the very ambiguity of expression here, the attempt to grasp meaning through a poor resonance with the gods of our earliest pantheons, that allows us a dim glimpse of another reality. Yet another example of this style is taken from J. R. R. Tolkien's *Fellowship of the Ring*:

It came to the edge of the fire and the light faded as if a cloud had bent over it. Then with a rush it leaped across the fissure. The flames roared up to greet it, and wreathed about it; and a black smoke swirled in the air. Its streaming mane kindled, and blazed behind it. In its right hand was a blade like a stabbing tongue of fire; in its left it held a whip of many thongs. "Ai! ai!" wailed Legolas. "A Balrog! A Balrog is come!" . . . the shadow about it reached out like two vast wings. It raised the whip, and the thongs whined and cracked. Fire came from its nostrils. But Gandalf stood firm. . . . The Balrog made no answer. The fire in it seemed to die, but the darkness grew. It stepped forward slowly on to the bridge, and suddenly it drew itself up to a great height, and its wings were spread from wall to wall; but still Gandalf could be seen, glimmering in the gloom; he seemed small, and altogether alone; grey and bent, like a wizened tree before the onset of a storm.[15]

That is a selection from perhaps the single greatest example of minimalist style in the fantastic literature. It is an image that remains fresh in my memory, though engraved there some twenty-seven years ago. But the Balrog is little more than a blade, a whip, and a pair of wings. What explains the enduring power of this image? I think it is the very sparseness and ambiguity of description that makes the Balrog a kind of projective test for the imagination.

Another acid test for my thesis is provided by authors' attempts to portray superhuman intelligence in science fiction. Here, for example, is an excerpt from Poul Anderson's "Brain Wave":

"Come in." He opened the door. She sat behind a littered desk, writing up some kind of manifest. The symbols she used were strange to him, probably her own invention and more efficient than the conventional ones. She still looked as severely handsome, but there was a deep weariness that paled her eyes. "Hullo, Pete," she said. The smile that twitched her mouth was tired, but it had warmth. "How've you been?" Corinth spoke two words and made three gestures; she filled in his intention from logic and her knowledge of his old speech habits: (Oh—all right. But you—I thought you'd been co-opted by Felix to help whip his new government into shape). (I have,) she implied. (But I feel more at home here, and it's just as good a place to do some of my work. Who've you got on my old job, by the way?)[16]

That is communication between the superintelligent? The only concession Anderson makes to the 400+ IQs involved here is that a greater portion of semantic content is transmitted by gesture rather than by words. But the semantic content itself is completely unremarkable. A similar difficulty in describing the supergenius occurs in Daniel Keyes's "Flowers for Algernon":

June 5. I must not become emotional. The facts and the results of my experiments are clear, and the more sensational aspects of my own rapid climb cannot obscure the fact that the tripling of intelligence by the surgical technique developed by Drs. Strauss and Nemur must be viewed as having little or no practical applicability (at the present time) to be the increase of human intelligence. . . . The surgical stimulus to which we were both subjected has resulted in an intensification and acceleration of all mental processes. The unforeseen development, which I have taken the liberty of calling the Algernon-Gordon Effect, is the logical extension of the entire intelligence speed-up. The hypothesis here proven may be described simply in the following terms: Artificially increased intelligence deteriorates at a rate of time directly proportional to the quantity of the increase.[17]

Since the protagonist in Keyes's story, Gordon, is initially of subnormal intelligence, our expectations for the brilliance of his writing are perhaps lower than for the superminds of "Brain Wave." Still, these diary entries convey no hint of wild human genius, let alone supergenius. In marked contrast is the depiction of superhuman intelligence in Thomas Disch's *Camp Concentration.* Here are some comments on God from Disch's syphilitic superman:

HEAVENLY REFRESHMENTS Intolerable foreword! That he cannot at once annihilate anything! The just pause before that which tends to non-being. Barb-tailed Scorpio, as Master Drer demonstrates, cannot annihilate anything. Therefore, come, tender little ones—to plash again! Introduce yourselves to my blood's Phlegethon. Ah, how nicely I burn now. Go it, guests! through all my talents! Now you listen, now you hear the flagellants' invisibly tiny griefs. I would not squander my lamps and oil. Annihilations. It would be so comforting like the "dead." Pale Venus, Pia Mater, accept these few spirochetes. . . . Ramiform, the column of fluid blasphemies ascended his spine, undergoing swift corruption. This neaptide of pus is not easy to extricate. . . . That mighty gallery, Anastomosis, primal forest of essential being that we call Heart's Blood. Obtunding, he descends on all that tends to non-being; he descends, and Frightfulness lurks alongside, who is born of Nothingness, and inhabits Here-and-Now. . . . It is enormous, of a sort without haecceity. Without prejudice to All-Maker's goodness, it may be called Slug Water. We must venture farther down, beneath God's lily, to the "Fathers" (Faust, q.v.) And without prejudice to his hairy palms, we are farctate with hatred and scorn. We thumb our noses. Plant life, water rills, quavers, enervations. Greenness reflects the most flagitious of them (God).[18]

Now this conveys much more of the sense of the superhuman. The text is wild and brilliant and nearly incomprehensible. Many of the terms are so obscure that they function almost like the neologisms of the *Necronomicon.* And so, ironically, even the well defined may be employed to generate the state of ambiguity essential to perception, albeit myopic, of the superhuman. Gene Wolfe likewise employs the obscure in the generation of mood, tone, and, ultimately, illumination in the *Shadow of the Torturer.* Here Wolfe writes of Master Gurloes, of the Guild of Torturers:

"His eyes were refulgent, brighter than any woman's. He mispronounced quite common words: urticate, salpinx, bordereau."[19]

Another characteristic superhuman trait is telekinesis or teleportation. Let us first examine a description of telekinesis from A. E. van Vogt's *World of Null-A*:

"The main point is, if we're right, your extra brain is an organic Distorter, and all that that implies. With the help of the mechanical Distorter, you should be able to similarize two small blocks of wood in three or four days, and that will be the beginning." . . . The ascendancy of mind over matter—age old dream of man. Not that he had done it without assistance. Every effort had been made to make the two blocks similar. And yet they would have changed slightly since then. So slightly. His body heat in the confined room would have affected them. Both the light beam and the surrounding darkness would have had a different influence on each block, despite the absorber tubes that lined the walls, despite the most delicate electron thermostat. Without the Distorter, of course, he wouldn't have succeeded this first time. It had similarized the blocks to nineteen decimal places. It quieted the molecular movement of the air, partially similarized the table on which the blocks rested, Gosseyn's chair, and Gosseyn himself.[20]

The preceding text exhibits all the verbiage of superscience: electron thermostats, atomic distorters, and matter exactly similarized to nineteen decimal places. But it is so overstated as to preclude any possibility of our sharing in the phenomenological experience of telekinesis. This is the major pitfall of what Gregory Benford refers to as stylistic blowout[21] in science fiction. In fascinating contrast is the vivid description of "jaunting" in the final pages of Alfred Bester's *The Stars My Destination*:

He was not blind, not deaf, not senseless. Sensation came to him, but filtered through a nervous system twisted and short-circuited by the shock of the PyrE concussion. He was suffering from Synaesthesia, that rare condition in which perception receives messages from the objective world and relays these messages to the brain, but there in the brain the sensory perceptions are confused with one another. So, in Foyle, sound registered as sight, motion registered as sound, colors became pain sensations, touch became taste, and smell became touch. He was not only trapped within the labyrinth of the inferno under Old St. Pat's; he was trapped in the kaleidoscope of his own cross-senses. He jaunted. He was aboard "Nomad," drifting in the empty frost of space. He stood in the door to nowhere. The cold was the taste of lemons and the vacuum was a rake of talons on his skin. The sun and the stars were a shaking ague that racked his bones.[22]

Now that is the way to describe the indescribable! There is little in the way of neologism here, but the text is wonderfully exotic. What could be more ambiguous and uncertain than to be synaesthetically adrift? The synaesthetic metaphor allows the substitution of a sense of internal dislocation (the *presque vu*) for the extreme external dislocation (the *jamais vu*) that must result from teleportation. And so our dim apprehension of the almost seen confers on us at least the flavor of that which we will never see. This is a far cry from Benford's example, "He sounded green down the analytic corridors." [23] Admittedly, the synaesthetic experience has been overused in science fiction, but my contention is that such trite usages (which now, at best, only summon a sense of the déjà vu) largely derive from Bester's accomplishment of no less than a literal description of the loss of all reference. And in so doing he communicates a terror comparable to that experienced by the first oxygen-drunk piscean terranaut. Bester employs a text-graphics mosaic in these passages that further contributes to the evocation of a mood of internal and external sensory chaos. What is completely remarkable here is that this commingling of word and image was accomplished in 1957, decades before the vaunted age of high-tech desktop publishing.

Perhaps the final test of this essay's thesis is the description of transcendence in science fiction. Let us first examine the transmogrification of Valentine Michael Smith in Robert Heinlein's *Stranger in a Strange Land*:

Mike continued to walk unhurriedly toward the crowd until he loomed up in the stereo tank in life size, as if he were in the room with his water brothers. He stopped on the grass verge in front of the hotel, a few feet from the crowd. "You called me?" He was answered with a growl. The sky held scattered clouds; at that instant the sun came out from behind one and a shaft of light hit him. His clothes vanished. He stood before them, a golden youth, clothed only in beauty—beauty that made Jubal's heart ache, thinking that Michelangelo in his ancient years would have climbed down from his high scaffolding to record it for generations unborn. Mike said gently, "Look at me. I am a son of man." . . . Through bruised and bleeding lips he smiled at them, looking straight into the camera with an expression of yearning tenderness on his face. Some trick of sunlight and stereo formed a golden halo back of his head. "Oh my brothers, I love you so! Drink deep. Share and grow closer without end. Thou art God!" . . . The mob opened up a little at that warning and the camera zoomed to pick up his face and shoulders. The Man from Mars smiled at his brothers, said once more, softly and clearly, "I love you." An incautious grasshopper came whirring to a landing on the grass a few inches from his face; Mike turned his head, looked at it as it stared back at him. "Thou art God," he said happily and discorporated.[24]

For all intents and purposes, this is simply an extremely pedestrian and simple-minded reiteration of the Crucifixion. For a considerably different approach, let us examine the climactic appearance of the over-gestalt in Theodore Sturgeon's *More Than Human*:

Gerry clapped his hands to his mouth. His eyes bulged. Through his mind came a hush of welcoming music. There was warmth and laughter and wisdom. There were introductions; for each voice there was a discrete personality, a comprehensible sense of something like stature or rank, and an accurate locus, a sense of physical position. Yet, in terms of amplitude, there was no difference in the voices. They were all here, or, at least, all equally near. There was happy and fearless communion, fearlessly shared with Gerry—cross-currents of humor, of pleasure, of reciprocal thought and mutual achievement. And through and through, welcome, welcome. . . . Their memories, their projections and computations flooded in to Gerry, until at last he knew their nature and their function; and he knew why the ethos he had learned was too small a concept. For here at last was power which could not corrupt; for such an insight could not be used for its own sake, or against itself. Here was why and how humanity existed, troubled and dynamic, sainted by the touch of its own great destiny. Here was the withheld hand as thousands died, when by their death millions might live. And here, too, was the guide, the beacon, for such times as humanity might be in danger; here was the Guardian of Whom all humans knew—not an exterior force, nor an awesome Watcher in the sky, but a laughing thing with a human heart and a reverence for its human origins, smelling of sweat and new-turned earth rather than suffused with the pale odor of sanctity. . . . He felt a rising, choking sense of worship, and recognized it for what it has always been for mankind—self-respect.[25]

Why is the Sturgeon piece so much more successful at transmitting a sense of the transcendent than Heinlein's? I think the answer lies in our Judeo-Christian expectations. Valentine Michael Smith is the Christ figure played to the hilt. He is completely in character, and ultimately boring. On the other hand, so to speak, is Homo Gestalt, or God the Father, as the next step in human evolution. But this is not the expected stern and paternal God of the Old Testament; this is a god that partakes of humanity "smelling of sweat and new-turned earth." And so our expectations of the sacrosanct are dashed. The novelty of this theology, in conjunction with an understated economy of description unique to Sturgeon, manages to maintain the mystery essential to even the most paltry perception of the superhuman. The sheer unexpectedness of the final integration with Homo Gestalt at the novel's conclusion serves only to intensify this essential mystery. Surprise can be an excellent route to the temporary suspension and transcendence of ordinary operating parameters. A much colder approach to transcendence is exemplified in Arthur C. Clarke's *Childhood's End*:

Something's starting to happen. The stars are becoming dimmer. It's as if a great cloud is coming up, very swiftly, over all the sky. But it isn't really a cloud. It seems to have some sort of structure—I can glimpse a hazy network of lines and bands that keep changing their positions. It's almost as if the stars are tangled in a ghostly spider's web.

The whole network is beginning to glow, to pulse with light, exactly as if it were alive. And I suppose it is: or is it something as much beyond life as that is above the inorganic world? . . .

Yes—I might have guessed. There's a great burning column, like a tree of fire, reaching above the western horizon. It's a long way off, right round the world. I know where it springs from: they're on their way at last, to become part of the Overmind. Their probation is ended: they're leaving the last remnants of matter behind. . . .

Now it looks exactly like the curtains of the aurora, dancing and flickering across the stars. Why, that's what it really is, I'm sure—a great auroral storm. The whole landscape is lit up—it's brighter than day—reds and golds and greens are chasing each other across the sky—oh, it's beyond words, it doesn't seem fair that I'm the only one to see it—I never thought such colors—. . . .

I can see clearly again. That great burning column is still there, but it's constricting, narrowing; it looks like the funnel of a tornado, about to retract into the clouds. . . .

The buildings round me, the ground, the mountains—everything's like glass— I can see through it. Earth's dissolving. My weight has almost gone. You were right—they've finished playing with their toys.[26]

And here is a final example from the literature of transcendence, from Greg Bear's *Blood Music*:

I am wiping my eyes, out of terror, awe, for I have seen nothing like this in all the hours we have been wandering over this nightmare land. Telephoto cameras showed us stockyards of Chicago. When we consider the enormous mass of living creatures—pigs, cattle—concentrated in those regions, perhaps we should not be surprised or shocked. But the largest moving creatures I have seen have been whales, and these exceeded in size the largest whale by I know not precisely how much. Great brown and white eggs, could they have been hovering? Perhaps just on the ground. Greater than dinosaurs, yet with no discernible legs, head, tail.

Not without features, however, extensions and elongations, tended or surrounded by polyhedrons, that is, icosahedrons or dodecahedrons—with insect-like legs, straight not jointed, legs that had to be two or three meters thick. The ovoid creatures or whatever they were could have easily spread across a rugby field. Yes— yes—we have been told . . . we have just been informed there are airborne life forms, living things and that we have narrowly missed a couple of them, resembling gigantic manta rays stretched out, gliders or bats, also white and brown. Flowing in a stream southwest, as if forming a squadron or flock.[27]

In these last two selections we see yet another strategy for the employment of ambiguity in science fiction. In both cases the description is perfectly straightforward. The ambiguity is in the physical or biological landscape itself. It is possible for even the jaded science fiction critic to apprehend directly the alien, the other than human, if the author has sufficient skill to avoid the hackneyed stereotypes (e.g., giant millipedes) that are rampant in the genre. This is probably the purest and the most difficult usage of the ambiguous and the obscure. There are no verbal tricks, no neologisms, no obscurantism. There is simply a bare description of the extraordinary. This could be called the style of zero filtration. But the extraordinary evolves rapidly in science fiction. The half-life of such definitions of the strange may be surprisingly brief, even as the too-apt neologism may be completely co-opted for standard usage (witness the conversion of Carroll's neologism *chortled* into standard English). After all, there was a time not too long ago when the notion of a Martian invasion was absolutely terrifying to a sizable proportion of the population. But as Brooks Landon has said, "the sustained fantastic becomes merely the ordinary."[28]

And so we have traveled from Dodgson through Hodgson to God's son and beyond. I think it is apparent that a major goal of science fiction, the empathic apprehension of that which is "more than human," is often facilitated by description through neologism, seldom-used language, and deliberate poverty of detail. The far more difficult task is to maintain a simplicity of expression and a plausible objectification of the alien, that yet does not impair the sympathetic transmission of that very alienness. Even so, a bandersnatch by any other name would hardly ever seem as strange!

Notes

1. Lewis Carroll, "Jabberwocky" (1872), in *The Complete Works of Lewis Carroll* (New York: Random House), pp. 153–54.
2. Henry Kuttner, "Mimsy Were the Borogoves," *Astounding Science Fiction* (February 1943): 52.
3. Larry Niven, *Neutron Star* (New York: Ballantine Books, 1968).
4. Roger Zelazny, *Sign of Chaos* (New York: Arbor House, 1987).
5. Kingsley Amis, *New Maps of Hell* (New York: Harcourt, Brace, and World, 1960).
6. James Clavell, *Shogun* (New York: Atheneum, 1975); Martin Cruz Smith, *Gorky Park* (New York: Random House, 1981).
7. K. W. Jeter, *Dr. Adder* (1984; New York: Penguin–New American Library, 1988), p. 194.
8. *The Thing*, dir. Christian Nyby (Winchester Pictures, 1951).
9. *The Thing*, dir. John Carpenter (U/Turman-Focter Productions, 1982).
10. John W. Campbell, "Who Goes There?" *Astounding Science Fiction* (August 1938): 60.
11. *Aliens*, dir. David Cameron (TCF/Brandywine, 1986); *The Fly*, dir. David Cronenberg (TCF/Brooksfilm, 1986).
12. David Gerrold, *A Matter for Men* (New York: Timescape, 1983), pp. 22–23.
13. H. P. Lovecraft, "The Dunwich Horror," in *The Best of H. P. Lovecraft* (New York: Ballantine Books, 1982), pp. 111–12.
14. William Hope Hodgson, *The House on the Borderland* (New York: Ace-Berkley, 1962), pp. 24–25.
15. J. R. R. Tolkien, *The Fellowship of the Ring* (New York: Ballantine Books, 1965), pp. 428–30.
16. Poul Anderson, "Brain Wave," in *A Treasury of Great Science Fiction*, 2 vols., ed. Anthony Boucher (New York: Doubleday, 1959), 2:45.
17. Daniel Keyes, "Flowers for Algernon," in *The Hugo Winners*, 6 vols., ed. Isaac Asimov (New York: Doubleday, 1962), 1:227–28.
18. Thomas Disch, *Camp Concentration* (1982; New York: Carroll and Graf, 1988), pp. 119–20.
19. Gene Wolfe, *The Shadow of the Torturer* (New York: Timescape, 1981), pp. 60–61.
20. A. E. van Vogt, *The World of Null-A* (1945; New York: Simon, c. 1952), pp. 163–64.
21. Gregory Benford, "Style, Substance, and Other Illusions," in this volume, p. 50.

22. Alfred Bester, *The Stars My Destination* (New York: Signet, 1957), pp. 178–79.

23. Benford, p. 50.

24. Robert A. Heinlein, *Stranger in a Strange Land* (New York: G. P. Putnam's Sons, 1961), pp. 399–401.

25. Theodore Sturgeon, *More Than Human* (New York: Ballantine Books, 1953), pp. 186–88.

26. Arthur C. Clarke, *Childhood's End* (New York: Ballantine Books, 1953), pp. 210–12.

27. Greg Bear, *Blood Music* (New York: Arbor House, 1985), p. 148.

28. Brooks Landon, "Styles of Invisibility: Sustaining the Transparent in Contemporary Prose Semblances," in this volume, p. 245.

Chapter 10

Camouflage and Sabotage:
Satiric Maneuvers in the Fantastic
Fiction of the German Democratic Republic

Stephanie Hammer

The boom in science fiction and fantasy writing in the German Democratic Republic in the 1970s and 1980s gave birth to a wide variety of types and styles of fiction—ranging from the comic-book simplicity of the *Kompass* novelettes intended for young readers to the highly intellectual musings of such recognized literati as Christa Wolf, who dabbled in fantasy.[1] But especially interesting to me is the satiric vein of fantasy literature that emerged in GDR writing of the late 1970s and early 1980s. Significantly, the authors who mingled fantasy and satire did not label themselves satiric or humorous, as several fantasy writers—notably Wolfgang Kellner—had done. Rather, they proposed seemingly innocuous stories whose interest lies in the supernatural-pseudoscientific aspects they bring to the fore. Not surprisingly, this seemingly harmless *Trivialliteratur* escaped the eyes of the censors and often proved far more subversive than writing that proclaimed itself *satirisch*. Thus we have the curious paradox that these patently un-realistic fictions provide insight—in a way that the "official" realistic literature of the country cannot—into the feelings and concerns of the people who lived in that major Soviet satellite that we disparagingly called East Germany.

With these ideas in mind, let us examine the satiric messages surreptitiously encoded in three remarkable short stories: Karlheinz Steinmüller's "Die Audienz" ("The Audience," 1979), Erik Simon's "Gespräche Unterwegs" ("Conversations en Route," 1979), and Klaus Möckel's "Die Brille" ("The Eyeglasses," 1980).[2]

Steinmüller's terse tale weaves an ironic märchen with a suspense story; it plays out a typical fairy-tale plot—the male protagonist with a mission who must miraculously overcome a series of seemingly insurmountable obstacles—while leaving us in the dark as to the identity of the narrator and the ultimate purpose of his quest. Steinmüller counterpoints the mysteriousness of the proceedings with his matter-of-fact first-person narrator, who, like the Mad Hatter, is extremely late for what is apparently a very important date with a mysterious person. His attempts to arrive in time for his interview become increasingly desperate as he runs an impossible gamut of bureaucratic red tape in a labyrinthine castle.[3]

Steinmüller's "palace" proves to be a modern office building that—with its myriad lettered entrances and exits, numbered offices, stopwatch-clutching officials, stamps, and infinite forms—reminds us strongly of Kafka's *Castle*. As time marches inexorably on, this postmodernist Herr K., the narrator of this tale, finds himself shuttled from department to department in a vicious circle because he has not presented his papers in the proper sequence; he then loses his way in the maze of offices, only to be shoved by a long-suffering clerk into the wardrobe department to change clothes for this important interview.

But as is true in most suspense stories, the author gives us a hint of where we are and with whom we are dealing in the very first sentence: " 'Aber du kennst mich doch, Marcel,' sagte ich zu dem Wachgrenadier" (" 'But Marcel, you *know* me,' I said to the guard on duty" [57]). The name Marcel leaps to our attention; it places us not in Germany but in France. We also file away the information that the narrator is well known to the guard and has therefore visited the palace at least several times before. At the bottom of the same page, the narrator notes that a "reorganization" of palace procedures has ruined what remained of his summer vacation; obviously then, the narrator works here. The word *reorganization* appears several times in the story, always negatively and always in reference to how difficult it has made the task of the narrator to arrive promptly for his interview. And in one particularly revealing moment halfway through the story the exasperated narrator exclaims to himself: "Thank God, I don't have to live in this dump any more!" ("Bloss gut, dachte ich, dass ich nicht mehr in dieser Bude wohnen muss!" [59]). A page later we discover that the audience in question is a royal one, and, in the final lines of Steinmüller's tale, we are told that the narrator is none other than the king himself; he is ostensibly Louis XVI, for he is dressed in full classical regalia, complete with a powdered wig. With this ironic twist we finally understand the significance of the term *reorganization,* which designates the French Revolution.

Thus, according to Steinmüller's satiric revision of history, the king of France has not been guillotined after all but has been sentenced to a punishment that is perhaps worse than death. Now a beleaguered state employee like everyone else, this monarch is doomed to endlessly run the bureaucratic gamut of the palace (which is, based on an oblique reference to a hall of mirrors, probably Versailles) and to play a political role devoid of meaning but whose symbolic stature no one seems to be able to dispense with. In this, Steinmüller gives us a French Revolution that does not overturn the existing power structure but instead effects a more subtle and ultimately insidious alteration—namely, a bureaucratic reordering of the same individuals into a paralyzing and paralyzed network of offices and departments.

Clearly, this fantastic portrait of a France that is an impossible and therefore comical amalgamation of eighteenth and twentieth centuries may be seen as an ironic commentary on the progress of so-called democratic revolutions in the capitalist West. But it also provides us with a symbolic picture of the GDR, whose own political revolution, Steinmüller obliquely suggests, may have occurred on the surface of things only. In the end, the palace of "Die Audienz" provides a disturbing commentary on the bureaucratization of all regimes, regardless of their ideology: modern states are all reshuffling themselves into gloomy masses of control and constraint—impersonal networks of power which remind us of the disciplinary systems envisaged by Michel Foucault in *Discipline and Punish.*

Foucauvian theory seems especially apropos in Erik Simon's longer story of 1979, for surveillance, examination, and control play an especially ironic role here. "Gespräche Unterwegs" promises us a relatively straightforward account of a starship crew's generations-long journey to Alpha Centauri. But we soon discover that nothing is what it appears to be.[4] Through the manipulation of three different standpoints, or perceptual levels, as Simon calls them, the story fools us not once but twice.

First Simon tricks us into sympathy for the *Sternschiff Eins* (*Starship One*) families, who believe they are on a trail-blazing expedition from which only their children will return, but who, as we discover in the second level of the story, are unknowing guinea pigs in a multidecade experiment at a nearby space station to test the psychological reactions of a human society deprived of its natural environment. The starship crew, whose ship, unknown to them, is attached to the space station, has simply been revolving around the earth for the past nineteen years.

Our sympathy for these misinformed space travelers grows during the Astronautics Office inspector's visit to the observation station that is monitoring the bogus mission. This impromptu visit has occurred because an official station observer (*Beobachter*) named Whiteby has expressly disobeyed orders and has tried to break into the phony starship to inform the space travelers that they have been the victims of a cruel hoax. A heated debate follows between the inspector and the station's psychologist, Sanchez. The former insists that the station personnel must be more rigorously and frequently tested in order to ensure their complete and unquestioning obedience. The latter expresses horror that hundreds of dedicated people must spend their lives unknowingly proving or disproving a scientific thesis of dubious merit:

Es ist schon ein Verdammt Komisches Gefühl, wenn man in einer der Beobacht-kabinen Dienst hat und sieht, wie hinter der Wand . . . Menschen leben, völlig isoliert von der Aussenwelt und in einer Weise betrogen, dass mancher lieber tot wäre als in diesem Titanzylinder.

It's a damned funny feeling to have your shift in one of those observation cabins and see that behind the wall . . . people are living completely isolated from the outside world and betrayed in a way; a lot of them would rather be dead than be in that titanium cylinder. (114–15)

However, the psychologist does not have the courage to condemn the inspector and his superiors outright. By the end of this conversation Sanchez has resigned himself to his unpleasant job, and he looks forward to another tour of duty elsewhere. He has no choice, it seems, but to obey.

But Simon has not completed our tour through his fictional hall of mirrors, for now Sanchez is summoned to a meeting on Earth at the central office for the starship project. Here the project director—who turns out to be none other than the rebellious Whiteby—asks that he pose as one of the official observers of the starship crew *and* that he attempt to organize a rebellion on the part of the observers in order to test their loyalty. It is at this point that we learn that the seemingly victimized crew of *Starship One* are indeed no more authentic than the journey itself. The spaceship next door to the station is empty, and the "hoodwinked space travelers" are in fact families of actors who have been taping scenes of starship life for the past thirty years. The purpose of this experiment thus reveals itself to be to examine not the astronauts but, of course, the examiners themselves.

As if this were not enough, Simon piles yet another irony onto this already absurdly Byzantine structure of falsehoods and deceptions. The director remarks laughingly that the whole Alpha Centauri project is ultimately academic; the office has no plans at present to actually launch such a program because the engineers have not yet ascertained whether this kind of mission is even technically feasible. Thus, what matters most to the central office is not the exploration of space but rather the strict surveillance of its own personnel with the ultimate goal of making the employees into unfeeling, mindless cogs in the institutional machine.

Simon underlines the importance and inevitability of deference to authority at the end of the story. True to form, Sanchez is at first outraged by this revelation of the facts and proudly refuses to undertake this act of espionage, but Whiteby responds to this defiance with a sinister bonhomie: "Sie müssen sich natürlich nicht sofort entscheiden. Wenn Sie noch eine Woche Bedenkzeit brauchen oder zwei. . . . Wir haben Zeit" ("Naturally, you needn't answer me right away. Take a week or two to think about it. We have time" [120–21]). In an organization in which every rebellion is itself an artificial mechanism to ensure obedience, the only possible answer to the chief's invitation clearly will be in the affirmative.

"Gespräche Unterwegs" records lies—false dialogues that do not so much exchange information as establish authority. These conversations are verbal ceremonies of power that will take the interlocutors about as far as the dummy spaceship will take the astronaut actors—that is to say, nowhere. Simon's satiric survey of a scientific institution interested in nothing but training its staff according to its own warped standards and norms of behavior at no matter what cost of time, money, and effort is both comic and grim, for this world in microcosm necessarily implies a society that works the same way, and the international proper names used in the story (Whiteby, Sanchez, Karel, Sveta, and Raoul) suggest the universality of Simon's critique. He is lambasting a world at large in which both the quest for knowledge and human compassion have been stamped out in favor of a nonthinking conformism. In the world of "Gespräche Unterwegs" there is nothing else to do but obey orders, no matter how absurd, no matter how counterproductive.

Klaus Möckel's short story of 1980 is the most overtly satirical of the three tales under consideration. Unlike the other two, it is clearly set in the

GDR, and it launches a fierce attack on the vanity of the country's literary endeavor—from both creative and critical points of view. In this sense it is a self-reflexive critique that ironically questions its own present effort and leaves us with a tantalizingly open ending.

"Die Brille" begins with an established literary critic's unfortunate fall from a ladder in his library and tells of his quest to repair his broken glasses in time to finish his book review of a state-approved author's new work. Told in a stuffy and inflated style and filled with impossibly lengthy and convoluted sentence structures for which the German language is rightly famous, "Die Brille" lays bare the absurdity of literary writing at its most pretentious and exposes its lack of moral conviction and intellectual courage. This point of view is signaled at the beginning:

Hans-Gerd Talhart, von Beruf Literaturkritiker (er lebte freilich vorwiegend von Gutachten, die er für verschiedensten Verlage anfertige), ereilte an einem Donnerstagvormittag ein dummes Missgeschick.

Hans-Gerd Talhart, literary critic by profession (of course, he really lived on the positive reviews he produced for the most diverse publishing houses), met with a silly mishap late on a Thursday morning. (40)

Möckel places his protagonist under a satiric lens by announcing Talhart's prestige—giving his full name and intellectual-sounding profession and then completely sabotaging the impression he has just created by revealing in a parenthetical aside that Talhart is in fact a hack who writes good reviews for every author who has been accepted by the government-controlled publishing companies.

The fall from the ladder, which neatly summarizes Talhart's unconscious fall from responsibility as a critic (and is also reminiscent of the fatal fall of Tolstoy's Ivan Ilych), precipitates him into a ludicrous mock-heroic search in an unnamed German city for an optician who, miracle of miracles, might be able to repair the broken glasses in less time than the usual two weeks. In what is clearly an ironic reworking of E. T. A. Hoffmann's supernatural occulist Dr. Coppelius in "Der Sandmann" ("The Sandman"), the seemingly professional white-coated optician in the corner shop is a strange and unearthly creature. Wearing a postmodernist sort of zoot suit underneath his coat, the optician undulates like a modern dancer, speaks like a foreigner, seems at some moments to be wearing a pair of yellow gloves, and most *unheimlich* of all, speedily repairs the glasses on the premises while Talhart waits.

But, of course, they are not the same glasses. On returning home, Talhart finds that he simply cannot complete the positive review he had begun, because on renewed inspection the book of prose and poetry entitled *Die Zukunft im Heute* (*The Future in Today*) seems an entirely different production than he had thought it was. Using a traditional satiric device—blame by praise—Möckel has informed us a bit earlier exactly what kind of book this is:

Die Zukunft im Heute von F. Gildenstein hatte hervorragende Menschen und ihre Ideen zum Mittelpunkt, Ingenieure, die gewaltige Werke planten, Seeleute, die Weltmeere durchkreuzten, Piloten, die Hohen-und Weitenrekorde aufstellten. Glückliche Menschen wurden besungen, ausgefüllt von der Arbeit und ihren Projekten, voller schöpferischer Unrast, mit Problemen, die sie überwinden, weil sie ans Morgen dachten. Man konnte im Grunde nur positiv zu diesem Buch aussern, das zwar etwas emphatisch geschrieben, poetisch überhöht und deshalb nicht leicht zu lesen war, aber "voller tiefer Gedanken und erregender Beispiele steckte" wie es im Klappentext hiess.

The Future in Today, by F. Gildenstein [Gildedstone], focused on exceptional people and their ideas: engineers who envisioned mighty factories, sea captains who crossed the oceans of the world, pilots who set records for high altitude and long-distance flying. Fortunate individuals were celebrated here, happy people filled to the brim with work and projects, chock-full of creative restlessness, people who easily overcame whatever problems they encountered because they always thought about tomorrow. One couldn't help but react positively to this book, which was so emphatically written, so poetically elevated, and consequently not easy to read, but which was so "full of deep thoughts and inspiring examples," as the jacket blurb put it. (42)

This unremittingly cheerful, ideologically correct picture of the GDR's present population is, Talhart now realizes, a tedious recapitulation of worn-out ideas. "I only wonder that no one has noticed it before myself!" exclaims the astounded critic ("Ich wundere mich nur, dass das vor mir noch keiner gemerkt hat" [43]). Under the influence of the demonic glasses Talhart can no longer blind himself to the true artistic merit (or lack thereof) of the works he reviews. He now embarks on an uncontrolled binge of truth telling; he lambastes the work he is supposed to tout and praises—appropriately enough—the darkly satirical poetry of an unpopular writer named Rudnickel.[5] Frightened by a critical acumen that he cannot control, his career on the brink of dissolution (for now his own reputation as a man of taste is in doubt), Talhart returns to the mysterious optician in the yellow gloves and demands his old glasses back. Admitting that he had indeed altered the prescription slightly, the optician explains cryptically that he only wanted to do Talhart a favor by giving him new, improved lenses. Suddenly, the literary critic finds himself lying on the pavement outside the optical shop, which is closed. After pounding on the door, he is given entry by an entirely different and unfamiliar salesperson, and he discovers that the mysterious optician is a photographed image on an advertisement for lenses entitled "WITH A SHARP LOOK INTO THE FUTURE" ("MIT SCHARFEM BLICK IN DIE ZUKUNFT" [54]). Equipped with his old glasses, Talhart retreats to his apartment to recover from his shock and to take up once again his critical—that is to say, noncritical—duties.

Like all good satire, Möckel's story ends with a question. Is high-quality innovative writing possible in the GDR, or is East German literature doomed to mediocrity by the judgments of self-proclaimed intellectuals who seek only to aggrandize themselves by pandering to government-sponsored organizations? The suggestion that Talhart's younger controversial colleague may be a standard-bearer of that new future referred to in the poster hangs on whether the younger critic really sees clearly or whether he too wears the artificially enlightening spectacles, which force the wearer, against his will, to see things as they are, but only for a time. Like the magical glasses of its title, Möckel's story forces its German readers to recognize the problematic state of their own literature, but it also obliges Western readers to consider the forces that, in a supposedly free society, also control the success and failure of writers. Whether such considerations are momentary disturbances which we can refuse and forget, as does Talhart, or whether we can accept this perspective and dare to act on it is in the end up to us. In this way, Möckel's story calls on us to say and write what we really think, while ironically pointing to the many real inconveniences that such a step usually predicates.

Through these tales Steinmüller, Simon, and Möckel show us the considerable complexity of GDR fantasy, and they provide us with exciting examples of a little-known national literature endowed with unsuspected sophistication and artistic merit. Most exciting of all, perhaps, for the Western reader is the fact that these authors' satiric focus is such a broad one. As I have indicated, Steinmüller's, Simon's, and Möckel's fantastic tales may certainly be read in a purely topical, nation-specific context. As such they both testify to the untenability of the socialist regime in Germany and point to its probable collapse. One might even go so far as to observe that the worlds of Steinmüller, Simon, and Möckel also neatly encapsulate in advance the chaos of postunification Germany—the enormous discrepancies between its idealistic promises and the grim economic realities with which its citizens (particularly those from the east) must live; in this context Steinmüller's ironic comment on the changes brought about by revolutions seems extremely apt.

I have also tried to show, however, that the relevance of these satiric critiques ultimately transcends cultural and ideological boundaries as well as historical moment. The three stories have something to say to all of us, no matter what our political agenda is. Just as we recognize ourselves in the remote universes of the *Satyricon* and the *Trip to the Moon*, so do we apprehend in the distorted mirror of GDR satiric science fiction the paradoxes, fears, and flaws that plague our own "free" societies. At the very least it should give us pause that in the subversive literature of a now-defunct socialist country we see reflected with such clarity our own individual failures of nerve in a social community that is, after all, no better than we ourselves are.

Notes

1. I am grateful to Dr. Olaf Spittel, whom I had the pleasure of meeting in Berlin in 1987. During numerous conversations he provided me with an overview of the science fiction scene in the GDR, and he introduced me to two of the writers I discuss here—Karlheinz Steinmüller and Eric Simon.

2. "Die Audienz," in Steinmüller, *Der letzte Tag auf Venus* (Berlin: Verlag Neues Leben, 1979); "Gespräche Unterwegs," in Simon, *Fremde Sterne* (Berlin: Verlag Das Neue Berlin, 1979); "Die Brille," in Möckel, *Die glasserne Stadt* (Berlin: Verlag Das Neue Berlin, 1980). All textual citations are from the West German short story collection *Die andere Zukunft*, ed. Franz Rottensteiner (Frankfurt-am-Main: Suhrkamp, 1982). As the GDR books are extremely difficult to obtain in the West, and particularly in the United States, the Suhrkamp edition provides a more accessible means to look at these tales.

3. During my visit with the Steinmüllers in Grunow the author related that he had gotten the idea for the story while shopping in the supermarket and that he had written it in one great rush. He also mentioned, somewhat cryptically, that the story is not typical of his writing.

4. This is precisely the author's intention, as he explained to me during my con-

versation with him. In particular, Simon is interested in playing with the expectations of the experienced science fiction reader, and for that reason he is fond of using and then twisting well-known science fiction situations and motifs.

5. Möckel reinforces this irony by having Rudnickel heatedly deny that his work is in any way satirical.

Chapter 11

Utopian Effect/Utopian Pleasure

Peter Fitting

What does the unhappily still unwritten history of the concept "pleasure" teach us about the fundamental aesthetic experience?
—Hans Robert Jauss, *Aesthetic Experience and Literary Hermeneutics*

The utopia anticipated by artistic form is the idea that things at long last ought to come into their own. . . . That is why the sensuous moment is so important: while it is riveted to the transitory here and now, it also points to that status of independence that every particular work has.
—Theodor Adorno, *Theory of Aesthetics*

The Utopian Effect

What reactions or feelings are stimulated by reading utopias? Are those reactions limited to an intellectual recognition of the outlines of an ideal society, or is there more? Recently critics have begun to examine the question of a "utopian effect": *How* does the utopia move the reader to act to bring about the ideal society presented in the utopian text? But these critics have not dealt with the related and often overlooked question of *why* or *what* leads the reader to actually continue reading. This is not as obvious a question as it might seem, especially since utopian novels are often described as lacking what most gives us pleasure in reading novels. "Reading for the plot," the enjoyment of the story, the identification with characters, and the pull of closure are usually diminished or even absent in most utopian fictions because the description of an alternate society weighs down and impedes the effects and processes of the novel. Although utopias are taxed as being boring and didactic, they do continue to be written and read, as the revival of English-language utopian writing since the 1970s has shown. In this essay I attempt to explain that popularity by offering a preliminary sketch of the modes and categories of utopian pleasure.[1]

For many the definition of contemporary utopian fiction begins with its status as a novel, to which an "extraneous" element has been added. This extra element is, of course, the presentation of an ideal society, and it is this addition that supposedly interferes with the pleasures and functions of the traditional novel form. In fact, the evolution of the utopian genre demonstrates a growing awareness of these charges. Utopian authors—in the dialogic context of a changing and expanding reading public—have increasingly sweetened their rhetorical strategies with fictional treats. One of the developments that contributed to the success of Edward Bellamy's *Looking Backward* (1888) was precisely the alteration in the techniques of persuasion. Along with the change in the intended audience (to the wider public of the newly formed middle classes in the United States) there was a shift from philosophic dialogue to utopian romance. This "novelization" of utopia involved a significant transformation in the construction of the reader: from the addressee in a philosophic dialogue who is persuaded through reasoned presentation, as in Thomas More's *Utopia*, to an emotional and experiential involvement with a fictional character whose changing attitudes and feelings are designed to increase the reader's own interest and concern. In utopian novels like *Looking Backward*, this process is most often conducted through the topos of the visitor from outside and his interest in the new society in terms of an erotic attraction to one of its citizens. Utopian novels often close with the visitor's realization that the utopian society is superior to his own (I say "his" because until recently, the visitor was usually a man), and with his decision to stay and live there with his newfound love.

In his *Reader in a Strange Land*, Peter Ruppert described how fictional utopias have evolved: "Literary utopias are no longer diatribes that harangue the reader into embracing utopian beliefs; rather, they are dialectical interrogations of social reality that *force* us to recognize the provisional nature of all social values and beliefs and of our own role in formulating them."[2] The experience of reading (as Roland Barthes demonstrated in *S/Z*) is unlike experiences of other artistic forms such as listening to music or looking at a painting or even watching a film: reading is a lengthy and often interrupted process, one to which, after each interruption, the reader *chooses* to return. To explain the utopian effect, one must explain this decision to return, which is not satisfied by Ruppert's explanation that utopias force the reader to do this or that. While Ruppert offered a valuable account of the changing "pragmatics" of utopia, he did not really acknowledge the reader's pleasure or explain why a reader returns to the text. On the other hand, some science fiction criticism does begin with the premise that the genre's specificity lies in a pleasurable feeling or effect, a "sense of wonder." Darko Suvin refined this sensation in his now-classic definition of science fiction as the "literature of cognitive estrangement," in which the effect of that strange newness (in Brecht's terms, as quoted by Suvin) "allows us to recognize its subject, but at the same time makes it seem unfamiliar."[3] This estrangement, or "defamiliarization," in turn leads—ideally—to a critical understanding of the "author's empirical reality." Indeed, the link between the initial estrangement and our understanding is crucial to Ruppert's description of the experience of reading utopias:

The efficacy of those utopian dreamworlds is not in the feasibility of their designs, nor in their therapeutic effects as heuristic models of peace and perfect harmony, but in their shocking and disturbing effects on readers who are now *forced* to think about the nature of their own lives and the socioeconomic system in which they live. (158; my italics)

Utopian and Other Pleasures: Some Distinctions

The text of pleasure, as Barthes put it, is not necessarily the pleasure of the text; this remark suggests some further qualifications of the utopian reader's experience. There may be passages in which some minor detail, like the taste of Marcel's *madeleine* in Proust's *À la recherche du temps perdu*, suddenly throws open the very personal gates of memory and joy. Despite its importance in a particular context or the intensity of the pleasure it might give, such a private reaction is not the sign of the utopian effect. I am seeking pleasures specific to utopias, pleasures shared by many readers.[4] In addition to such individual flashes of delight, there are also pleasurable moments shared by many readers—a happy phrase or a moving scene, an amusing anecdote or a particularly successful character or situation, and so on—elements that may be found in any novel and thus are not specific to the utopian dimension.

There is too the simple reality—so often forgotten—of the mediation of words and writing: these characters and their experiences, like the worlds they are reacting to, are imaginary. They are mediated through language and the conventions of literature—phantoms summoned up by marks on a piece of paper. We must avoid the temptation to simply fold reading pleasure into reading about pleasure. On the other hand, this does not mean that we must shun all mention of a character's bliss and wonder, although it may be but a fictional representation of the pleasure I am claiming for the reader of utopias. Nonetheless, our response may be determined by and coterminous with representations of a character's pleasure, despite Barthes's dictum. The reader's reactions are to some extent already inscribed in the text, insofar as characters are used to stand in for the reader as intermediaries for the changed experience of daily life in a different society.

To this extent some of the enjoyment of reading utopias is enacted in the gratification and delight that the characters experience. But there are also other pleasures, including effects that are pleasurable insofar as they themselves anticipate the joy and freedom from anxiety of utopia. But it is perhaps the very deviation of the utopian form from the narrative conventions and expectations of the novel that points (as well) to its pleasures—namely, the alternate world of the utopia. Following Suvin—in particular his description of contemporary utopian fiction as a sociopolitical subgenre of SF—we might say that whereas in the latter the "strange newness" (novum) may be drawn from a variety of possibilities and alternative realities, in utopian fiction that "cognitive novelty" lies specifically in the depiction of a different society.

Thus I am arguing that the novum of the "alternate society" not only provides the cognitive dimension of the utopia but also the pleasure. This fictional pleasure can best be seen in the extraordinary success of some fantasy novels with elaborate and detailed imaginary worlds—Arrakis, Oz, Earthsea, Narnia, and Middle Earth, or the Cimmeria of the Hyborian Age. Their attraction derives from a pleasure produced by the evocation of the imaginary world itself, one that can be seen as well in the many accompanying materials that spring up around these novels: maps, glossaries, encyclopedias, costumes, fan conventions, and so on. Accordingly, I argue that the popularity of all utopian writing may be understood, at least partially, in these terms. For along with its other characteristics, More's *Utopia* (for instance) may also be read in the context of the growing popularity of travel narratives, which, regardless of their contents or ultimately their veracity, were avidly consumed by seventeenth- and eighteenth-century readers.[5] The popularity of travel literature and imaginary voyages prior to the emergence of the novel as the dominant form of narrative in Europe in the eighteenth century attests to pleasures distinct from those of reading for the story or the characters which so dominate discussions of the enjoyment of reading novels today. The enjoyment of travel narratives is itself a little-examined area, but in one of the most important examinations of the genre, Percy Adams's *Travel Literature and the Evolution of the Novel*, the author does mention "the *ancient and perennial thirst for exact details*— whether recognizably real, merely marvellous, or obviously fantastic." [6]

Given this general fascination with the depiction of other worlds, what are the differences between reading utopias and reading fantasy and SF, or even travel literature? We have already seen that as a sociopolitical subgenre of SF, the specificity of utopian fiction lies in the situation of the novum in the depiction of an alternate reality. In terms of fantasy, Suvin argues that the essential difference between SF and other "estranged" (or nonnaturalistic) forms like fantasy lies in the latter's "anti-cognitive" stance, which depends on the metaphysical nature of the imaginary worlds depicted. As opposed to the neutrality of our physical environment, the natural world of the fantasy novel is invested with good and evil, and the outcome of the hero's adventures is predetermined. In Jean Pfaelzer's terms, "The fantastic confronts us with situations that do not conform to the ground rules of the world, rules that we empirically assume; it calls into question our very modes of perception. . . . Utopian works by contrast, stimulate feelings of optimism and possibility." [7] In terms of travel literature, on the other hand (whether about real or imaginary places), there is no necessary difference, for some of it is in fact utopian (from Vairasse's *Histoire des Sevarambes* [1675–79] to Diderot's *Supplément au voyage de Bougainville* [1773]). Again, the distinction lies in the purpose or function of the novum—in what might be seen as an opposition between strangeness for its own sake (exoticism) versus the cognitive aims of attempting to imagine and describe a better society: "The particular essential novum of any SF tale must in its turn be judged by how much new insight into imaginary but coherent and this-worldly, that is, *historical*, relationships it affords and could afford." [8]

The success of the fantasy novel also depends on the reader's identification with the characters, a point to which I now turn because it has played a crucial role in the "novelization" of utopian writing. There is an important distinction to be made here between positioning and identification. By *positioning of the reader* I mean the conventions of character through which our apprehension and understanding unfold from a particular perspective or point of view. *Identification*, on the other hand, is the temporary merging of the reader's identity with that of the fictional character and the attendant psychological processes through which the text replays, as it were, buried or repressed fantasy scenarios.[9] This distinction is central to the device of the utopian visitor, who stands in for the reader as the new world is gradually revealed. Thus there is a crucial difference between the practice of depicting the new world through the eyes of a wondering outsider and the attempt to seduce the reader by linking the beauty and attractiveness of the alternative society to a person with whom the visitor falls in love.

This feature of identification is (perhaps) most evident in the ending, and the difference may be seen in novels in which the reader's seduction is confirmed by the visitor's ability to choose to remain in the new society. Other utopian novels reject such comfortable endings by refusing this satisfaction to the reader. Nor is this a new development, as can be seen by the ending of William Morris's *News from Nowhere* (1890), which was written as a reply to *Looking Backward*, and in which Bellamy's happy ending is rejected as the visitor is told he must return to his own reality.

No, it will not do; you cannot be of us; you belong so entirely to the unhappiness of the past that our happiness even would weary you. Go back again, now you have seen us, and your outward eyes have learned that in spite of all the infallible maxims of your day there is yet a time of rest in store for the world, when mastery has changed into fellowship—but not before. Go back again, then, and while you live you will see all round you people engaged in making others live lives which are not their own, while they themselves care nothing for their real lives—men who hate life though they fear death. Go back and be the happier for having seen us, for having added a little hope to your struggle. Go on living while you may, striving, with whatsoever pain and labour needs must be, to build up little by little the new day of fellowship, and rest, and happiness.[10]

While I do not have time to develop further examples of the rejection of the pleasures of identification and closure in detail here, let me at least quickly mention some recent examples.[11] The refusal of the traditional happy ending is perhaps most explicit in Marge Piercy's *Woman on the Edge of Time* (1976), in which the heroine is not only returned to her own world but is faced with personal humiliation and defeat. A second form of the refusal of identification can be seen in the polemics and direct address of Joanna Russ's *The Female Man* (1975). And there is the nonhero of Delany's *Triton* (1976), in which Bron's unhappiness and particularly his egotism and selfishness confound our attempts at identification and lead us to reflect on our own needs and the resulting shape of utopia.

Thus, although there has been an increasing novelization of utopias since the nineteenth century, they still maintain some distance between the reader and the imaginary society and its characters. Because of their didactic and intentional characteristics, utopias need a thinking reader. The more complete the identification, one might argue, the more dulled our critical faculties. While the reader is usually positioned vis-à-vis the imaginary world and the unfolding events through the perspective of the visitor, in many recent utopias identification and the imaginary release of closure are deliberately blocked. We must look elsewhere for utopian pleasure.

Pleasure and Cognition

Significant modern SF, with deeper and more lasting sources of enjoyment, also presupposes more complex and wider cognitions: it discusses primarily the political, psychological, and anthropological *use and effect of knowledge, of philosophy of science,* and the becoming or failure of new realities as a result of it. . . . Once the elastic criteria of literary structuring have been met, *a cognitive . . . element becomes a measure of aesthetic quality, of the specific pleasure to be sought in SF.*[12]

To recapitulate my argument thus far, the first mode of utopian pleasure lies in the discovery of the new world itself, in our thrill and fascination with newness and otherness. This form of enjoyment has a rich literary history, as I have already suggested, both in contemporary fantasy and in the earlier popularity of travel narratives and imaginary voyages. But the value of the novum of the alternative society lies not in its otherness or strangeness per se, but in the "insights" they afford.

In this way I now return to the dialectic between pleasure and cognition; in attempting to chart utopian pleasures, I am forced to recognize that these two functions cannot be separated. Here is a brief passage from Morris's *News from Nowhere* in which the thrill of discovery is not simply the result of a "thirst" for otherness but springs from a delight in a world shaped by the utopian principles of "generosity and abundance of life": "This whole mass of architecture which we had come upon so suddenly from amidst the pleasant fields was not only exquisitely beautiful *in itself,* but it bore upon it the expression of such generosity and abundance of life that I was exhilarated to a pitch that I had never yet reached. I fairly chuckled for pleasure" (203; my italics).

In the same way, there is a category of utopian pleasures that might be called "foretastes" of utopia—brief moments of textual pleasure in which disalienation and the end to repression are figured in some libidinal transcendence of our physical limits, as in fictional scenes of flying, from Arthur's adolescent experiences in T. H. White's *The Once and Future King* to the dragon hunt in Samuel Delany's *Stars in My Pocket Like Grains of Sand*.[13] Again, what is specifically utopian about these happy moments seems to lie in the *purpose* of these representations of pleasure. In the Delany example, for instance, there is a connection between the pleasure of this account of the dragon hunt and a larger utopian purpose because the sensation of flying, of union with the dragon's sensorium, is both the expression of a moment of libidinal unbinding in a "shared" experience (I take all such expressions of shared happiness as utopian, as juxtaposed to expressions of private pleasure) and also—in the very notion of a dragon *hunt*—a rejection of what we think of as hunting in our own world: tracking and killing some life form different from our own.

This physical exhilaration can be found as well in the "wind-riding" of Sally Gearhart's utopian novel *The Wanderground*. Again this is not simply delight in a sensation for its own sake but also an experience that arises from and embodies the new relationship of the Hill Women to Nature and the body of Earth: "With a new exhilaration she dived and swooped some more. . . . She looped above the trees in wider and wider arcs. She relearned the handling of pitch, a throwing up and downward of her legs; she rehearsed the secrets of direction." [14]

In this same vein, I argue for a more intellectual utopian pleasure, one we obtain from seeing how the ideals and promises of freedom and equality might be realized, from seeing how an author goes about working out the structures and details of an imaginary society that would make possible a realm of human freedom. In this category, my favorite example is Ursula K. Le Guin's attempt to show Marx's vision of a communist society in which the regulation of general production would "make it possible for me to do one thing today and another tomorrow, to hunt in the morning, fish in the afternoon, rear cattle in the evening, criticize after dinner, just as I have a mind, without ever becoming hunter, fisherman, shepherd or critic." [15] Le Guin's DivLab is, of course, far more than this, and the novel is a defense of Kropotkin's anarchism as well a critique of authoritarian communism. But Shevek's assertion that "work is done for work's sake. It is the lasting pleasure of life," [16] is a strong reaffirmation of this goal. Ideally the Div-Lab computers fit jobs and people together, but in the harsh conditions of Annares, this is not always possible.

A slightly different form of this more intellectual pleasure can also be found in newer modes of reading which more explicitly involve the reader in the production of meaning. While Le Guin's *Always Coming Home* (1985) does not demand as much of the reader as, for example, the experimental French novels of a few years ago which came unbound and without page numbers, through its many nonnarrative sections the book does involve the reader in the fictional construction of a new society far more than do traditional utopian narratives. The reader approaches the text (and the accompanying audio tape) a bit like a kit that must be assembled.

Conclusion

So finally the right to a specific pleasure, to a specific enjoyment of the potentialities of the material body—if it is not to remain only that, if it is to become genuinely political, if it is to evade the complacencies of "hedonism"—must always in one way or another also be able to stand as a figure for the transformation of social relations as a whole.[17]

I began my search for those pleasures specific to utopia with the reader's decision to continue reading works that have often been described as lacking the pleasurable features of the traditional novel. After some distinctions, I concluded that there was an indissoluble link between pleasure and cognition. And yet I do not want to overinstrumentalize that bond. Pleasure is not simply the manifestation of the *absence* of pain and suffering; it is not simply the emblem of the transition from the realm of necessity to a realm of freedom. Utopian pleasure cannot simply be reduced to the useful or the cognitive; it is in itself an important component of the utopian, as is suggested in William Morris's review of *Looking Backward*, in which he complained of Bellamy's "scheme of the organization of life; which is organized with a vengeance."[18] Just as recent so-called ambiguous or critical utopias have tried to leave room for individual happiness and pleasure, in contrast to earlier works which stressed the complete organization of life in the new society, so may one speak of pleasurable elements that escape or exceed the pragmatic and descriptive functions of the utopian text— although these latter features are what guarantee and make possible our happiness and delight.

Let me speak, then, of utopian pleasures that *exceed* cognition or the performative dimension, and which provide through that very excess an anticipatory experience of the hoped-for new world. Let me speak of a "surplus" pleasure that goes beyond the needs and demands of a critical explanation of the utopian work—an excess evident, for instance, in Olaf Stapledon's 1937 novel *Starmaker* (I have deliberately chosen a philosophical SF novel with very minimal plot and characters whose pleasures are seemingly few). This visionary work, with its depiction of a universe swarming with a multitude of species and fantastic forms of sentient life, may be read—in familiar utopian terms—as the critique of the author's own empirical reality, and as a sketch of new collective forms and possibilities. Yet the profusion and variety of worlds and beings presented in the novel exceed any such explanation; and even a reading that focuses on this multitude and diversity of life forms still cannot explain the function or necessity for this abundance of description (in which several generations of readers have nonetheless found wonder and enjoyment).

The critical tendency to explain the usefulness and function of every detail of a literary work is a reflection of the increasing management and commodification of our leisure time as our desires are manufactured and regulated to meet the demands of the market and of the state's attempts to control its citizens. But this must be resisted. The pleasurable discovery and the experience of a fictional world may exceed, but they do not contradict or deny cognition precisely insofar as they allow us to glimpse the possibility of an alternative which only cognition can help us comprehend. Understanding and the decision to act may follow this sensation, but the actual discovery and pleasure in otherness are themselves a promise of a world to come.

I am faced with two dilemmas in my discussion of the utopian effect. My hope for utopias that would move their readers to act is tempered by my desire that any such decision be based on reason, on an intelligent choice. Unlike advertising and political campaigns in the United States, which are interested in compelling or causing people to think or act in a certain way, we should present people with the materials to allow them to make up their own minds. The other dilemma is between hedonism and utopia, between a reading pleasure without any consequences and one that (ultimately) leads the reader to act to change his or her society. While arguing against the dangers of instrumentalization, of the critical reduction and assessment of utopias in terms of their effectiveness or usefulness, there is, of course, an opposite danger, which lies in advocating pleasures that do not outlive the immediacy of the instant. Many of the pleasures of our contemporary culture leave the reader or spectator just as he or she was before. My argument has been for a pleasure that somehow combines these elements; while retaining their pleasurable characteristics, utopias also point to a human community that does not now exist but which could be. My dream of an art able to link the experience of beauty with the need to act is summed up by the poet Rilke in his celebrated sonnet "Archaic Torso of Apollo," in which the headless torso "binds you with its grace": "For every part of this commanding form holds you in its gaze [the poem concludes]. You must change your life."

Notes

1. A version of this paper was given at the annual meeting of the Society for Utopian Studies in Boston in October 1988 and has appeared in the selected proceedings: *Utopian Studies 2*, ed. Lise Leibacher and Nicholas Smith (Lanham, Md.: University Press of America, 1991). I thank Robert Philmus and Darko Suvin for their helpful comments on that first version, comments I have only begun to develop here.

2. Peter Ruppert, *Reader in a Strange Land* (Athens: University of Georgia Press, 1986), p. 52; my italics.

3. Darko Suvin, *Metamorphoses of Science Fiction* (New Haven: Yale University Press, 1979), p. 6.

4. By mentioning the madeleine I have chosen an ambiguous example. On the one hand, I am referring to Marcel's "involuntary memory" triggered by a taste/smell from his childhood which would not have the same effect on anyone else. Yet memory, and especially Proust's descriptions of Marcel's reconstruction of his past, plays an essential role in the utopian theories of Herbert Marcuse, particularly in his *Eros and Civilisation* (New York: Vintage, 1955), p. 213. See also Hans Robert Jauss, *Aesthetic Experience and Literary Hermeneutics* (Minneapolis: University of Minnesota Press, 1982).

5. See the seventy-four titles published by Charles-Georges-Thomas Garnier in his "Voyages imaginaires, Songes, Visions, et Romans cabalistiques" (1787–1789), which are listed and described in Pierre Versins, *Encyclopedie de l'Utopie et de la Science Fiction* (Lausanne: L'age d'Homme, 1972), pp. 944–46.

6. Percy Adams, *Travel Literature and the Evolution of the Novel* (Lexington: University of Kentucky Press, 1983), p. 113; my italics.

7. Jean Pfaelzer, *The Utopian Novel in America, 1886–1896* (Pittsburgh: University of Pittsburgh Press, 1984), p. 16.

8. Suvin, p. 81.

9. See "Interaction Patterns of Identification with the Hero," in Jauss (152–88); as well as Simon Lesser, *Fiction and the Unconscious* (New York: Vintage, 1962).

10. William Morris, *Three Works* (London: Lawrence and Wishart, 1977), p. 401.

11. This refusal of identification and closure, as I and others have argued, is characteristic of many of the "critical" utopias of the 1970s. See Peter Fitting, "Positioning and Closure: On the Reading-Effect of Contemporary Utopian Fiction," in *Utopian Studies 1*, ed. Gorman Beauchamp, Kenneth Roemer, and Nicholas D. Smith (Lanham, Md.: University Press of America, 1987), pp. 23–36. See also Tom Moylan, *Demand the Impossible* (New York: Methuen, 1986).

12. Suvin, pp. 14–15.

13. For a discussion of flying as a "physical analog to liberation from societal gravity and oppressively closed social relationships" in early SF, see D. Suvin, *Victorian Science Fiction* (Boston: G. K. Hall, 1983), pp. 412–13. See also the theme of "flying" in Tom Disch's 1979 masterpiece, *On Wings of Song*.

14. Sally Gearhart, *The Wanderground* (Watertown, Mass.: Persephone Press, 1978), p. 107.

15. Karl Marx and Friedrich Engels, *The German Ideology*, ed. C. J. Arthur (New York: International Publishers, 1970).

16. Ursula K. Le Guin, *The Dispossessed* (New York: Avon Books, 1974), p. 121.

17. Fredric Jameson, "Pleasure: A Political Issue," in his *Formations of Pleasure* (London: RKP, 1983).

18. Quoted by A. L. Morton in his introduction to Morris, *Three Works*, p. 25.

Part 4

STYLE AND STRUCTURE

Chapter 12

The "Missing Middle"
of Science Fiction

Charles Platt

Here's a simple test. See if you can guess the American author of the following quote: "When dawn broke over the capital city of Walden, the sight was appropriately glamorous. There were shining towers and curving tree-bordered ways, above which innumerable small birds flew tumultuously. The dawn, in fact, was heralded by high-pitched chirpings everywhere." Not much to go on, is it? But it does contain some clues. First, the name of the city is a literary reference. This is relatively unusual; most science fiction writers still show little or no interest in literature outside their field. We can presume, for instance, that Isaac Asimov didn't write this quote, or Lin Carter, or Gordon R. Dickson, or any others of their age and ilk.

Second, the quote shows a reasonably broad vocabulary. The word *tumultuously*, for instance, wouldn't be used this way in the work of a bread-and-butter author churning out prose. Thus we can safely assume the quote wasn't written by a high-volume wordsmith at the low end of the literary scale.

Third, there's ironic detachment. The sight being described isn't just glamorous, it's "appropriately" glamorous, and the climactic sentence—talking about "high-pitched chirpings"—is a sardonically contrived stylistic pratfall. The author is describing a lyrically beautiful scene, but he isn't being lyrical. He's stylistically self-aware. He thinks straight lyricism is a bit corny.

This really narrows things down. Very little American science fiction is written with ironic detachment, and stylistic self-awareness is generally the preserve of a few "literary" types such as Thomas M. Disch or Gene Wolfe, or maybe Philip K. Dick or Robert Silverberg.

But the author of the above paragraph isn't any of those people. Here's another quote from the same source: "He'd been a misfit at home on Zan because he was not contented with the humdrum and monotonous life of a member of a space-pirate community. Piracy was a matter of dangerous take-offs in cranky rocketships, to be followed by weeks or months of tedious and uncomfortable boredom in highly unhealthy re-breathed air." Now we've gone beyond irony, into satire. The rest of the paragraph (too much text to include here) goes into specific details explaining why space piracy, as depicted in thousands of old science fiction sagas, is a silly idea that wouldn't work. This sounds modern—a bit like Douglas Adams or Terry Pratchett, except that the author is American. So could it be Harry Harrison? No; the light irony of the previous quote isn't characteristic of Harrison. He didn't do it.

One last extract before I reveal the author's name:

"There's no question about the crime," observed the ambassador. ". . . You proposed to improve a technical procedure in a society which considers itself beyond improvement. If you'd succeeded, the idea of change would have spread, people now poor would have gotten rich, people now rich would have gotten poor, and you'd have done what all governments are established to prevent. So you'll never be able to walk the streets of this planet again in safety. You've scared people.

"Do you realize . . . that a culture in which nothing unexpected ever happens is in what is called its Golden Age? That when nobody can even imagine anything happening unexpectedly, they later fondly refer to that period as the Good Old Days?"

This is beyond satire. The tone is light, yet there's an undercurrent of anger. Could it be written by a libertarian? Unlikely; few libertarian science fiction writers show the humor or detachment of the earlier quotes. Someone like Keith Laumer? No, Laumer is verbose, and although this quote is unpretentiously written, it's succinct in a way that suggests some feeling for economical prose.

In fact, all three quotes are unusually literate compared with most modern American science fiction. They seem nicely balanced between satire and seriousness, light entertainment and wordplay.

You may be surprised, then, to learn that they were written by Murray

Leinster. They came from his novel *The Pirates of Ersatz*, serialized in *Astounding Science Fiction* in February, March, and April 1959—just over thirty years ago.

Some of you, I suspect, have never heard of Leinster (whose real name was William F. Jenkins). He started selling science fiction in 1919, was a regular contributor to *Astounding Science Fiction* in the 1950s and 1960s, and died in 1975. Not much of his work remains in print because he wasn't highly regarded compared with other writers of his time. If we look him up in *The Encyclopedia of Science Fiction*, we find he rates a rather disparaging entry (written by John Clute), which uses phrases such as "a juvenile series." The best that Clute can find to say about poor old Leinster is that his work shows "craftsmanship and consistency."

Well, fair enough; Leinster wasn't at the bottom of the barrel, but he wasn't at the top, either. He could turn out fluent, readable stories with interesting ideas, but he never produced a classic. His books are gone and forgotten.

Why, then, am I quoting him? Because today, thirty years after the above extracts were first published, they look so surprisingly good. The novel that they are taken from is full of ideas, is compulsively readable, has little twists of irony, and manages to make gentle fun of adventure fiction while telling a strong, fast adventure story. Overall, it's surprisingly, impressively competent.

How can it be that a writer who was thought of as mediocre in his time now seems so much better than average? The answer must be that *average* has changed its meaning over the past thirty years. Fairly decent writers of the 1950s now look like grand masters compared with their modern equivalents. Even their prose (which some of us used to criticize as being glib and trite and shallow) looks better. A modern writer such as Jack Chalker, who works at a level of ambition roughly equivalent to Leinster's level in the 1950s, is abysmally clumsy and shallow by comparison. Chalker shows no detachment from his own work—hence, no self-criticism. His use of the English language is rudimentary; his stories exist on one level only: as simplistic mass entertainment.

I'm not suggesting that all science fiction of the 1950s was better written than science fiction of the 1980s. That would be foolish, and wrong. Our best modern writers, such as William Gibson and Lucius Shepard, have mastered a broader range of techniques and are considerably more sophisticated than anyone who wrote science fiction thirty years ago. Back then, Ray Bradbury was considered a "literary stylist," but by today's standards his work seems clumsy and naïve.

I'm not saying, either, that the crudest science fiction is worse now than it was then. Juvenile adventures are probably much the same as they ever were. The techniques in Flash Gordon and Perry Rhodan are, no doubt, eternal.

It's middlebrow, unpretentiously entertaining science fiction that has deteriorated. The stories and novels that Murray Leinster wrote didn't break new ground, weren't nonconformist, and had a broad appeal. Yet work written at a similar level of ambition today is crude, junky, and dumb by comparison.

It's easy to blame the readers for this. We can say, oh, kids these days don't know any better. They just want cheap thrills. TV has ruined their ability to appreciate subtlety in form or content. They don't get a decent education in the English language. They don't even want to read.

Maybe there's a little truth in these clichés. But according to a recent Gallup poll, less than a quarter of the American science fiction audience is under twenty-five. We can't blame "wasted youth" for the deterioration of a literature that is mostly consumed by their parents.

Who, then, can we blame? Personally, I pick the editors. Maybe this sounds too simplistic; but in the past thirty years there has been a radical shift in the way that science fiction is edited and published in the United States.

In the 1950s, magazines were the focus of science fiction, and their editors defined it in a way that is unknown today. John W. Campbell, who edited *Astounding Science Fiction*, literally told his writers what to do and how to do it. He insisted on original ideas, rigorous plausibility, and science that made sense—or at least seemed to. Likewise, Horace Gold of *Galaxy* magazine played an active role in the development of science fiction that used the "soft" sciences. Anthony Boucher of *Fantasy and Science Fiction* molded writers of yet another school. And so on.

Today, magazine editors aren't very important. More and more novels are being published, and book editors are the arbiters of taste. Unfortunately, book editors seldom have the time to make demands on their authors. They may ask for a small rewrite here and there, but editing, say, forty-eight novel-length manuscripts a year is much more time-consuming than editing a monthly magazine—especially since science fiction editors may have to deal with other categories of fiction as well, and they spend at least half their time going to meetings or grappling with the art department or going over figures from the sales department.

Worse still, many modern book editors aren't even interested in getting their writers to try harder for plausibility and accurate science. Someone like Jack Chalker can use simplistic ideas that don't make much sense because there's no one telling him to do otherwise. Likewise, he's free to write sloppy prose because no one has time to edit him. And if his work sells well (which, in Chalker's case, it certainly does), an editor will actually be reluctant to mess with it in any way. In purely commercial terms, why should anyone want to mess with a winning formula?

In fact, from this perspective, in purely commercial terms, editors of the 1950s were wasting their time trying to make science fiction better than it really needed to be. Most of the readers wouldn't have been able to tell the difference between authentic science and pseudoscience. Most of them were deaf to nuances of ironic detachment. I myself, as a wide-eyed teenager looking for escapist kicks, might have been just as happy in the 1950s if someone had given me Jack Chalker instead of Murray Leinster.

Today, I can see the difference very clearly between these two writers and the periods they represent. I find Leinster subtler, funnier, more readable, and more thought provoking. He tried harder, he had a broader range of knowledge, and he had integrity.

But my taste isn't typical. In purely commercial terms, therefore, publishers should ignore cantankerous old critics like me and give the majority of readers what they want—or at least what they'll put up with.

This is exactly what publishers seem to be doing, and as a result, I find that middle-range adventure fiction has become unreadable. Well, that's my hard luck; if I don't like it, I can always go back and reread some more stuff by Murray Leinster. After all, he did write a lot of books. And in purely commercial terms, as I'm well aware, my opinion is completely irrelevant anyway.

Chapter 13

"Born of *Misery*": Stephen King's
(En)Gendered Text

Sharon Delmendo

Recently Stephen King has begun to move away from generic horror fiction toward a new textual territory located in a developing mythic system geographically centered on Salem's Lot in Maine and the Overlook Hotel in Colorado. He has begun to experiment with new forms: a pseudo–children's fable in *The Eyes of the Dragon* and the more ambitious mythic project *The Gunslinger*, the first installment for the larger series *The Dark Tower* (starring a protagonist named Roland). Between these two departures from the "simple" horror story is *Misery*, a novel about one best-selling author's struggle with his own creative impulses and identity as author and critical and popular receptions of his work. For Paul Sheldon, a successful author of popular romance novels who has become literally entrapped by his own success, questions of literary genre and value become questions of survival. Constructed through typically postmodern fragmentation, self-referentiality, the use of doubles, and a mixture of styles, genres, and media centered on a basic Scheherazade theme, *Misery*—both the stimulus and product of *Misery's Return*—becomes the uneasy resolution of mutually antagonistic genres, a bastard child born of the tortured mixing of "high art" and the vulgar best-seller.

Misery tells the story of Paul Sheldon, an author whose best-selling romance series featuring Misery Chastain subsidizes his more serious art (he "wrote novels of two kinds, good ones and best-sellers").[1] Paul has killed off Misery in his recent *Misery's Child* in order to pursue a serious literary career. Celebrating after finishing his masterpiece *Fast Cars*, Paul cripples himself in a car crash, from which he is rescued by his "number one" psychotic fan, Annie Wilkes. Annie imprisons Sheldon in her home, addicts him to codeine-based Novril, and forces him to resurrect Misery in another *Misery* novel written just for her. The rest of the novel plots out Sheldon's struggle against Annie: he must write the novel to stay alive and kill Annie before she kills him or, perhaps worse, his creative faculty.

Yet, opening *Misery*'s cover to begin the novel, the reader finds not the title page to the novel he is expecting[2] but a false cover for *Misery's Return*, by Paul Sheldon, bearing a typical romance-novel picture of a man embracing a beautiful woman. But the man looks not at his passionate partner but at the reader—and the man has Stephen King's face. This false cover immediately disorients the reader: it is not *Misery*, by Stephen King, it seems, that we are reading; we are reading someone else's novel . . . or is it? Turning to the opposite inside page, one reads: "Misery's eyes, that gorgeously delicate shade of cornflower blue, had fluttered open. They passed from Ian to Geoffrey, who saw only puzzlement in those eyes. 'Where am I?' she asked." This excerpt is printed in large pica type, but the *es*, *n*s, and *t*s are handwritten in. Below this excerpt is another, which says, "Dear Reader: If there is puzzlement in *your eyes,* please be assured that you are reading an excerpt from the manuscript of MISERY'S RETURN by Paul Sheldon as it appears in the #1 Bestselling Novel MISERY by STEPHEN KING" (italics King's), followed by the invitation to "Read on . . ."[3] Accepting this invitation, the reader passes the title page and credits and an introductory section heading "goddess / Africa" to section 1, titled "Annie" and bearing the epigraph by Nietzsche: "*When you look into the abyss, the abyss also looks into you*" before finally reaching the novel's first paragraph. Before the narrative proper even begins, King problematizes the normally axiomatic assumption of authorial identity and integrity. *Misery* is inseparable from *Misery's Return*, a combination of King's manuscript and Paul Sheldon's. Breaking down the usual barriers between an author's visible separation from his text (in the sense that the author is visually obscured by the work), King also breaks down the voyeuristic separation between the reader and the text. The novel depends on a mutual gaze between the author and the reader (and the abyss) first established by King's knowing gaze at the reader from *Misery's Return*'s false cover and eventually carried out by the reader as he fills in the blank letters dropped by Paul's typewriter.

These levels of collaborative and symbiotic textuality and authorship are at the heart of *Misery*, which is essentially a work in progress that depends on Paul's developing manuscript. Compiling both the novel's action proper (i.e., the story of Paul's captivity) and excerpts from Sheldon's *Misery's Return* as a work in progress, *Misery* is a symbiotic text in that the movement from internal to external plot simultaneously makes up and breaks up the narrative, until the "internal plot" becomes inseparable from the "external plot." The novel cannot complete itself until Paul's novel completes itself—for the completion of Paul's novel will bring *Misery*'s plot to a conclusion as well, culminating in either Paul's death or Annie's.[4]

The mixing of texts is both *Misery*'s crux and its matrix. Intertextuality is not only structural and thematic but sexual as well, both in terms of textuality itself and Sheldon's author-muse/captive-captor relationship with Annie. Paul killed off Misery to get out of writing enormously successful, but essentially feminine, romance novels so that he could pursue a more masculine, "higher" art.[5] At Annie's command Paul resurrects Misery, who died in *Misery's Child* giving birth to an illegitimate baby. At first Paul tries to appease Annie with a caricature of his own Misery novels, a ridiculously exaggerated sequel to his other melodramatic books. Annie rejects his initial effort as not "authentic" because his resurrection of Misery is not believable; the resolution of a melodramatic cliff-hanger (such as Misery Chastain's ostensible death), she insists, doesn't have to be "realistic" as long as it is "fair" (109). Paul goes back to *Misery's Return* more seriously and becomes trapped in his own narrative, eventually blending the typical romance melodrama with literary elements from his "serious art." *Misery's Return* grows into a literary monstrosity, both dark epic and bastardized Gothic, revolving around a mythic African tribe (Africa being the symbol for Paul's captivity) led by a Bee Goddess who mirrors Annie, the psychotic bitch goddess/murderous muse who first called the narrative to life. The bastard child of gendered genres, "feminine" romance and "masculine" art, *Misery's Return* outgrows both gender and genre categorization.

This central theme of en-gendering texts revolves around an inversion of the Scheherazade myth, in which prostitution, survival, and obsession coalesce into story making. Writing, for Paul, is a sexualized activity, and writing "feminine" novels threatens his "masculine" creativity. Paul killed off Misery Chastain to end his prostitution to a female audience, but he prostitutes himself to stay alive by writing *Misery's Return*: "Fast Cars *was about not being a whore. That's what killing . . . Misery was about, now that I think about it. I was driving to the West Coast to celebrate my liberation from a state of whoredom. What you* [Annie] *did was to pull me out of the wreck when I crashed my car and stick me back in the crib again.*"[6] Like Scheherazade, Paul tells a story that must become his audience's obsession if he is to save his life. Annie reads Paul's manuscript as he writes it, and "so began the thousand and one nights of Paul Sheldon" (149). His manuscript appeases Annie's addiction to the Misery Chastain saga, but Paul has his own addiction to the drugs Annie gives him for his crippling injuries. As he begins *Misery's Return*, Paul and Annie feed each other's addictions at almost an even level of exchange; Paul's only hope for survival is to tip the economy in his favor. But Paul also addicts himself to his own story—becomes his own Scheherazade—in order to find a reason to live. Annie's mental torture makes him increasingly psychotic, and her progressive amputation of parts of his body as an added incentive to write physically shrinks him.[7] Ironically, the manuscript itself reflects Paul's psychological deterioration as the typewriter loses more and more keys, until it becomes more efficient for Paul to write his story by hand; thus Paul's manuscript charts his mental decomposition inversely as his narrative composition grows. But the narrative obsession grows despite the increasing difficulty in producing the physical manuscript—for Paul, Annie, and, ultimately, the reader—and the narrative surges uncontrollably to its conclusion, which will inevitably end both Misery's saga and either Paul's or Annie's life.

The text, in *Misery*, is the sexualized bargaining chip between Paul and Annie. The novel begins with Annie's "raping" Paul back to life (after he had gone into respiratory arrest as a result of the drugs she had given him) with "the breath she had forced into him the way a man might force a part of himself into an unwilling woman" (5). Annie forces Paul to burn his masterpiece *Fast Cars* to divorce him from his masculinized "high" art and acquiesce to writing another Misery sequel, and Paul ultimately retaliates by trying to kill Annie by choking her with the ostensible manuscript of *Misery's Return*, "lying squarely on top of her like a man who means to commit rape, . . . thinking *I'm gonna rape you, all right, Annie. I'm gonna rape you because all I can do is the worst I can do. So suck my book. . . . Suck on it until you fucking* CHOKE" (317; italics King's). This scene is the novel's "climax." By choking Annie with the book she forced him to write, Paul obtains not only his sexual revenge but his artistic revenge as well, as, unbeknownst to Annie, Paul has saved the real manuscript of *Misery's Return* and chokes her with a dummy manuscript of blank sheets and first-draft debris. *Misery's Return* becomes a blockbusting best-seller, the artistic and financial means for Paul to begin his life again.

The autobiographical relationship between an author and his work is always hazardous ground. King's personal and professional auto-biographical relationship with *Misery* inevitably comes up; King forces the issue by displaying his own face on the false cover for *Misery's Return*.[8] By supplying his own face for an illustration of one of Paul Sheldon's char-acters, King raises the question of whether Paul Sheldon is Stephen King's fictional character or Stephen King is Paul Sheldon's. Playing out the auto-biographical question King forces on us, the distinctions between "real" and "fictional" author disappear as imperceptibly as do the distinctions between the "real" and "fictional" texts.[9]

The issue of King's authorial identity, and the fictionalization of that identity, was raised in 1985 by Steve Brown's discovery that Stephen King had published five early novels (*Rage*, *The Long Walk*, *Roadwork*, *The Running Man*, and *Thinner*) under the pseudonym Richard Bachman. In "Why I Was Bachman," the introduction to the reprinted edition of *The Bachman Books*, King offers this partial explanation for his use of a pseudonym: "I think I did it to turn the heat down a little bit; to do something as someone other than Stephen King. I think that all novelists are inveterate role-players and it was fun to be someone else for a while" (viii). Beyond playacting, however, King hints that his use of a pseudonym allowed him to escape the literary stereotyping that confined him to writ-ing "out-and-out horror stor[ies]" (ix)—that, like Paul Sheldon, Stephen King wrote "two kinds of books." Unlike Sheldon's categorization of his work into mutually exclusive "good [books] and best-sellers," King re-verses his narrative categories into Stephen King's best-sellers and Richard Bachman's "just plain books . . . the paperback book publishing world's equivalent of trench warfare. . . . or cannon [canon?] fodder" (x). King discusses the possibility that he used a pseudonym because he had over-published under his own name: "I didn't think I was overpublishing the market . . . but my publishers did. Bachman provided a compromise for both of us" (xi). He continues, "My 'Stephen King publishers' were like a frigid wifey who only wants to put out once or twice a year, encouraging her endlessly horny hubby to find a call girl. Bachman was where I went when I had to have relief" (ix). King's metaphor here for a compulsive need to publish as analogous to sexual satisfaction, combined with his Bachman productions described in metaphorical terms of warfare, reflects the same association of writing with sexual tension/prostitution and antagonism manifested in *Misery*.

King built Bachman from a narrative outlet into a literary alter ego with an elaborate fictive biography including a wife, a child who died in "an unfortunate accident," a near (surgical) escape from cancer, and a "bogus author photo on the back of *Thinner*."[10] The problem with developing the fiction so far was that Bachman's viability blurred the distinctions between Stephen King the "real" author and Bachman the "fake" author— like the authorial confusion between King and Paul Sheldon in *Misery*— until, "like Mickey Mouse in *Fantasia*. . . . things are never the same." King has been "getting letters asking me if I was Richard Bachman from the very beginning" (vii–viii).

King explicitly reveals the relevance of the Bachman issue to *Misery* when he states, "I had intended Bachman to follow *Thinner* with a rather gruesome suspense novel called *Misery*" (xi). King reveals his anxiety about the literary value of his own work during his Bachman years by admitting, "I was . . . young enough in those days to worry about that casual cocktail-party question, 'Yes, but when are you going to do something *serious*?" and it is this anxiety that King self-reflexively allegorizes in *Misery*. And, King asserts, it was *Misery* that "might have taken 'Dicky' onto the best-seller lists" (xi). "Of course," he reflects, "we'll never know now. . . . Richard Bachman, who survived the [fictitious] brain tumor, finally died of a much rarer disease—cancer of the pseudonym" (xi). By staying alive long enough to complete *Misery's Return*, which combines his "female" best-sellers and "masculine" art, Sheldon—one fictional author—reconciles his "two kinds of books." Ironically, Stephen King couldn't keep his own fictional "author" alive long enough to complete *Misery*. Published under Bachman's name, *Misery* would have, by "tak[ing] 'Dicky' onto the best-seller lists," reconciled King's "two kinds of books."[11]

Ultimately, the false cover of *Misery's Return* is the matrix for a series of narrative bifurcations: the gendering of literary categories, such as "female" pop fiction and "male" high literature; the authorial confusion between Stephen King as *Misery*'s author and Paul Sheldon as the author of *Misery's Return*; and the autobiographical confusion between Stephen King and Richard Bachman. And true to the central theme of Scheherazade, the spinning of stories is a matter of survival: in an appropriately ironic twist, King kept Sheldon alive long enough to finish *Misery's Return* and kill Annie, yet he was unable to keep Bachman alive long enough to finish *Misery*. Outside the narrative world Bachman succumbed to the same threat faced by "his" novel's protagonist: Bachman was "killed" by one of his readers. King's metafictive problematizing of these narrative bifurcations integrally involves a drive toward sexual and authorial legitimacy, and ultimately fails to achieve that legitimacy without enormous cost: Sheldon regains his masculinity and *author*ity at the cost of a foot, a thumb, a good part of his sanity, and Annie's life; and King, bereft of narrative recourse to Bachman, has yet to be accepted as writing "high" fiction.

Notes

Appropriately enough, given the postmodern doubleness and intertextuality of King's novel, my own analysis of it has also, in some sense, been "written" by its readers. I am particularly indebted to Neil Schmitz and Andrew Hewitt, both of SUNY-Buffalo, for their suggestions and comments on this project.

1. Stephen King, *Misery* (New York: Signet New American Library, 1987), p. 7.
2. The reader's gender, and his or her expectations, are very much an issue for Sheldon, given his determination to escape his "prostitution" to *Misery*'s female audience. *Misery* and King's description of a recurring nightmare on which the novel's plot is modeled both reveal an anxiety about a castrating female critic (see n. 8 below). I am currently examining this central tension between gender, the popular reader, and the empowered reader-critic in another version of this paper.
3. This invitation to participate in the text is significant if one remembers the traditional horror myth, popularized by Bram Stoker's *Dracula*, that evil must be invited in. In this interesting inversion, the reader becomes partially culpable for the story: in being invited into the text, the reader assumes the position of evil; in being a collaborative author, he unwittingly helps create the novel's events.
4. Annie also produces her own unfinished "manuscript": the scrapbook "Memory Lane," made up of the newspaper accounts of her victims up to and including Paul, who is listed as "reported missing" (*Misery*, p. 201). But this "text," like everything else in the novel, must wait on the completion of Paul's manuscript to find its own completion (or, in the case of Annie's scrapbook, its definitive incompletion).
5. *Fast Cars* opens with the lines, " 'I don't have no wheels,' Tony Bonasaro said, walking up to a girl coming down the steps, 'and I am a slow learner, but I am a fast driver.' " *Fast Cars* is stereotypically male oriented in its male

protagonist, the "dirty" (i.e., "unladylike") language to which Annie objects, and Bonasaro's assumption that a fast car provides the means for the sexual attainment of the girl.

6. *Misery*, p. 72; italics King's. Being "stuck back in the crib" also calls up maternal images, and Annie is identified at various points as a punishing/nurturing (anti)mother.

7. In the course of the novel Annie amputates one foot and a thumb but refrains from castrating Paul—although the idea occurs to both Paul and Annie—either in deference to the traditional association between the penis and the pen or to keep castration in reserve as the (pen)ultimate threat.

8. The autobiographical question becomes even more insistent when one reads King's description of a recurring dream in *Danse Macabre* (New York: Berkley, 1981):

> [In a dream] which has recurred at times of stress over the last ten years—I am writing a novel in an old house where a homicidal madwoman is reputed to be on the prowl. I'm working in a third-floor that's very hot. A door on the far side of the room communicates with the attic, and I know—I *know*—she's in there, and that sooner or later the sound of my typewriter will cause her to come after me (perhaps she's a critic for the *Times Book Review*). At any rate, she finally comes through the door like a horrid jack from a child's box, all gray hair and crazed eyes, raving and wielding a meat-ax. And when I run, I discover that somehow the house has exploded outward—it's gotten ever so much bigger—and I'm totally lost. On awakening from this dream, I promptly scoot over to my wife's side of the bed. (84–85)

With remarkably few alterations, King's nightmare works itself into *Misery*, with Annie as a combination of the ultimate critic and the madwoman in the attic, and Sheldon, trapped in the house by his injuries, the weather, and his drug addiction, standing in for King. Even the sound of the typewriter as the stimulus for punishment translates into *Misery*'s plot, as Annie cuts off Paul's thumb because he complains about the typewriter with which she has supplied him.

9. Michel Foucault, "What Is an Author?" in *Textual Strategies: Perspectives in Post-Structuralist Criticism*, ed. and trans. Josue V. Harari (Ithaca, N.Y.: Cornell University Press, 1979), pp. 141–60; Stephen King, "Why I Was Bachman," in *The Bachman Books* (New York: Signet New American Library, 1985), pp. v–xiii. Subsequent page numbers in the text all refer to this article.

   I am indebted to Foucault's "What Is an Author?" Both "author" and "work" are problematic terms which in some sense mutually define each other, but ultimately the author's name is not "a pure and simple reference, . . . it is the equivalent of a description . . . [which] performs a certain role with regard to narrative discourse, assuring a classificatory function" (Foucault, pp. 146–47). Both Foucault and King discuss the historical phenomenon of how the author's name affects the literary value of his work in interestingly similar terms (see Foucault, pp. 148–51; and King, "Bachman," pp. xi–xii).

10. "Bachman," p. viii. King's choice of the pseudonym Bachman irresistibly recalls Johann Sebastian Bach, the prolific master of the fugue. The doubling, labyrinthine intertwining of *Misery* and *Misery's Return*, the "real" versus "fictive" authors, the reader's role in authorship, and sexual satisfaction and warfare as metaphors for fictional production appropriately resemble a narrative fugue.

11. In "Why I Was Bachman" King relates a Beatles anecdote:

> In 1968 or 1969, Paul McCartney said a wistful and startling thing in an interview. He said the Beatles had discussed the idea of going out on the road as a bar-band named Randy and the Rockets. They would wear hokey capes and masks à la Count Five, he said, so no one would recognize them, and they would just have a rave-up, like in the old days.
>
> When the interviewer suggested they would be recognized by their voices, Paul seemed at first startled . . . and then a bit appalled. (vi)

King's Bachman masquerade ended because, like the Beatles, he couldn't obscure his "voice."

Chapter 14

Styles within Styles,
or "Death of a Hack Writer":
Herovit's World Reconsidered

Reinhart Lutz

This is pitiful. Truly pitiful, Lothar finds himself thinking and thinking then for the twenty-ninth time that if only Colonial Survey had not been so authoritarian he would have had his last slave-voyage several moons ago. He hopes that this thinking is not an omen of worse things to come but suspects that as always his mood is a good barometer of what will follow.

As Lothar's speculations might indicate, Barry Malzberg's 1973 science fiction novel, *Herovit's World*,[1] is a grim, sarcastic examination of the (end of the) world of a once-successful and immensely prolific mass-market science fiction writer. Unable to complete novel number ninety-three, Jonathan Herovit is set on a mental obstacle race, in the (downward) course of which he reexamines his life in the "field" of science fiction. Burdened beyond his breaking point, Herovit first assumes the identity of Kirk Poland, his all-American pseudonym (under which he has published the *Survey* series), a writer-persona he has crafted from the scrap heap of his own aspirations and the stringent commercial requirements of the "field." Alas, Kirk's tragicomic attempt at straightening out the life he inherits from Herovit collapses in a bitter series of defeats hardly surpassed in literature. Herovit next takes the ultimate step prescribed by the logic of schizophrenia when

181

he identifies himself with his creation, "pulp" hero Mack Miller, and embarks on a suicidal rampage which ends when he is run over in the streets of New York City.

As a novel about the writers of mass-market science fiction and the conditions in which they operate—under which both the best and the worst works of the genre have been produced—*Herovit's World* is exceptional in its clear-eyed and merciless revelation of the nightside of human suffering among the creators of a form of writing—of art?—that has long suffered from peculiarly downgrading modes of production.

Rather than lecturing to its readers in the vein of Frederic Wertham's 1954 *The Seduction of the Innocent, Herovit's World* uses science fiction itself to present the idea that writing it can be hazardous to your mental health if you are too aware of the paradoxes and ironies of the genre. Locking firmly onto his target, Malzberg creates a fictional triptych, three stylistically different interlocking texts-within-the-text which interact to make a literary-artistic statement on the style, form, and economics of a genre which is nevertheless dear to the heart of its assailant. Thus, within *Herovit's World*, we find, first, excerpts from Kirk Poland's science fiction novels; second, the "realist" story of Herovit's fall; and, third, the grand finale of Mack Miller's hostile takeover.

Within the strategic network of the novel, intratext number one—the excerpts from *Survey Sirius*, the yet-to-be-completed twenty-ninth novel in the "Mack Miller" series Herovit writes under the pseudonym Kirk Poland—fulfills the double functions of making the reader a silent accomplice in the hack writer's desperate struggle to finish his book and of cannily exposing the prevailing rottenness of the excerpts' "real-life" counterparts, science fiction stories and novels. To set these excerpts apart visually, Malzberg has made use of what Harlan Ellison in *Dangerous Visions* (1967) calls "typographical tricks": they are set in a typeface that mimics the look of a typescript (rather than a printed text), and they come complete with graphic flaws (presumably caused when the paper got caught in the typewriter) and with occasional negligence about capitalization and spacing. The excerpts look like messy typescript and read like "pulp."

Herovit admits to never rewriting a page, and his typescript abounds with sentence fragments and the occasional misplaced adverb. For example, this is how Mack perceives the alien:

As it ate up the ground with surges of pure physical energy, flashes of power volting from its brutal and strangely shaped head. . . . He could hear the hoofs and greenish spurs of the Meldebaranin" (25–26).

But if the style here approaches levels of subliteracy strongly reminiscent of genuine pulp fiction, it nevertheless also approximates language used in such generally acknowledged masterpieces of the genre as Heinlein's *The Puppet Masters*. Consider, for example, Heinlein's description of the goings-on on Venus: "The slugs were moving in to stay. . . . It is sure that Mary saw her parents being placed in suspended animation—for later use in the invasion of Earth? Possible."[2]

What makes *Herovit's World* transcend satire or parody, however, is the existence of the second intratext—the center panel of the triptych—which is essentially an exegesis of the fragments of *Survey Sirius*. In this, Herovit's musings on the conditions, conventions, and mechanics of the science fiction field make him his own literary critic and produce an aura of self-referentiality. In a typical instance, Herovit, looking at page 21 of his ordeal, realizes that he "must establish the physical-science basis for the plot at this point . . . explaining the mysterious substance that one hundred and fifty-nine pages later will signal [the aliens'] doom" (11). The ominous typescript promptly reappears in the text, giving the musings of the first mate: "is there such a thing as tanamite or is it a fool's construct?" (11).

Of course, Malzberg is not the first to spike his text with literary self-consciousness: he taps into a long tradition. Just among contemporary novelists, for example, in the title story of his *Lost in the Funhouse*, the narratological asides of John Barth's intrusive fictional author preview Malzberg's maneuver: "The boy's father was tall and thin, balding, fair-complexioned. Assertions of that sort are not effective; the reader may acknowledge the proposition, but . . . his imagination is not engaged."[3]

Traces of Eugene Ionesco and Samuel Beckett are noticeable in Malzberg's work. But what, then, makes the stylistic manipulations of *Herovit's World* special? Do they do more than merely reflect the influence of absurdist fiction and (post-) modern theory, with its dictum "the text is all there is"?

Firstly, *Herovit's World* was not written in an intertextual vacuum. In its field it *is* innovative, and it certainly exceeds the typical level of self-reflexivity, former heights of which can be observed in Robert A. Heinlein's *Stranger in a Strange Land* (1961), in which Jubal Harshaw (Heinlein's alter ego) asserts that "if I turned down a free feed, they'd toss me out of the Author's Guild."[4] Secondly, genuine to *Herovit's World* is its special focus on the material conditions under which text/product and author/manufacturer exist. This is a new direction, and it moves beyond Barth, who in *Funhouse* still concerns himself with the *art* of the novel.

Thus, on an ontological level, through *Survey Sirius*, *Herovit's World* comes up with a radical proposition and screams it at the reader: "science fiction *is* because its authors want to make money." Before even looking at the field itself, the text warns us that to enter the artistic one-way street of writing science fiction for what seems like easy money will result in irre- versible artistic decay brought on by years of underutilization of talent and massive exploitation . . . and not even much financial reward.

Furthermore, this quagmire offers little in terms of artistic satisfaction; if there are any redeeming values, we learn from *Survey Sirius*, they have to lie somewhere else. Yet even different aspirations—that science fiction can work as "applied social science" or "fictional futurology"—are mer- cilessly exploded by the second ("realist") intratext's cynical presentation of Herovit's final marital battle with Janice. Her enraged, subjective, but genuine voice makes short work of such myths as "[science fiction] fore- told the splitting of the atom": "Like hell it did. It was just a lot of crap, all of it, and a couple of lucky guesses" (158).

For the moment, stripped of any redeeming literary, sociological, or sci- entific values, the writing and reading of science fiction are reduced to a simple economic exchange: in order to provide subliterate and underdevel- oped brains with some escapist material—to be consumed "on busses and in public rest rooms" (7)—the "hack" is given a meager fee.

A prime problem with this equation, however, is that it violates power- ful cultural perceptions which have idealized the act of writing; and the second intratext picks up its cue when Herovit, who has now assumed the persona of Kirk Poland, his erstwhile pseudonym, meets his "artistic" counterpart, a nameless prostitute. After all, the act of taking money for a service is not questionable—car mechanics and dentists do it every day and thrive in the process. On the other hand, to profane the sacred by com- mercialization leads directly to cultural ostracism and the destruction of self-esteem in the perpetrator, whether hack or whore. In Herovit's case, baiting his muse with money comes close to an act of literary simony—and the trouble is that the text insists on its character's self-knowledge of that degradation, an insight that leads to Herovit's self-destruction.

By holding up the mirror for its protagonist in his encounter with the streetwalker, *Herovit's World* breathes new life into the tired cliché about prostituting one's talents by literalizing the metaphor in an original fashion for the field of science fiction. Both Herovit and the whore provide plea- surable escapist activity which moves to a clearly defined terminal climax; further, the duration of the plot is determined by the amount of money spent by the "trick" or reader. In the same way that Herovit reflects on his methods, so does the prostitute offer her deal. "Put it together at 15,000 words," he says, "and sell it to Steele; string it up to 60,000 and go for the book rights" (7). "It's twenty dollars," *she* says, "but it can be fifteen, I suppose, if you don't want a long date" (125). In the absence of artistic inspiration or textual complexity (or mutual sexual enjoyment) as motivating forces for the plot, the crudeness of the monetary motive comes as an insult to the reader (or "trick"), who wants to believe anything but that the text (or intercourse) exists only to fulfill a commercial contract.

Consequently, both "providers," hack and whore, try to cheat as much as possible—"perhaps he can get away with forty-two thousand if he uses wide margins and lots of dialogue" (20)—and try to terminate the act as soon as possible. "I need it," says the prostitute, "need it so badly, make it hard and make it quick" (134). She mechanically repeats the crude credo of commercialism: "time is money." Likewise, Herovit's notes to himself further reveal how devoid of artistic aspirations his products have become and how desperately he needs to conserve his energy: "Lothar speaks repetitively," he writes, "don't forget this to fill out word count" (141). The poignancy and accuracy of this aside are confirmed by even a brief look at the real pulp science fiction where Herovit's commercial rules operate. Just consider, for example, the style of C. M. Kornbluth's story "The Words of Guru": "The place we were in next was lit with red lights, and I think that the walls were of rock. Though of course there was no real seeing there, and so the lights only seemed to be red, and it was not real rock."[5]

The cruelest, most disillusioned analogy comes at the end of Herovit-Kirk's encounter with the whore. Just as bought sex does not offer "love," so something is missing after finishing a *Survey* novel: "You held off the ending until the proper time and then you sprung it and another two thousand dollars was yours. What the hell did they want for their two thousand dollars: sense? Resolution? 'Screw this,' [Kirk] murmurs" (113). Thus commercial fiction has been proved to be as empty of meaning as a can of Bud Light is of food value; from here, the only alternative can be to get away from all pretensions and embrace the depravity of which you convict yourself.

It is ironically significant that in their crucial encounter, the prostitute refers to Herovit first as "Johnny"—the affectionate form of his own name, Jonathan—and then, on his insistence that she "individualize" him, as "Mac"—the name of Kirk Poland's pulp protagonist. Never, however, does she address him as "Kirk"; thus, she refuses the name he has chosen for himself in his attempt at writing his own text, in defiance of the realist world of Jonathan Herovit and the fictional world *created for him* as Mack Miller.

Kirk thus fails to take control of Herovit's world. His logical next step is to look at the protagonist of his fictional text, *Survey Sirius*, the product not primarily of his genuine imagination but of his necessarily slavish adherence to the requirements and ideological paradigms of the field. To be a hero of mass-market science fiction, Mack Miller has to be a destroyer: "Killing was a necessary part of the job and he had no guilt. No sense in taking chances on a strange planet with its record of brutal slaughter . . . Mack . . . was not an Establishment member, had no truck with sociology, and could recognize danger when he saw it" (25–26).

Consider *The Puppet Masters* again, for a brief check on the veracity of *Survey Sirius*: "What the President needed to do the Old Man had already figured out—declare a national emergency, fence off the Des Moines area, and shoot anybody who tried to slip out. . . . Use the radar screen, the rocket boys, and the space stations to spot and smash any new landings" (20).

Of course, the idea that nearly all science fiction up to the New Wave of the 1960s comes close to protofascism is not original with Malzberg. Yet *Herovit's World*, like Norman Spinrad's *The Iron Dream* (1972; a novel written by the Adolf Hitler of a parallel universe), is a powerful commentary from within the field rather than a sociological study or a mainstream text featuring a quick dismissal of unread material. Writing Mack Miller into existence has had its effects on Herovit. In the absence of love and art, violence becomes a viable alternative, and the author is finally ready to enter the world he has written up according to the guidelines laid down by a culture which first feeds and then forsakes the hack.

Thus, the third intratext functions ultimately to unify *Herovit's World*, for the narrative conveys the last moments of the protagonist, and by completing the story, unifies it. As Mack, Herovit has internalized the message of his medium to the fullest and lives accordingly. We notice how his violence is presented in terms of achievement:

At the first alien intersection, Mack attacks and knocks unconscious with a blow a male alien; . . . he *manages* to inflict injury upon several others. But by weight of numbers the pursuers . . . wear him down. . . . An alien vehicle hits him with terrific force, striking through his armor. . . . "It isn't fair," Mack says, . . . and then says no more. (208–9; my italics)

With this third intratext, which conveys the ideology of the genre and its lethal dangers if applied directly to human intercourse, *Herovit's World* concludes its painting of a nighttime of human suffering—a world where the gap between global pretensions ("foretold the splitting of the atom[!]")

and violent ideology cruelly clashes with the reality of the shoddy, besotten, mundane, and mediocre lives of its creators. The texts produced in Malzberg's inferno are bad prose at best, and self-destructive if taken seriously. Is *Herovit's World*, then, the swan song of science fiction?

The answer, I think, is no. Despite all the acid Malzberg's novel pours on the aspirations, pretensions, and illusions of the genre, his text is the product of a relationship that includes love as well as hate. First, *Herovit's World* transforms a science fiction writer into a genuinely tragic American hero of the rank of Arthur Miller's Willy Loman and Saul Bellow's Thommy Wilhelm. Thus it refuses to cast aside the genre and its authors as utterly meaningless and negligible. After all, the subject is elevated to a level of self-consciousness, critical analysis, and dramatic experience which is not usually bestowed on culturally irrelevant matters.

Secondly, on a biographical note, it is interesting to consider that the author performs his merciless scrutiny of the science fiction field using material borrowed from his dabblings in a neighboring genre. Even though Malzberg started his science fiction career as "K. M. O'Donnell," proudly bearing the initials of Kirk and Mack, he never, even at his worst, wrote science fiction of Kirk Poland's *Survey* series type—but he did produce fourteen Lone Wolf crime novels, all published between 1973 (the year of *Herovit's World*) and 1975, and all issued under the pseudonym Mike Barry. Their titles carry alliteration—as seen in Kirk Poland's *Survey Sirius, Survey Starlight, Survey Sunlight*—to its logical self-referential conclusion. The titles follow roughly alphabetical order: *Chicago Slaughter, Desert Stalker, Havana Hit, Los Angeles Holocaust*, and *Miami Marauder* form a neat series. Interestingly enough, as Francis M. Nevins, Jr., points out in *Twentieth Century Crime and Mystery Writers*,[6] Malzberg's character Burton Wulff (the "Lone Wolf" of the series), is a more paranoid version of Donald Pendleton's "Executioner," Mack Bolan, a one-man commando fighting organized crime—and Malzberg worked for Pendleton's literary agency, Scott Meredith. In an act which ironically mirrors the fall of Mack Miller/Jonathan Herovit, Burton Wulff finally loses all sense of moral distinction and turns into a killing machine, thus personifying the genre's ideology.

Suddenly, then, the text of *Herovit's World* frees itself from any one particular genre; it has universal reference. But there is another aspect to be taken into consideration. This borrowing across genres in a sense pays silent homage to the *potential* of science fiction, in which Malzberg still believes, no matter what his fictional writer does with and to the genre by working in the most debased forms it offers—for when Malzberg wants real trash, he doesn't reach for science fiction. Part of the silent anguish which makes *Herovit's World* more than a mere declaration of war on science fiction comes from its exquisitely felt pain over the transformation and abuse of this potentially most radical form of fiction, a form that brought forth such genuinely revolutionary and prophetic masterpieces as George Orwell's *1984* (1948). At its best, the genre refuses to frolic in a dime-store cosmos ruled by a warped and violent ideology.

In all powerful love-hate relationships, it is difficult to know when to quit. Malzberg's love-hate relations with the genre of science fiction produce a text that loads the dice by also presenting the reader with two characters who have freed themselves from the field, but only to the point of becoming phony exploiters of unmerited fame. First, there is V. V. Vivaldi—labeled "dean of science fiction" by the fandom—who has ceased writing in favor of founding and administering Process Religion (a not-so-subtle allusion to L. Ron Hubbard's *Dianetics*); in truth, he is a cantankerous alcoholic who passes out on Herovit and causes his expulsion from the Science Fiction Writers' Guild shortly before it ceases to exist altogether. Then there is Herovit's friend Wilk, who has escaped from writing by accepting a nontenured professorship at a small eastern college; through him, academia and the "art" of analysis, or critical discourse, are revealed as phony, self-serving, painful, and thoroughly absurd alternatives to writing, which at least has some dignity and creative courage. (Note Malzberg's bias: he once claimed that he started writing science fiction to avoid becoming an unpublished assistant professor.)

In a scene reminiscent of the nightmare world of Woody Allen's deeply sarcastic *Stardust Memories* (1980), Herovit dreams that he is lured into bed by a coed only to be examined physically and verbally by academics of Kafkaesque proportions. There is a close analogy here to Allen's burnt-out comedian Sandy Bates, who vainly tries to escape the analytic rage of fans and critics, including those who continue their critique in his bed. What destroys both Herovit and Sandy Bates is the unbridgeable gap between the pretensions of their crafts and the realities of their lives. While Herovit's science fiction characters breeze through a vast cosmos, their writer-creator suffers in a claustrophobic study—a converted maid's chamber; likewise, the jolly comedian Bates lives in an apartment—mirror of his soul—which he has decorated with gigantic photos of war atrocities.

It is exactly this vicious gap between glamorous pretensions and mundane reality that stands at the center of *Herovit's World*. The text is not—

as critics have charged—a vitriolic rejection of the genre but a warning by a writer who perceives a pathological paradox at the bottom of all classic science fiction. Nine years later, Malzberg said that this dark behemoth—one of the forces behind *Herovit's World*—is created by "the megalomaniacal, expansive visions being generated by writers who increasingly [see] the disparity between Spaceways and their own hopeless condition."[7]

So—is there hope left at the end of *Herovit's World*? Or does its warning come too late to prevent the inevitable crash of the genre? Like John Barth, Barry Malzberg has continued to write, and in *The Destruction of the Temple* (1975) he created a genuine masterpiece of science fiction. And from the vantage point of 1982, he also delivered a kind of epitaph to Herovit, when his fictional author Ruthven—the Herovit of "Christmas Come" in *The Engines of the Night*—delivers an address to his fans: "We tried . . . I want you to know that, that even the worst of us, the most debased hack, the one-shot writer, the fifty-books series, all the hundreds and thousands of us who ever wrote a line of this stuff for publication: we tried" (197).

In the end, the act of writing transcends its criticism and its destruction, and stories continue to be spun to delight, educate, and satisfy their readers, who pay a tribute of one kind or another to the creators. The triptych of intratexts in *Herovit's World* offers a painful exposure of inadequacies and suffering, but it is not the swan song of science fiction.

Notes

1. Barry Malzberg, *Herovit's World* (New York: Random House, 1973). All further references are to this edition and are cited by page number within the text.

2. Robert A. Heinlein, *The Puppet Masters* (New York: Signet Books, 1951), p. 148. All further references are to this edition and are cited by page number within the text.

3. John Barth, *Lost in the Funhouse* (Garden City, N.Y.: Doubleday, 1968), pp. 75–79.

4. Robert A. Heinlein, *Stranger in a Strange Land* (New York: Putnam, 1961), p. 244.

5. C. M. Kornbluth, "The Words of Guru," *Starring Science Stories* (June 1941).

6. John M. Reilly, *Twentieth Century Crime and Mystery Writers*, 2d ed. (New York: St. Martin's Press, 1985).

7. Barry Malzberg, *The Engines of Night* (Garden City, N.Y.: Doubleday, 1982), p. 189. All further references are cited by page number within the text.

Part 5

TROPES AND AESTHETIC TECHNIQUE

Chapter 15

Landscapes of British Science Fiction

Patrick Parrinder

Landscape has a special importance in the literature of science fiction and fantasy for several reasons. Any place described or evoked in words becomes an imaginary, or at least an imagined, place, a *logotopia* existing not in physical space but in verbal space. The implied reader of such a description is usually absent from the place described or unable to experience it fully and directly. When a *strange* world is to be evoked, the descriptive task is made considerably more difficult. The places characteristically evoked in science fiction and fantasy are both imaginary and strange. The strange places compose or form part of strange worlds, and these worlds frequently present a natural spectacle—a "countryside" or "wilderness"—since even "hard" science fiction is not all technological marvels and hermetically sealed cityscapes. In his history of the country and the city in literature, Raymond Williams wrote that "out of an experience of the [industrial] cities came an experience of the future." But though science fiction is the vehicle of this experience of the future, the genre has a strong pastoral element, as Williams noted. Civilizations are shown as having evolved beyond their urban and technical phases, or as having regressed backward or followed some alternative, nonmetropolitan course of growth; and many writers have a strong emotional investment in these developments.[1]

There is frequently a dialectic of appearance and reality in these texts. A strange world in science fiction operates as a kind of coded message. Either the fictional world or the protagonist's response to it contains the key to hidden truths, so that description and revelation are interrelated. The protagonist is often an explorer or adventurer who encounters the fictional world for the first time, and for whom its landscapes provide the visible evidence of an ecological process—of a new and unforeseen relationship between human beings (or some other form of intelligent life) and their environment. Just as a modern landscape historian deduces social history from the hidden archaeology of the landscape, so the science fiction writer can use landscapes to disclose, or hint at, the strange nature of an imagined world.

The ideas of logotopia and verbal space imply that landscape descriptions in science fiction and fantasy do not differ in principle from such descriptions in other forms of writing. In particular they resemble the descriptions of travel writing, in which strange and exotic landscapes are often the norm. I begin this essay on British science fiction landscapes with a single example from an actual British traveler, Charles Dickens, whose *American Notes* (1842) records his first triumphant tour of the United States. Dickens traveled down the Ohio River and up the Mississippi to St. Louis by steamboat. He was then taken a few miles eastward to the village of Lebanon, Illinois, to see a prairie. His American hosts were anxious to find out what effect this strange landscape, known as Looking-Glass Prairie, would have on him, but Dickens was not impressed: "There it lay, a tranquil sea or lake without water, (if such a simile be admissible)." "I felt little of that sense of freedom and exhilaration which a Scottish heath inspires, or even our English downs awaken. It was lonely and wild, but oppressive in its barren monotony."[2] Like almost every nineteenth-century English traveler in the Midwest, Dickens begins by comparing the prairie landscape to a seascape. But then it becomes apparent that he is the kind of traveler who takes England (and Scotland) with him wherever he goes. Gazing into the mirror of Looking-Glass Prairie, he finds nothing that he can recognize as significant; it is not a meaningful landscape like the Scottish heaths or the English downs. Luckily things are different when he reaches the inn at Lebanon, where he is to spend the night. "In point of cleanliness and comfort it would have suffered by no comparison with any English alehouse, of a homely kind, in England," he observes, managing to produce a sentence that contains both "England" and "English," with "homely" in between.

For Dickens, it seems, if an exotic landscape is to give pleasure it must also (paradoxically) be familiar. In British science fiction, too, it is not difficult to find examples of the emphatic familiarization of the exotic. In *Moreau's Other Island*, by Brian Aldiss, the hero is a castaway on a Pacific island on the eve of a nuclear war. Looking out from the fortified research laboratory to which he has been taken after his capture by two of the islanders, he sees a lagoon, palm trees, a landing stage, and what appears to be a native village. "It was such a typical view that I wondered if I had seen it before, perhaps in some previous reincarnation," he reflects.[3] The view is, of course, doubly familiar: it is both the typical tropical island of book illustrations and travel posters and the island of H. G. Wells's Doctor Moreau. Aldiss's Pacific island is Wells's Pacific island one hundred years later. By the end of the novel a chain of weird and grotesque events will have made the island far less familiar than it looks; nevertheless, the first impression is of familiarity, not of strangeness.

Admittedly, science fiction—even British science fiction—contains many landscapes that seem wholly defamiliarized at first sight. The lunar landscapes discovered by Wells's oddly assorted pair of explorers, Mr. Bedford and Mr. Cavor, are a famous example:

It was absolutely unreal. . . . About us the dream-like jungle, with the silent bayonet leaves darting overhead, and the silent, vivid, sun-splashed lichens under our hands and knees, waving with the vigour of their growth as a carpet waves when the wind gets beneath it. Ever and again one of the bladder fungi, bulging and distending under the sun, loomed upon us. Ever and again some novel shape in vivid colour obtruded. The very cells that built up these plants were as large as my thumb, like beads of coloured glass. And all these things were saturated in the unmitigated glare of the sun, were seen against a sky with a few surviving stars. Strange! the very forms and texture of the stones were strange.[4]

The first rule of describing an unfamiliar landscape—a rule that Wells here seems to have learned from Edgar Allan Poe—is to reiterate words such as *unreal, dreamlike, novel,* and *strange* in describing it. But this strange landscape is put together from some familiar elements. There is sunlight (mentioned four times in the quoted extract), even though this light appears different on the moon—despite the sun's glare, the sky is bluish black and a few stars are still visible. The sun could suggest a tropical landscape, and Bedford is standing amid a "dream-like jungle," full of "vivid colour," but the forms of the vegetation are not tropical but lunar forms, produced by a set of physical conditions not found on Earth. *The First Men in the Moon* takes account of the severity and length of the lunar night and of the necessity for vegetation to grow and die back within the fourteen-day period of lunar daylight, as well as of the lower gravitation. Vegetation grows both very much faster and very much larger, so that the description is based on speedup and magnification effects. The result in the passage just quoted is an enormously distended rock garden—a rock garden seen from the point of view of a stationary ant. The huge forms are lichens, cacti and succulents, and fungi; and "the very cells that built up these plants were as large as my thumb." The colors, olive green and vivid orange, might be found in a rockery as well as in a jungle.

Clearly, it was the unfamiliarity of this landscape that originally caught our attention. But I would argue that this initial estrangement is much less common, in British science fiction, than its opposite—an apparently familiar landscape that becomes stranger the more we get to know it. Certain landscape types recur in British novels, and especially in British science fiction. The island is one of these, for obvious reasons. In novels from Richard Jefferies's *After London* to Christopher Priest's *Fugue for a Darkening Island*, Britain is the imaginary island (a sinking or a darkening one); but British writers have also loved to invent and seek out other islands, which have the advantages of the British Isles but not the disadvantages. The advantages stem from a combination of inland fertility and plenty of seashore—the ideal or idyllic island, we could say, is a garden surrounded by a beach. The disadvantages or things to be avoided—to judge by the number of writers who have imagined themselves in the situation of lone castaways on tropical islands—are not only the British climate but the rest of the British people. The Robinsonade, or tropical island romance, began with the real-life adventure of the Scottish sailor Alexander Selkirk, whose cave on the beach of Robinson Crusoe Island in the Juan Fernandez group is still shown to visitors. "The climate is mild, the vegetation rich, and there are plenty of wild goats—and some tourists" (I quote from a current guidebook).[5] Beginning with Thomas More's *Utopia* there are many such invented islands, some of them the austere "desert islands" of the popular imagination, others liberally supplied with gardens and beaches.

The word *castaway* is frequently applied by British writers to characters marooned in places that are not islands in the strict sense. Cavor rather disingenuously describes himself and Bedford in *The First Men in the Moon* as "poor terrestrial castaways."[6] The moon and the planets are easily viewed as metaphorical islands. There is a clear logic in such a comparison, since, as Charles Darwin discovered in the Galápagos, an island may possess its own self-contained ecosystem. But there are other sorts of metaphorical islands besides the alien planet, as J. G. Ballard memorably demonstrated in his sequence of novels from the mid-1970s: *Concrete Island*, *High-Rise*, and *The Unlimited Dream Company*. Of these, *Concrete Island* stands out as an exemplary island novel, a self-conscious Robinsonade set in a self-enclosed piece of land formed by an intersection in the inner London motorway system. (The title *Concrete Island* is in fact a partial misnomer, since we are concerned with a stretch of overgrown derelict land, not with what is known as a "traffic island.") The highways are steeply embanked, and Robert Maitland, the "castaway" whose car has plunged down the embankment, is marooned by his apparent inability to climb the steep slopes due to a broken leg. Eventually Maitland discovers that the "island" has two other inhabitants, both of them social outcasts, but they do not regard it as an island since they freely come and go from their hideaways. In a mode every reader of Ballard will recognize, Maitland's "concrete island" surrounded by expressways is revealed as an island of the mind, and his car crash and subsequent sequestration fulfill a deep psychic need. It is not by chance that a road accident has brought him to the island.

The Crusoe parallels in *Concrete Island* are in fact very deliberate. At first, Maitland uses the resources of his shipwrecked car to keep himself alive, drinking the windscreen-washer fluid and using the cigarette lighter and pieces of glass from the shattered windscreen to start a fire. Then, when he struggles to the top of the embankment, he even discovers a human footprint left in the mud at the edge of the road. Once he has made contact with the other inhabitants, he ruthlessly sets out to dominate them and to become master of his island, as Daniel Defoe's hero (the archetypal colonist) did in *Robinson Crusoe*.

Concrete Island does not merely offer a contemporary urbanized version of the castaway and the island as sanctuary. The island has beaches (the embankments and soft road verges), but its interior is also a garden—in fact, we have here the characteristic British landscape motif of the ruined garden, the garden full of ruins. The highway intersection where Maitland crashes his car has only just been built, so the contractors have not yet finished "landscaping" the site. Maitland's "island" has an appearance of dereliction, and it turns out that the intersection has been built over what was once a residential district, and the foundations of demolished Victorian houses and the sites of their gardens are still visible. The more Maitland explores the island, the more it becomes a fantastic landscape of ruins, including a former churchyard, an air-raid shelter from the Second World War (comparable to Alexander Selkirk's cave), and, most marvelous of all, a ruined underground cinema. Both the shelter and the cinema are inhabited.

The concrete island, a successor to Robinson Crusoe's island, therefore leads us to consider the ruined garden, which, if anything, has a still richer literary and social history. The greater part of Wells's *Time Machine* is set in a ruined garden. When the Time Traveller arrives in the future, he sees first the weatherworn White Sphinx and then the garden-city landscape of great dilapidated buildings: "The whole earth had become a garden,"[7] he observes, though all that he has seen of it is the area of Kew Gardens and Richmond Park in southwest London (which is pretty much like a garden today). Later on, he goes cross-country to the Palace of Green Porcelain, a vast, ruined counterpart of the London museums that Wells knew from his student days in South Kensington. David Y. Hughes has related Wells's garden landscapes to T. H. Huxley's famous metaphorical garden in his *Evolution and Ethics*;[8] but, while Wells must have noticed the garden metaphor in Huxley and Darwin, it is equally relevant that his own father had been a professional gardener at one of the great English country houses. To write of ruined gardens in an English setting is, indeed, necessarily to allude to the art of landscape gardening, which in the eighteenth century transformed the "views" and "prospects" seen from the drawing-room windows of the English aristocracy.

Landscape gardening is (perhaps unconsciously) evoked in another recent postcatastrophe story, Angela Carter's *Heroes and Villains*, when Marianne, the professor's daughter who is roaming the countryside with the barbarians, comes across a riotously overgrown country house:

Before her, she saw a beautiful valley of lush pasturage around a wide river hemmed with flowering reeds. On the other bank of this river . . . there lay a house of a kind Marianne had never seen before, though she had seen enough photographs and engravings to identify portions of the house's anatomy and give them their historical names. This house was a gigantic memory of rotten stone, a compilation of innumerable forgotten styles now given some green unity by the devouring web of creeper, fur of moss and fungoid growth of rot. Wholly abandoned to decay, baroque stonework of the late Jacobean period, Gothic turrets murmurous with birds and pathetic elegance of Palladian pillared facades weathered indiscriminately together towards irreducible rubble. The forest perched upon the tumbled roofs in the shapes of yellow and purple weeds rooted in the gapped tiles. . . . The windows gaped or sprouted internal foliage, as if the forest were as well already camped inside, there gathering strength for a green eruption which would one day burst the walls sky high. . . . Upon the balustrade of the terrace were many pocked and armless statues in robes, or nude and garlanded. These looked like the petrified survivors of a malign *fête-champêtre* ended long ago, in catastrophe.[9]

Echoing the words of Brian Aldiss's protagonist in *Moreau's Other Island*, we could say of this gloriously decadent prospect that "it was such a typical view that I wondered if I had seen it before."

This applies not only to the wildly eclectic architecture but to the state of ruin into which the house has fallen. The idea that "nature" will one day take its revenge on the "art" of building and landscaping is the subject of Alexander Pope's famous lines,

> Another age shall see the golden ear
> Embrown the slope, and nod on the parterre,[10]

and it is implicit in the taste for the picturesque ruin, one of the most familiar features of eighteenth-century landscape gardens.

The connections between landscape gardening and British science fiction and fantasy are more extensive than one might think. Brian Aldiss argues that science fiction is "characteristically cast in the Gothic or post-Gothic mode,"[11] and we should recall that at least two of the original Gothic novelists, Horace Walpole and William Beckford, were also architects and shapers of the landscape. Both are readily associated not only with exotic fiction but with picturesque architectural follies and purposely built ruins. Beckford, author of *Vathek*, built the towering edifice of Fonthill Abbey, a cross between country house and mausoleum in which he himself lived although the architect's specification stated that it was to be "partly in ruins."[12] Beckford himself was financially ruined by the building of this extravagant folly, and in any case, soon after his death the great central tower collapsed and Fonthill Abbey was left entirely in ruins. Half a century earlier, Horace Walpole had invented both the Gothic novel (with *The Castle of Otranto*) and the neo-Gothic country house (Strawberry Hill; he called himself the "Abbot of Strawberry"). The grounds of Strawberry Hill were too small for any very ambitious ruins or follies, but Walpole's correspondence shows that he spent many happy hours praising and condemning the "designer ruins" of his friends and contemporaries.[13] The type of building described in Angela Carter's novel as the sign of a new barbaric age—a "memory of rotten stone," with its "Gothic turrets murmurous with birds" and windows that "gaped or sprouted internal foliage"—might actually have been glimpsed, brand-new, from the windows of many an eighteenth-century mansion.

The picturesque ruin is one element in the fantasy landscape of the English country gentleman's park. This landscape is what has been known since the eighteenth century as the English garden, or *jardin anglais*. There is much evidence that, far from being native to the British Isles, the *jardin anglais* was itself an exotic importation, a fantasy of elsewhere; so that the ruined garden of the English imagination involves both time travel—taking us back to the feudal and Gothic past—and, if not exactly space travel, at least travel to the extremes of the known world. Of the two probable sources for the English garden, one is the landscape painting of Claude and Poussin, but the other is the classical Chinese garden, with its artificial hills and lakes, deep grottoes, and labyrinthine paths, which became known to seventeenth-century Europe through the reports of Jesuit missionaries. Sir William Temple in his essay *Upon the Gardens of Epicurus* (1685) was perhaps the first to suggest that these exotic models should be taken seriously. The British landscape architect who bears most responsibility for developing a wilder and freer style of garden design is William Kent (1684–1748), who had traveled in Italy and had also doubtless seen the set of prints of Chinese gardens acquired in 1729 by his patron, Lord Burlington.[14] The name *jardin anglais* is an abbreviation of the *jardin anglais-chinois*, or Anglo-Chinese garden,[15] so it is fitting that at least two impressive examples—Kew Gardens in London and the Englische Garten in Munich— are adorned with pagodas, which tower over the trees like one of John Wyndham's triffids or H. G. Wells's Martians. There is surely a link between the sensibility that domesticated the Chinese garden in England and the sensibility that has given birth to such quantities of science fiction and fantasy.

The garden is primarily a cultural image reflecting an ideal of healthy and civilized living. There is a direct line from the eighteenth-century gentleman's park to the garden suburbs, urban parks, and recreation areas of the nineteenth and twentieth centuries, not to mention the more or less utopian ideal of the "garden city." I would stress here the contrast between the iconography of the garden, which is a place to live in (or to be surrounded by), and that of my final category of science fictional landscapes—beach landscapes. Nobody (except perhaps Californians) dreams of living on a beach; on the whole, beaches are more barren even than deserts. In science fiction and fantasy we find the beach associated not with gracious living but with the beginnings and endings of life.

There is, as I suggested earlier, a topographical connection between gardens and beaches, since both are attractive features of island landscapes. The *jardin anglais* owes much to the insular British climate, whose generous rainfall allows gardeners to produce green grass all the year round. An island, if inhabitable, ought to have lush vegetation; but within its restricted bounds the vegetation can be brought under control. An inhabited island is much more a garden than it is a wilderness or forest. The island's boundary, or coastline, is likely to include beaches if it is possible for visitors to land; uninhabited islands, of course, don't need them. The beach in science fiction is conceived of as a landing stage or a place of departure; and much of this fiction alludes to the scientific belief that biological life began in the sea and eventually emerged or crawled onto dry land. The beach had to be crossed, and a beachhead established, for civilized life to develop. The eventual biological decline and fall can therefore be symbolized by life retreating back into the ocean. Such a scenario is present at the end of Wells's *Time Machine*: life has devolved back through giant land crabs to a final sinister cephalopod glimpsed out at sea.

Toward the end of Carter's *Heroes and Villains* there is a beach scene, near the site of a drowned and ruined town, in which we realize that the future barbarians are close to extinction; one of them attempts suicide by wading into the sea. The undisputed master of "terminal beach scenes" in modern British science fiction is, again, J. G. Ballard. In his story "The Reptile Enclosure," primitive, self-destructive mechanisms are triggered off in everyone's mind by satellite transmissions, and the whole population gathers on the beach and starts marching down into the sea. Ballard's beach is usually a metropolitan or "concrete" beach. His story "The Terminal Beach," for example, takes us to the concrete island of Eniwetok, which was used in the 1950s as a nuclear testing ground.

In Ballard, the beach as edge of survival refers not only to the marine origins of life and to the possibility of a retreat from civilization back to the sea; it also implies (in a heavily ironic mode) that travel and migration into space might constitute a new frontier for "life," comparable in significance to the biological migration from the sea to the land. The claim that landing on a new planet might constitute a step for humanity of the same magnitude as the arrival of marine life on the beach is made in a number of Ballard's short stories. Here, for example, is the beginning of "The Cage of Sand":

At sunset, when the vermilion glow reflected from the dunes along the horizon fitfully illuminated the white faces of the abandoned hotels, Bridgman stepped on to his balcony and looked out over the long stretches of cooling sand as the tides of purple shadow seeped across them. Slowly, extending their slender fingers through the shallow saddles and depressions, the shadows massed together like gigantic combs, a few phosphorescing spurs of obsidian isolated for a moment between the times, and then finally coalesced and flooded in a solid wave across the half-submerged hotels. . . .

As Bridgman watched, his lean bronzed arms propped against the rusting rail, the last whorls of light sank away into the cerise funnel withdrawing below the horizon, and the first wind stirred across the dead Martian sand. Here and there miniature cyclones whirled about a sand-spur, drawing off swirling feathers of moon-washed spray, and a nimbus of white dust swept across the dunes and settled in the dips and hollows. Gradually the drifts accumulated, edging toward the former shoreline below the hotels. Already the first four floors had been inundated and the sand now reached up to within two feet of Bridgman's balcony. After the next sandstorm he would be forced yet again to move to the floor above.[16]

Like Angela Carter's, Ballard's work takes a good deal of its meaning from its romantic and decadent landscapes. We can note how his richly poetic details are just—but only just—held within his lingering sentence structures, and how intricately intertwined in the passage are the various levels of metaphorical intimation of the floodtide of a forthcoming disaster. Moreover, since this is science fiction, very little in the landscape is what it seems to be at first sight.

To start with, it is not a Martian landscape, despite the reference to the "dead Martian sand." Ballard's abandoned holiday resort is located not on Mars but near Cape Canaveral, Florida. At the height of the space age it was found necessary to replace the weight of material taken from Earth to Mars with millions of tons of Martian topsoil brought back to Earth as ballast—a typical piece of Ballardian pseudoscientific fictive sophistry (though no worse, perhaps, than some of the crackbrained ideas that from time to time take hold of the actual scientific community). The sand, which turned out to contain a virus lethal to terrestrial plant life, was dumped just off the Florida coast. There is no sea and no literal incoming tide in the landscape that Bridgman surveys from his balcony, only the sand dust blown in by the wind and the lengthening shadows cast by the ridges of the dunes. The actual shoreline is ten miles away. It is sunset, however, and the symbolic decline from day into night is projected forward on two different time scales: first there is the steady inundation of the abandoned hotels by the drifting sand, and then there is the gradual return of the ocean itself—"Slowly the Atlantic was driving the shore back to its former margins"[17]—overwhelming the dead zone of the artificial dunes, but also threatening to inundate Cape Canaveral, the first "space beach," itself.

Ballard has written other Cape Canaveral stories reflecting the same "vermilion glow," notably "Memories of the Space Age." The protagonists in these stories are haunted survivors and beachcombers who (like Maitland in *Concrete Island*) are fulfilling some psychic need by returning, often as fugitives, to an area of ruins that has been abandoned and placed in quarantine. Bridgman, a former architect of Martian cities that were never built, is the Ballardian "last man"—or rather, the member of a last human group of two men and a woman—lurking at bay on a poisoned beach that is the historic site of what should have been one of humanity's great leaps forward but is now a deserted no-man's-land. It is curious that in "The Cage of Sand" we are told that space travel has, in fact, continued—passenger rockets are "supposed to be as safe as commuters' trains"—and it is merely the state of Florida, that "corner of Earth that is forever Mars," [18] that has been evacuated and placed off-limits. In Ballard's story this ongoing world of technological mastery is an entirely peripheral presence: what preoccupies him is the beach landscape to which his veteran protagonists return to mourn their dead past, like doomed warriors licking the wounds of defeat on the concrete beaches of some new version of the Celtic Twilight.

Not only is Ballard a consummate landscape artist, but he draws our attention to the eschatological resonances of science fiction landscapes. To the extent that they set themselves against mundane, everyday experience, science fiction and fantasy necessarily attempt to evade or defamiliarize the suburban and metropolitan surroundings in which most modern people actually live. Perhaps the landscapes of such fiction correspond in some way to our changing notions of the beginning and ending of life. Traditionally, in Christian civilization, human life has been conceived as a grand procession from the Garden of Eden to a metropolis, which might turn out either to be the Heavenly City (a crowded concert hall in which the angels have only just enough elbow-room to play their harps), or the other "populous and smoky city," a Hell much like London (as Shelley described it in "The Mask of Anarchy"). Today's skeptical scientific humanism conceives of human evolution not as a march of progress from the garden to the city but as an inextricable mixture of culture and nature, without a God to preside over it and ensure a linear, or bifurcated, outcome. If we try to speak of human origins or human destiny in modern terms, we are torn between cultural and natural metaphors; the concept of the nuclear winter is one example of such a mixed metaphor. By focusing on the British tradition, I have tried to show how science fiction and fantasy reflect this mixed state of understanding through their powerful evocation not so much of cityscapes or wildernesses, but of metaphorical landscapes such as concrete islands, ruined gardens, and poisonous and derelict beaches in which the natural and artificial elements are finally indistinguishable from one another.

Notes

1. Raymond Williams, *The Country and the City* (London: Chatto and Windus, 1973), pp. 272, 276.

2. Charles Dickens, *American Notes* (Harmondsworth: Penguin Books, 1972), pp. 225–26.

3. Brian Aldiss, *Moreau's Other Island* (London: Triad/Panter, 1982), p. 33.

4. H. G. Wells, *The First Men in the Moon* (London and Glasgow: Collins, 1954), pp. 94–95.

5. John Brooks, ed., *South American Handbook* (1989; London: Trade and Travel Publications, 1988), p. 429.

6. Wells, *The First Men in the Moon*, p. 96.

7. H. G. Wells, *The Time Machine* (London: Heinemann, 1895), p. 49.

8. David Y. Hughes, "The Garden in Wells's Early Science Fiction," in *H. G. Wells and Modern Science Fiction*, ed. Darko Suvin and Robert M. Philmus (Lewisburg, Pa.: Bucknell University Press; London: Associated University Presses, 1977), pp. 48–69.

9. Angela Carter, *Heroes and Villains* (Harmondsworth: Penguin Books, 1981), pp. 31–32.

10. Alexander Pope, "Moral Essays (IV): Epistle to Burlington."

11. Brian Aldiss, *Billion Year Spree: The History of Science Fiction* (London: Weidenfeld and Nicolson, 1983), p. 8.

12. Martin S. Briggs, *Goths and Vandals: A Study of the Destruction, Neglect and Preservation of Historical Building in England* (London: Constable, 1952), p. 144.

13. Barbara Jones, *Follies and Grottoes*, 3d ed. (London: Constable, 1974), p. 56n.

14. William Howard Adams, *Nature Perfected: Gardens Through History* (New York: Abbeville, 1991), pp. 156–57, 166, 205–6; and information from a lecture by Richard Bisgrove, Department of Horticulture, University of Reading.

15. Jones, *Follies and Grottoes*, p. 111.

16. J. G. Ballard, "The Cage of Sand," in *The Best Short Stories of J. G. Ballard* (New York: Holt, Rinehart, and Winston, 1978), pp. 189–90.

17. Ibid., p. 191.

18. Ibid., p. 202.

Chapter 16

In the Palace of Green Porcelain:
Artifacts from the Museums of Science Fiction

Robert Crossley

Recall these scenes from a short list of science fiction masterpieces: a twenty-first-century Englishman, the last human being on Earth, finds relief from loneliness in studying "the Diorama of ages" in the monuments, libraries, and galleries of Rome. A traveler, seeking his stolen time machine, takes an afternoon off to explore the darkened corridors and ruined exhibits in a derelict museum. An unhappy mathematician feels his imagination disturbingly liberated as he walks through a preserved ancient house of the nineteenth century, "completely enclosed in a glass shell" like an enormous museum exhibit. Ten million years from now a crew of engineers in Siberia unearths a vast underground archive of scientific and historical records carved on stone tablets by the survivors of an ancient atomic disaster. A former graduate student, having escaped a devastating plague in North America, wanders the stacks of a deserted university research library, reverently handling its books. A stowaway on an intergalactic starship is given a guided tour of the local city museum of an alien world, with special attention to a gallery of art reproductions and natural history models from Earth. In an era of profound climatic change, a pirate in a white suit hauls treasures up from the tropical waters covering the cities of Europe and installs them in his own floating museum. A visiting professor of physics from the moon, touring a museum of decorative arts in a sophisticated capital on the mother planet, sickens at the sight of a royal ceremonial garment made from the tanned skins of human beings. A self-taught reader in an illiterate future America sits in the film archive at New York University painstakingly deciphering the printed speeches of twentieth-century silent films. A visionary in a postindustrial tribal society examines the stone pillars that once supported a vanished cathedral before an atomic detonation destroyed Canterbury hundreds of years before. A twenty-first-century Australian in a world impoverished by the cumulative effects of the greenhouse phenomenon steps into the museum of Melbourne's cinematographic society and views the slapstick comedies of his great-grandparents' culture.[1]

This preliminary catalog of artifacts from the museums, libraries, and archives of science fiction describes variants—and I suspect they could be multiplied—of a scene that is reconstituted with astonishing frequency in science fiction narratives. The spectacle of an observer examining an artifact and using it as a window onto nature, culture, and history permits that convergence of anthropological, prophetic, and elegiac tonalities that science fiction handles more powerfully than any other modern literary form. The building itself, as much as the artifact, is important in such scenes. A museum, designed for the contemplation of publicly displayed exhibits, is an inherently social place. Eric Rabkin's revealing study of the epiphanic paintings, photographs, and pictures in fairy tales, stories of the preternatural, and other subgenres of the fantastic that emphasize private experience does not identify any text centered on the observation of a visual artifact in a museum.[2] This is hardly surprising, especially in fantastic forms that celebrate timelessness and subjectivity. But the museum is a locale particularly valuable to science fiction, arguably the most social and the most time-specific of all forms of fantastic literature. When a science fiction protagonist experiences an epiphany in a museum, the event enacts in a very precise way the preoccupation of the genre with time, particularly with the relationship between the past and the future, and with humanity at large rather than the private self.[3]

Every public museum is a repository of some portion of the past and an act of faith in the future; it is a laboratory for humanistic or scientific research; it is an organized record of cultural differences and continuities; it stands as a secular and populist alternative to the private collections of churches and social elites. Similarly, science fiction is especially concerned with time and change, with the representation and analysis of cultural difference, with experimental constructions of hypothetical realities, with the intersections of natural history and human history, and with the development of countercultural and popular audiences. In all these respects it has functional affinities with the museum. Above all, both the museum and the science fiction text have a paradoxical relationship to time. A museum is never wholly a monument to the past any more than science fiction is narrowly or exclusively a literature of the future. While the museum represents the past, its interest in preservation makes it profoundly committed to the future; and while science fiction is usually oriented to the future, it rarely looks ahead without also glossing the present and the past. A museum may not be precisely a time *machine,* but it is a contrivance that collapses linear time and encourages the tourist who visits it to shuttle back and forth imaginatively among temporal worlds. I will return for a closer look at the uses of such temporal disjunctions in a few of the fictional scenes in museums summarized in my preliminary list, but first I want to sketch a very brief institutional history of the museum as it bears on the aesthetic concerns of science fiction.

The development of museums as public buildings rather than private "cabinets of curiosities" roughly parallels the historical rise of science fiction. Both the public museum and the genre of science fiction are emblems of the nineteenth century's experiment in the democratization of culture. It is true that one may find suggestive anticipations of science fiction in Lucian or Milton or Swift, and so too there are prefigurings of the modern museum in ancient and Renaissance collections of natural objects and cultural artifacts. Nevertheless, most historians of science fiction find that the genre achieved its authentic identity only in the nineteenth century—either with Mary Shelley if you follow Brian Aldiss's account of Gothic origins, or sometime in the latter third of the century if you accept Mark Rose's argument that the genre is emphatically postromantic;[4] similarly, most cultural historians see the public museum as essentially a nineteenth-century creation. Ancient collections with limited access such as those housed in the library at Alexandria are more akin to the private holdings of the royal houses of Europe than to the museums and libraries of the past two centuries. The treasure hoards of feudal lords have far more in common with the contemporary market for "collectibles" as a form of investment than with the museum's functions of conservation, arrangement, and public display of artifacts. Of other possible prototypes for the modern museum perhaps the most viable is the medieval cathedral, which in its architecture and crafts—if not always in its jealously guarded manuscripts and art treasures—could claim to be in fact as well as in principle "people's buildings."[5]

When the first London College of Antiquaries was founded in 1572, its members viewed their personal collections of rarities—often the loot from so-called voyages of discovery—more as trophies of wealth and as hobbies to be shared with fellow antiquarians than as bases for museums of science or art, but in the eighteenth century a reformed Society of Antiquaries began to articulate the principles on which future public museums would be established. Collectors of scientific and artistic curiosities, the society maintained in initiating its journal, *Archaeologia*, in 1770, might help prevent the darkness of ignorance from descending on a future age:

The only security against this and the accidents of time and barbarism is, to record present transactions, or gather the more ancient ones from the general wreck. The most indistinct collection has this merit, that it supplies materials to those who have sagacity or leisure to extract from the common mass whatever may answer useful purposes.[6]

By the end of the eighteenth century the connoisseur was in the ascendancy over the indiscriminate collector, although not every putative rarity could live up to the society's grand claims. While the century could boast Sir Hans Sloane's extraordinary 100,000 specimens, which eventually formed the core collection of the British Museum, there were also such fantastic and whimsical items as Pontius Pilate's wife's chambermaid's sister's hat in the collection of James Salter—an interesting reminder that the connoisseur and the con artist often roam the same territory.[7] But the Society of Antiquaries, while championing the scholarly value of even "the most indistinct" of its members' holdings, was not proposing to open the collections to any but those few suitable people of "sagacity or leisure."

The Ashmolean, inaugurated at Oxford in 1682, is widely recognized as the first modern museum. In it natural history specimens, antiquities, and various "curiosities" were arranged for display, for teaching, and for public inspection at a charge of sixpence, so that even "country folk" on market day could crowd in to examine Roman burial urns, Saint Augustine's crozier, or the famous stuffed dodo.[8] In fact, the *Oxford English Dictionary*'s first two recorded usages of *museum* in its modern sense of "a building or portion of a building used as a repository for the preservation and exhibition of objects" are references to the Ashmolean.[9] But the Ashmolean was hardly typical of eighteenth-century museums, and its location in a university town ensured that its primary audience would be a scholarly one. Museums as institutions open for general visitation are the product of post-Enlightenment democratic tendencies in societies at

large. The British Museum, though established in 1759, took nearly a century to begin to admit the public in any significant numbers on a regular
basis.[10] The model public art museum in the early nineteenth century was
the Louvre—which managed to combine the populist principles of the
Revolution with the rich plunder gathered during the Napoleonic wars.[11]
In London the reopening of the British Museum in 1829 at its present location in Bloomsbury, the completion of the great domed reading room in
1857, the wonders of the Crystal Palace and its dinosaur sculptures built
at mid-century, and the establishment of the Natural History, Science, and
Victoria and Albert museums in the district of South Kensington in the
second half of the century may be taken as vital signs of the coming of age
of the public museum.

The dramatic potential for the emerging museum as a locale in science fiction can be illustrated by comparing two nineteenth-century futurist texts,
one published when the fascination with museums was just beginning to
catch the public imagination and one published late in the century when
museums were enjoying their heyday.

The final scenes of Mary Shelley's 1826 eschatological novel *The Last
Man* are played out in the palaces and churches of Italy as Lionel Verney
and a diminishing circle of companions seek consolation for the impending
extinction of humanity by contemplating "master-pieces of art," "galleries
of statues," and other "antiquities."[12] Arriving in Venice, the survivors
climb the tower of San Marco for a prospect of the tumbledown condition
of the city's famous buildings, the paintings defaced by salt water and mud,
and the seaweed draped over marble artifacts. "In the midst of this appall-
ing ruin of the monuments of man's power," Verney writes with romantic
gloom, "nature asserted her ascendancy, and shone more beauteous from
the contrast" (319). When Verney is finally alone after his two remaining
companions die during a storm, he takes a grim satisfaction in imagining how, if the earth should ever be repopulated by some other intelligent
species, our artifacts might offer a window onto human civilization and
"we, the lost race, would, in the relics left behind, present no contemptible
exhibition of our powers to the new comers" (331).

Verney's ultimate destination is "Rome, the capital of the world, the
crown of man's achievements" (335). Its "storied streets, hallowed ruins,
and stupendous remains" (335) make the whole city *the* great outdoor exhibit of European culture. Wandering among the sculptures of Phidias and
Praxiteles, touring the Coliseum and the temple of Jupiter, Verney wants
to validate the grandeur of human aspiration and achievement. But when

he sees a buffalo walking along the ancient Roman avenues he understands that the age of human dominance is gone, that already other creatures are beginning to occupy the space we called "Rome." He takes to sheltering in an abandoned palace where he can soothe his sleepless nights with splendid paintings; in a Keatsian gesture he embraces and kisses the cold marble of statues representing passionate lovers; and mimicking papal pomp he solemnly ascends the steps of St. Peter's to carve the number 2100 in stone, the date of humanity's last year. In the absence of any social context, both the artifacts and the beholder appear ludicrous or pitiful. At the end Verney harbors no more illusions about "eternal Rome"; he feels himself a living anomaly, his body "a monstrous excrescence of nature" (340), and Rome becomes both physiologically and psychologically a deathtrap: a breeding place for malaria and a shrine to the dead end of human aspiration.

Few of the buildings Shelley's Verney visits can properly be called museums. The power of this climactic scene resides in its focus on monuments, urban architecture, and artifacts that belong to the public perception, even myth, of imperial and ecclesiastical Rome. It is the consciousness of Verney rather than the design of a curator that organizes these disparate artifacts and displays them to the reader as a lesson in the glory and the boundaries of artistic achievement. When H. G. Wells attempted a similar didactic episode seventy years later in *The Time Machine*, he was able to do it with greater concentration and a more impressive art because he could draw on the idea of the public museum and the experience of museumgoers in ways not yet available to Shelley. "At the first glance," the time traveler says when he walks with his Eloi companion, Weena, through the main door of an imposing though crumbling building 800 millennia from now, "I was reminded of a museum." [13] The familiarity of the design of its entrance ("the customary hall, a long gallery lit by many side windows" [80]) leaves him in no doubt about the building's use and signals to the reader that the function of this episode will be in some way analogous to our familiar museum experiences.

In these two instances, as in so many others in the early history of science fiction, Shelley and Wells deliver a one-two punch: she pioneering an intellectual strategy, and he discovering its most streamlined narrative form; she articulating the archetype, and he imagining the fictional prototype. If Shelley found a way to turn all Italy into a museum as a way of fabricating a memento mori for the human species, Wells succeeded in creating the most memorable of all science fictional museums, the eerie, deserted, ruinous Palace of Green Porcelain.

Inside that vast structure of metal, glass, and tile the traveler explores galleries of paleontology, mineralogy, botany, zoology, chemistry, military history, ethnography, industrial history, and many others unspecified in the course of a long and wearying afternoon. Excepting some sketchily described futuristic machines in one gallery, all of the exhibits might have been found in London in 1895. Wells's Palace is almost certainly a composite of several English museums as they existed at the close of the nineteenth century: notably, the British Museum in Bloomsbury and the complex of museums in South Kensington near the Normal School of Science where Wells had been a student in the 1880s. In uniting these separate museums into one "palace" Wells was accomplishing in fiction and in the future what was dreamed of by Prince Albert in the nineteenth century: a single grand institution that would acknowledge the interdisciplinary nature of anthropological study and that would not separate "natural history" from human artifacts in the study of culture. Surviving photographs suggest that some details of Wells's palace are drawn directly from the Victorian museums he knew: the enormous fossil of a brontosaurus at the entrance to the Palace is reminiscent of the brontosaurus that dominated the East Dinosaur Gallery of the Natural History Museum, and "the old familiar glass cases of our time" (80) duplicate those that the trend-setting British Museum had just installed in its ethnographic galleries. The cracked and smashed "white globes" (82) the traveler sees hanging from the ceiling of one of the interior galleries undoubtedly reflect the recent installation of electrical lighting in the museums in Bloomsbury and South Kensington.[14]

Many commentaries on *The Time Machine* either ignore chapter 8, view it as a kind of interlude in the narrative, or give it short shrift as a supply depot out of which the traveler can arm himself to recover his machine and so advance the plot to its proper culmination in the year thirty million.[15] But Wells and his traveler have to go out of their way to get to the Palace of Green Porcelain—eighteen miles the traveler estimates—and there certainly were more convenient ways to get fire and a club into the time traveler's hands if that was all Wells was after. The Palace is a locale central to the aesthetic and moral design of *The Time Machine*, I suggest, because Wells saw the institution of the museum as an immediately accessible icon for the narrative's philosophical concerns with nature and culture, time and change. In what he calls "this ancient monument of an intellectual age" (81) the traveler, alternately exhilarated and dismayed, receives a vision of mortality, of the inexorable processes of time, of the frailty of human culture that is second in power only to his more famous apocalyptic vision in the year thirty million. If that later vision of the end of the world offers the definitive view in *The Time Machine* of the hostility of the cosmos to terrestrial life, the epiphany in the Palace of Green Porcelain is the book's most concentrated lesson in the vanity of human wishes and the brevity of intellect.

Any catalog of artifacts from science fiction's many museums would have to give pride of place to the contents of Wells's Palace: the sealed camphor and matches, the bulky corroded machinery, the Eloi necklaces fashioned out of fossilized bones, the dummy dynamite caps, the inoperable guns, and the easily vandalized stone idols arranged in what the time traveler names "the ruins of some latter-day South Kensington" (80). But the most spectacular moment in the Palace of Green Porcelain comes when the traveler enters a room hung with "brown and charred rags" (84). At first thinking them decayed military banners, he quickly grasps that he has found the museum's library and that the rags are all that remain of its books. Staring at the empty bindings, he wryly places the fate of his own seventeen published scholarly papers on optics into the framework of a universal disintegration of texts: "They had long since dropped to pieces, and every semblance of print had left them. But here and there were warped boards and cracked metallic clasps that told the tale well enough. Had I been a literary man I might, perhaps, have moralized upon the futility of all ambition" (84). In his epiphany in the museum, Wells's traveler, not for the last time in the narrative, marks the end of a world. The "somber wilderness of rotting paper" in the Palace's library (84) furnishes an elegiac commentary on the fantasy of the triumph of will over time, of art over nature. Precisely because the time traveler does not speak out of the wishful sensibilities of "a literary man," the episode amounts to a matter-of-fact repudiation of the sentiments that open Shakespeare's fifty-fifth sonnet:

> Not marble nor the gilded monuments
> Of princes shall outlive this pow'rful rhyme.

Tellingly, what survive best in the Palace are the means for destruction—sulfur and camphor and matches, rusty hatchets and a mechanical lever recycled into a mace; the works of mind and imagination are only as durable as their materials. Poetry, philosophy, criticism, scholarly journals, scientific romances, the printed words you are reading right now: these are far more fragile.

Wells's successor as historian of the future, Olaf Stapledon, imagined more durable textual artifacts surviving time's processes, but he foresaw an equivalent fragility in the mental and moral stability of those future users of the materials preserved in archives from the past. One entire stage of *Last and First Men* can be described in terms of a pair of crucially placed archives. Stapledon's Patagonians, struggling to construct a human civilization some 100,000 years from now, are psychologically devastated when a team of archeologists examining the basement of a derelict building in China discover metal plates from which twentieth-century books were printed. Decoding this futuristic Rosetta stone, Patagonian linguists and cultural anthropologists realize that their own culture, at a stage roughly equivalent to the European Renaissance of the sixteenth century, had been long since overshadowed, and that their human ancestors had not been primitive but highly and dangerously developed, that everything they thought they were discovering and inventing was in fact a rediscovery and a reinvention. Some of the Patagonians find this revelation depressing; they become reactionaries incapable of facing the future because they are paralyzed by the past. Others find in this evidence of an advanced civilization reason to hope that such a level of material comfort and intellectual vigor might be achieved again.

In the upshot this "progressive" mentality wins out, though the triumph is as problematic and as compromised as that of twentieth-century human culture. The Patagonians achieve a new civilization at the price of nationalism, warfare, economic rivalries, class stratification, squandering of planetary resources, and at last the unleashing of the djinn in the bottle of atomic energy. A chain reaction scalds the planet and destroys all but thirty-five members of the human species in Siberia, and thus the ruined Chinese depository of printing blocks predicts the cycle of human risings and fallings central to the aesthetic and psychological design of *Last and First Men*. The artifacts miraculously preserved from the twentieth century serve only to stimulate the cataclysm of the hundred-thousandth century. Out of that cataclysm the Siberian survivors, before sinking after several generations into subhuman barbarism, create a stone archive preserving as much knowledge of the Patagonian civilization as they can on carved tablets, along with a pictorial dictionary and grammar. The project falters when newer generations begin to resent "the hardship of engraving endless verbiage upon granitic slabs." [16] Inevitably, several million years later, that stone museum is unearthed, its artifacts are decoded, and its ideals are recycled into the evolved human species Stapledon calls the Second Men. The condition of the literary artifacts in Wells's Green Palace and the uses made of the historical records removed from Stapledon's archives testify to both the grandeur and the ironies in the human dream of composing imperishable monuments, whether in stone, metal, or words.

In George Stewart's *Earth Abides* the library at the University of California at Berkeley has a similarly pivotal role in defining an attitude toward civilization. Initially, Isherwood Williams cherishes the library as a cultural temple and a bulwark against a reversion to barbarism in the aftermath of a global epidemic. "Here rested in storage the wisdom by which civilization had been built, and could be rebuilt," we are told after Ish carefully breaks into the building.[17] But as a new arcadian society begins to form, the library's treasures, invested with a taboo status by Ish, actually come to seem largely irrelevant to the future. Books, after all, will be "mere wood-pulp and lampblack" (268) in an unlettered culture. When a great fire burns most of the San Francisco Bay area near the end of the novel, the elderly Ish observes among the gutted buildings of the university campus the still-intact library, its million volumes amazingly spared from the flames. He feels he should rejoice in this preservation but instead decides that the accumulated wisdom of earlier ages will probably matter little to the culture of the future. He worries that he will suffer nightmares born from his betrayal of the literary and scientific culture embodied and entombed in the library: "Will I dream of a million books passing in endless procession, looking reproachfully upon me because after so long I have begun to have doubts in them and all they stood for?" (309).[18]

As Ish stands in the reader's near future pondering a more distant future he loses confidence in the ability of a bankrupt past to offer any usable guidance for those who will shape the new society. "History repeats itself," according to one of the central aphorisms in *Earth Abides*, "but always with variations" (176), and therefore the relation of past and future will always be problematic. In a later postcatastrophe novel which imagines a less attractive illiterate society than the neo-Amerindian one Stewart projected, Russell Hoban designs an epiphany in the closest thing to a museum to survive the nuclear holocaust that ended twentieth-century civilization. At "Cambry Senter" Riddley Walker finds the entrance to a crypt that once sat beneath Canterbury Cathedral. As he enters the hole in the ground where, as it seems to him, stone trees grow out of the earth, he is shaken by his perception of a saner ancient world whose artisans carved pillars with such cunning art and out of an instinctive sense of the wholeness of things:

It come to me what it wer wed los. It come to me what it wer as made them peopl time back way back bettern us. It wer knowing how to put ther selfs with the

Power of the wood be come stoan. The wood in the stoan and the stoan in the
wood. The idear in the hart of every thing.

If you cud even jus only put your self right with 1 stoan. Thats what kep saying
its self in my head. If you cud even jus only put your self right with 1 stoan youwd
be moving with the girt dants of the every thing the 1 Big 1 the Master Chaynjis.
Then you myt have the res of it or not. The boats in the air or what ever. What
ever you done wud be right.

Them as made Canterbury musve put ther selfs right. Only it dint stay right did
it. Somers in be twean them stoan trees and the Power Ring they musve put ther
selfs wrong.[19]

In *Riddley Walker* these relics from medieval culture outline the tragedy of
Riddley's world and ours, but they also define the aesthetic of the artifact
Riddley is making as he writes the autobiographical-anthropological narrative that we read, a text in which Riddley attempts to put himself—and
us—right again.

In Arthur C. Clarke's *Childhood's End* the epiphany takes place on
another world, although, as in *The Time Machine*, from the moment the
protagonist enters the alien building of the Overlords there is no doubt in
his mind that the structure must be a museum. Stowaway Jan Rodricks,
stunned by the radical strangeness of daily life on another planet, gets "a
much needed psychological boost to find himself in a place whose purpose
he could fully understand." [20] But if he finds the physical layout of the inter-
stellar museum familiar and reassuring, Jan does not find his actual tour of
the museum an antidote to culture shock. Far from it. In an interview with
the curator for Earth he is distressed at how few of the terrestrial specimens
he can identify and at the magnitude of his ignorance of human culture.
His pride chastened, he then is given a further jolt when he sees the model
of an enormous eye of a "cyclopean beast" from a distant stellar system
(197), an eye so frighteningly alien that it further reduces the stature of
human beings in the midst of a nature infinitely inventive and profoundly
inhuman.

J. G. Ballard's *The Drowned World* is enacted on our own planet, but
its physical environment is in many ways as alienating as anything in
Childhood's End. The most spectacular site in *The Drowned World* is the
submerged London planetarium, to which the biologist Robert Kerans descends in diving gear, but the essential museum locale in the novel may be
Strangman's "treasure ship," a mobile monument to kitsch and rapacity.
Strangman, the leader of a gang of vandals who plunder the abandoned

cities of Europe, has installed meretricious pseudo-art in the form of fake marble columns, peeling gilt banisters, and gold-colored draperies and tassels that, we are told, give the ship's decor the look of "a bad film set of Versailles."[21] The ship's cataloging room contains an assortment of good and bad pieces looted from museums: stone limbs and torsos, an ornamented altarpiece, stacks of gilt-framed pictures, pairs of huge cathedral doors, pieces of armor, equestrian statues, ceremonial inkstands, and other miscellaneous bric-a-brac. Strangman, walking his visitors through the storeroom, identifies each object with a single identifying phrase about its original home: "Sistine Chapel" or "Medici Tomb." One of the tourists on this pirate ship murmurs, "Aesthetically, most of this is rubbish, picked for the gold content alone" (93). Another member of the party says of the museum relics simply, "They're like bones" (93). And two black sailors from Strangman's crew turn this into a derisive chant: "Bones! Yes, man, dem's all bones! Dem bones dem bones dem . . !" (94).

Strangman, as Mark Rose has indicated, is the pivotal figure in *The Drowned World*, and his project to drain the water from London and re-expose the artifacts from the city's lost museums is a ghoulish activity.[22] The museums in Ballard's narrative are the tombs of the past, and the effort to reclaim the past—whether by acquisitive madmen like Strangman or by Kerans's scientific expedition into the sunken planetarium—leads to revulsion, nightmare, and flight. Ballard's museums, presided over by the spookily elegant skeletons of Delvaux paintings and the surreal images of Max Ernst, have an elegiac function like the Palace of Green Porcelain, the Rome of *The Last Man*, and the ruins of Canterbury Cathedral, though where Wells, Shelley, and Hoban emphasize the achievements that have been lost, Ballard highlights (even more emphatically than George Stewart) the dilapidation of Western culture and (with Clarke) dramatizes the alienation of the museum visitor from the artifacts. Ballard's science fictional museum becomes either a sterile memento of a world well drowned, as in the underwater planetarium, or a cultural rummage in which artistic accomplishment is inextricably linked with vulgarity, robbery, and racism.

I end as I began with Wells and Shelley. Almost the time traveler's last act in the Palace of Green Porcelain, a gesture that from one perspective is the most trivial in the whole narrative, occurs when museum fatigue has left him with a waning interest in the silent galleries he has been exploring. He enters a room full of ancient totems from a great cross-section of planetary cultures and pauses before a massive figure carved in soapstone: "And here, yielding to an irresistible impulse, I wrote my name upon the nose of a steatite monster from South America that particularly took my fancy" (86). This piece of apparently gratuitous vandalism, this desire to announce his presence and even to claim possession of the artifact, not only makes an incongruous link between Wells's self-consciously proper Victorian and Ballard's sleazy Strangman, it also stands as one of the most provocative commentaries on the recurrence of museums in science fiction. Wells's traveler, anonymous to us, in an act of mischief carves his signature into an ancient artifact encountered 800,000 years from now. Every reader of *The Time Machine* remembers the pair of flowers the traveler brings back from the future to his dinner guests in 1895, but the impulse to leave behind some graffiti in 802,701 is an equally eloquent—and perhaps a more revealing—gesture. Although no one will ever read it, the traveler cannot forgo the self-important announcement that Kilroy was here. Mary Shelley's Lionel Verney does much the same sort of thing in his final days. With white paint taken from a deserted shop, he inscribes his name in three languages on a conspicuous place in each town he passes through on his way to Rome: "Verney, the last of the race of Englishmen." Beneath this flamboyant obituary he adds as postscript, this time only in Italian, a more homely cri de coeur addressed to the figment of another survivor: "Deh vieni! to aspetto!" (Come, I beg you. I am waiting for you! [332]).

To these self-focusing flourishes we might add Ish's discovery of his own name written on the checkout slip of a geography book in the Berkeley library (268), Kerans's startled vision of himself in a mirror in *The Drowned World*'s planetarium (106), and Jan Rodricks's irrational and overwhelming conviction that that single, gigantic, artificial eye is staring at *him* (196). In all these instances we are reminded that in the showcases of science fiction's museums *we* are what is chiefly on display. The artifacts in the museums may be historical, extraterrestrial, or futuristic; they may be the most elegant products of a refined civilization, the unfathomable evidences of a totally alien mind, the shameful testimony of human crimes, the poignant relics of a vanished splendor, or junk indiscriminately preserved by time's accidents. Whatever its source, whatever the predilections or deficiencies of its curators, the science fiction museum invites the reader to become a tourist and to peer into the glass case in wonder, or alarm, at an object that collapses distances of time and space, disorients and displaces the observer, and ultimately requires us to put ourselves right again. In science fiction's museums, if we look closely enough, we will at last and almost inevitably see with unmistakable clarity an object inscribed not only with Kilroy's name but with ours.

Notes

1. The events summarized come from these novels, in order: Mary Shelley, *The Last Man* (1826); H. G. Wells, *The Time Machine* (1895); Yevgeny Zamiatin, *We* (1922); Olaf Stapledon, *Last and First Men* (1930); George Stewart, *Earth Abides* (1949); Arthur C. Clarke, *Childhood's End* (1953); J. G. Ballard, *The Drowned World* (1962); Ursula K. Le Guin, *The Dispossessed* (1974); Walter Tevis, *Mockingbird* (1980); Russell Hoban, *Riddley Walker* (1980); and George Turner, *Drowning Towers* [English title: *The Sea and Summer*] (1987).

2. Eric S. Rabkin, "Fantastic Verbal Portraits of Fantastic Visual Portraits," *Mosaic* 21 (Fall 1988): 87–97.

3. Compare Karl Kroeber's recent suggestion that "virtually all the best science fiction is, explicitly or implicitly, a kind of time travel" (*Romantic Fantasy and Science Fiction* [New Haven: Yale University Press, 1988], p. 27).

4. See the opening chapters of Brian Aldiss, *Trillion Year Spree: The History of Science Fiction* (New York: Atheneum, 1986), pp. 25–52; and Mark Rose, *Alien Encounters: Anatomy of Science Fiction* (Cambridge, Mass.: Harvard University Press, 1981), pp. 1–23.

5. For an account of the rise of the modern science museum out of private libraries and "cabinets of curiosities" see Silvio A. Bedini, "The Evolution of Science Museums," *Technology and Culture* 6 (Winter 1965): 1–29. The most complete survey of the development of the modern "public service" function of the museum is in Alma S. Wittlin, *The Museum: Its History and Its Tasks in Education* (London: Routledge and Kegan Paul, 1949).

6. Introduction to volume 1 of *Archaeologia, or Miscellaneous Tracts Relating to Antiquity, Published by the Society of Antiquaries of London* (1770), p. ii.

7. On the collections of Sloane and Salter see Arthur MacGregor, "The Cabinet of Curiosities in Seventeenth-Century Britain," in *The Origins of Museums: The Cabinet of Curiosities in Sixteenth- and Seventeenth-Century Europe*, ed. Oliver Impey and Arthur MacGregor (Oxford: Clarendon, 1985), pp. 157–58. For the growth of institutional collections in the eighteenth century as a transition from the private "cabinets of curiosities" of earlier periods to the rise of truly public museums see, in addition to MacGregor's article (pp. 147–58), Michael Hunter, "The Cabinet Institutionalized: The Royal Society's 'Repository' and Its Background," in ibid., pp. 159–68.

8. For reports of early tourists to the Ashmolean, including continental scholars scandalized by the open admissions policy, see Martin Welch, "The Ashmolean as Described by Its Earliest Visitors," in *Tradescant's Rarities: Essays on the Foundation of the Ashmolean Museum, 1683*, ed. Arthur MacGregor

(Oxford: Clarendon, 1983), pp. 59–69. A general account of the Ashmolean in the history of modern museums is in Kenneth Hudson, *Museums of Influence* (Cambridge: Cambridge University Press, 1987), pp. 21–22.

9. There are useful discussions of the early history of the word *museum* in English in Wittlin, *The Museum*, pp. 1–8, and in Hunter's appendix to "The Cabinet Institutionalized," p. 168.

10. On the discontent in the 1820s over the limited public access to the collections and the reading room at the British Museum, see Edward Miller, *That Noble Cabinet: A History of the British Museum* (London: Andre Deutsch, 1973), pp. 122–24.

11. On public access to the Louvre from its opening in 1793 see the discussion in Helmut Seling, "The Genesis of the Museum," *Architectural Review* 141 (February 1967): 109–10.

12. Mary Shelley, *The Last Man*, introduction by Brian Aldiss (1826; London: Hogarth, 1985), p. 313. Further references to this edition are given parenthetically.

13. H. G. Wells, *The Time Machine* (1895; New York: Bantam, 1968), p. 80. Further references to this edition are given parenthetically.

14. For a discussion of Prince Albert's ideal of a unified museum see Hudson, *Museums of Influence*, pp. 69–70. Photographs on pp. 27 and 71 show, respectively, the new glass cases at the British Museum and the brontosaurus skeleton in the Museum of Natural History. In *A Social History of Museums: What the Visitors Thought* (New Jersey: Humanities Press, 1975), Hudson points out that electricity was installed in the 1880s at South Kensington and at the British Museum in 1890 (p. 79). Cf. Stephen Prickett's discussion of the Victorian fascination with the dinosaur park at the Crystal Palace and its impact on late-century fiction in his *Victorian Fantasy* (Bloomington: Indiana University Press, 1979), pp. 82–89.

15. In *The Definitive Time Machine: A Critical Edition of H. G. Wells's Scientific Romance* (Bloomington: Indiana University Press, 1987), Harry M. Geduld sees the visit to the Palace as one of several "autonomous" episodes in which the author "is depicting scenes rather than developing plot" (p. 12). My own earlier commentary on the Palace in *H. G. Wells* (Mercer Island, Wash.: Starmont, 1986) is limited to describing it as a place where the traveler "procures weapons" (p. 26). An important exception to the neglect of chapter 8 in studies of *The Time Machine* is John Huntington's detailed reading of this episode as an example of Wells's mediation of opposites; see Huntington, *The Logic of Fantasy: H. G. Wells and Science Fiction* (New York: Columbia University Press, 1982), pp. 46–47.

16. Olaf Stapledon, *Last and First Men* (1930; New York: Dover, 1968), p. 95.

17. George R. Stewart, *Earth Abides* (1949; New York: Fawcett, 1971), p. 116. Further references to this edition are given parenthetically.

18. Ish's doubts are counterpoised throughout the novel by the unambivalent attitude of Em, the new Eve of the emergent arcadian society. Drawing on her perspectives as a woman and as an African American, Em refuses to mourn the vanished "cultural literacy" of the past. See, for instance, her mordant observations on the "communication" that resulted from earlier European voyages of exploration (p. 174) and on the "angry" male God of Judeo-Christian tradition (p. 258). To Ish's persistent anxiety that the society of the future will not be as creative as its predecessors, Stewart contrasts Em's provocative questions about the catastrophic failures of imagination in Euro-American cultural history.

19. Russell Hoban, *Riddley Walker* (1980; New York: Washington Square Press, 1982), pp. 161–62.

20. Arthur C. Clarke, *Childhood's End* (1953; New York: Ballantine Books, 1974), p. 194. Further references to this edition are given parenthetically.

21. J. G. Ballard, *The Drowned World* (1962; New York: Penguin, 1965), p. 92. Further references to this edition are given parenthetically.

22. See Rose's excellent commentary on *The Drowned World* in *Alien Encounters*, pp. 127–38.

Chapter 17

Words of Wishdom:
The Neologisms of Science Fiction

Gary Westfahl

While many earlier works now regarded as science fiction offered *visions* and *narratives* of the future, only the literature of the twentieth century has presented the *vocabulary* of the future. Modern readers may take for granted that a story set in future times will include examples of futuristic language, but this has not always been the case: two future tales of the early nineteenth century—Mary Shelley's *The Last Man* and Edgar Allan Poe's "Mellonta Tauta"—have no neologisms to speak of, and even two stories from around 1900—Rudyard Kipling's *With the Night Mail* and H. G. Wells's *When the Sleeper Wakes*—contain relatively few of them. To explain the great flowering of neologisms in twentieth-century science fiction, one must, of course, acknowledge the work of nineteenth-century linguists who revealed language as a constantly changing and evolving phenomenon and discussed how words can be created and altered. But credit must also go to Hugo Gernsback, the first science fiction writer who manifestly loved coining new words and demonstrated how to employ and explain unfamiliar terms in the context of a science fiction story. Indeed, should we choose to regard linguistic extrapolation, like scientific extrapolation, as a key element in science fiction, then we have yet another reason to regard Gernsback as the true father of the genre.[1]

When I began to explore the lexicon of science fiction, I limited myself to imagined extensions of the English language as it may be spoken in some future time; thus I bypassed the fascinating subjects of alien languages in science fiction and the jargon developed and used by science fiction fans—*fiawol, egoboo,* and the like—since these coinages never appear in the literature. And while some major writers attempted to construct a complete language of the future—notably George Orwell in *1984* and Anthony Burgess in *A Clockwork Orange*—I restricted my study to authors whose limited creativity was more typical of the genre. Specifically, I examined eight novels about a technologically advanced, urbanized future Earth, representing the four major eras of modern science fiction: Hugo Gernsback's *Ralph 124C 41+: A Romance of the Year 2660* and Philip Francis Nowlan's *Armageddon 2419 A.D.*, examples of the fiction of the Gernsback era; Robert A. Heinlein's *Beyond This Horizon* and Isaac Asimov's *The Caves of Steel,* two novels by major writers of John Campbell's Golden Age; Philip Jose Farmer's "Riders of the Purple Wage" and John Brunner's *Stand on Zanzibar,* two leading works of the New Wave movement; and William Gibson's *Neuromancer* and Bruce Sterling's *Islands in the Net,* novels by two prominent cyberpunk authors.[2]

The nature of the futuristic language employed by these, and most other, authors of science fiction, I submit, has never been properly described. I liken them to an Englishwoman of the nineteenth century who spends some time living in Kenya: while she continues to speak and write the English she mastered as a child, and never learns Swahili, she finds her language increasingly infused, or contaminated, with borrowed Swahili terms she has picked up during her visit; and she finds herself repeatedly using those terms when she returns to England and describes her experiences to her friends. Similarly, I cast science fiction writers as visitors to an imagined future who, after returning to tell their stories, essentially maintain the structure and grammar of contemporary English while including samplings of futuristic vocabulary.[3]

In failing to understand the nature of science fiction language, those few commentators who have discussed neologisms in the genre have inappropriately characterized writers as either attempting too much or attempting too little. On the one hand, Walter Myers's "The Future History and Development of the English Language" accuses a few science fiction writers of committing fundamental blunders in describing the future evolution of their language. Though Myers's particular complaints may be valid, I argue that most writers are not seeking to develop and describe a complete language of the future, making Myers's criticisms inapplicable to most works. On the other hand, L. Sprague de Camp's *Science Fiction Handbook* understates the phenomenon of linguistic creativity when observing that science fiction writers "must represent the speech of [future] time in understandable English, but . . . may indicate futurity by a few made-up words or expressions" (147). Yet in the eight works I examined I found a total of 869 neologisms, or an average of 109 new words per work; furthermore, many of these words are used not once but several times, in their original form or transformed in some fashion.[4] Thus there are far more than "*a few* made-up words or expressions"; indeed, I suggest that neologisms constitute a basic, and powerful, element in the style of science fiction. The examples in the glossary at the end of this essay demonstrate that science fiction writers reveal a remarkable energy and creativity in crafting new words, indicating that such inventions are an important part of their writing, one that cannot be dismissed as merely ornamental.

The neologisms of science fiction can be fruitfully examined from at least three different perspectives. Linguists should find any collection of coinages interesting in themselves, and those developed in science fiction could serve as an excellent data base for studying how words are created and transformed and why certain neologisms become standard while others vanish. Cultural historians could look in detail at the meanings of the neologisms as a concrete record of the expectations and fears of science fiction writers—and by extension, their society—regarding future developments and possibilities. Here, along with some comments regarding these other concerns, I explore neologisms primarily in my role as a critic of science fiction, using the nature, context, and distribution of these words in the eight works as a method for gaining a better understanding of the characteristic techniques of the genre and its evolution in the twentieth century.

One straightforward way to classify neologisms is by part of speech; and as table 1 shows, in all eight works an overwhelming majority of the new words are nouns, although significantly larger numbers of adjectives and verbs do appear in the more recent four works. In a way, this result is surprising: one might expect to find nothing but nouns in Gernsback's novel, since much of that story, after all, consists of rather static tableaux introducing and explaining marvelous new inventions; but even in the kinetic, frenetic, happening world of Brunner's *Stand on Zanzibar*, about three-fourths of the new words are nouns. This might reflect the simple fact that most coined words are nouns, and in particular that most words borrowed from other languages are nouns. Thus the preponderance of nouns supports my claim that science fiction writers typically borrow words from an imagined future English, and do not actually create a new language.

Table I. Neologisms in Science Fiction Works Classified by Part of Speech

Author	Nouns	Adjectives	Verbs	Others (adverbs, pronouns, interjections)
Gernsback	96 (87)	1 (1)	1 (1)	2 (2)
Nowlan	87 (73)	11 (9)	2 (2)	0 (0)
Heinlein	85 (61)	10 (7)	6 (4)	0 (0)
Asimov	91 (74)	7 (6)	1 (1)	0 (0)
Farmer	75 (54)	14 (10)	8 (6)	3 (2)
Brunner	74 (164)	12 (27)	11 (24)	4 (8)
Gibson	81 (95)	11 (13)	7 (8)	1 (1)
Sterling	77 (99)	17 (22)	6 (8)	0 (0)
Average of all words	81 (707)	11 (95)	6 (54)	1 (13)
Average of authors' percentages	83	10	5	1

Note: In tables 1, 2, 3, and 5, the first number is the percentage of neologisms; the figure in parentheses is the actual number. Percentages may not total 100 due to rounding off.

But one could also suggest that the dominance of nouns reveals that science fiction is above all a literature of objects that revels in and celebrates objects, and even to an extent reduces human beings to objects—clones, cyborgs, and computer-linked "cowboys." In particular, such data could be used to support Dennis Etchison's claim, in his talk at the Eleventh Eaton Conference, that science fiction practices "reductionist objectification."

I next attempted to classify these neologisms by their construction. Although linguists have devised various categories of word construction, I felt these could be safely reduced to four basic types. First are "bound-morpheme constructions," new words containing at least one prefix, suffix, or root which is not itself a word (*menograph, zymoveal*). Second are "free-morpheme constructions"—either existing words given a notable new meaning (*exchange, Personal*), or two or more words combined to form what is sometimes called a self-evident compound (*diet-negative, tanglegun*). Third are "reduced-morpheme constructions," words containing at least one morpheme which has been shortened in some way; these include clipped words (*zeck*), abbreviations used as words (*C/Fe*), acronyms (*emp*), and blended or portmanteau words (*tempoxy*). Finally, I set up a fourth category of "other constructions" consisting of echoic words (*huftymagufty*), imitations of baby talk (*fuzzy-wuzzy*), and words I could

not meaningfully analyze, which I designated "possible root constructions" (*zock*).

The first three categories are reflections of the three classes of people who
coin words: bound-morpheme constructions are the typical creations of
scientists, scholars, and other intellectuals; free-morpheme constructions
are the simple expressions of common people; and reduced-morpheme constructions are the usual argot of the members of various underclasses—
artists, rebels, criminals, and the like. As inventions move from the laboratory to become familiar and finally overly familiar objects, one often sees
a progression of terminology down through these three categories: thus,
"cinematograph" becomes "motion picture" or the "big screen," which
becomes "movie" or "flick"; and "television" becomes the "small screen,"
which becomes "TV" or the "telly." Given that twentieth-century science
fiction steadily shifted from a focus on scientist-protagonists to more average characters to outcasts and rebels in the first three eras of the genre
that I studied, I expected to find a preponderance of one word category
in each era; and I sought results on the cyberpunk writers as one way to
characterize this controversial literary movement.

As table 2 shows, this is not exactly what I found. True, there is a larger
percentage of bound-morpheme constructions in works of the Gernsback-
era writers and a steady decline in the percentage of such words in works of
later writers; and there is a marked increase in the percentage of reduced-
morpheme constructions in works of the new wave writers. The trend that
emerges most strongly, however, is significant numbers of free-morpheme
constructions even in the early works; and in the other six works, such
words constitute a plurality—or even a majority—of all neologisms. These
results may simply reflect authors' decisions to employ words that will
look most familiar to their readers; but since words of other types can also
be readily understood, I tentatively suggest that the frequent use of these
words may reveal a rarely voiced judgment about the typical readership of
science fiction.

In the popular tradition of science fiction criticism there are three basic
opinions about the proper audience for science fiction. Gernsback saw science fiction as literature for everyone; he hoped that "every man, woman,
boy and girl, could be induced to read science fiction" ("Science Fiction
Week," 1061). Later, John W. Campbell, Jr., envisioned science fiction as
essentially written for a scientifically educated elite: "No average mind can
either understand or enjoy science-fiction; it takes an amount of imagination beyond the average man" ("Science-Fiction," 37). Finally, Harlan

Table 2. Neologisms in Science Fiction Works Classified
by Type of Word Construction

Author	Bound morpheme	Free morpheme	Reduced morpheme	Other constructions
Gernsback	53 (48)	37 (34)	8 (7)	2 (2)
Nowlan	49 (41)	39 (33)	11 (9)	1 (1)
Heinlein	42 (30)	53 (38)	4 (3)	1 (1)
Asimov	42 (34)	42 (34)	16 (13)	0 (0)
Farmer	32 (23)	40 (29)	22 (16)	6 (4)
Brunner	21 (47)	40 (90)	31 (69)	8 (17)
Gibson	23 (27)	50 (58)	24 (28)	3 (4)
Sterling	23 (30)	47 (61)	22 (29)	7 (9)
Average of all words	32 (280)	43 (377)	20 (174)	4 (38)
Average of authors' percentages	36	44	17	4

Ellison announced links between science fiction and the counterculture, claiming that "speculative fiction has grown to be one of the most potent sources of stimulation for an entire generation of concerned and anxiously seeking individuals" ("Brinkmanship," 21), and "the mad dream of the fantasists [are] the secret whimseys [*sic*] on which our thoughts fasten when, like Winston Smith in *1984*, we are thrown into whatever Room 101 the System thinks will whip us in shape" ("Science Fiction," 80). Certainly, if the *protagonists* of science fiction are examined, one finds support for the claims of Campbell and Ellison; that is, heroes and heroines are typically either scientists and intellectuals or criminals, rebels, and artists. On the other hand, the apparently average protagonists of novels like *Beyond This Horizon* and *The Caves of Steel* ultimately emerge as unusually intelligent and talented, and truly average men and women are most often the object of ridicule, as in the satirical stories of the 1950s.[5] However, the types of neologisms employed in science fiction—its characteristic language, as it were—indicate that the genre is indeed, as Gernsback argued, addressing everyday men and women; and the growing popularity of the genre in the twentieth century further suggests that while science fiction writers may posture as spokespersons for intellectuals or outcasts, they are in fact writing for an audience of average people.

Table 3. Percentages and Numbers of Neologisms Introduced by Sympathetic and Unsympathetic Characters in Science Fiction Works

Author	Narrator	Sympathetic character	Unsympathetic character	Neutral character
Gernsback	68 (62)	29 (26)	2 (2)	1 (1)
Nowlan	81 (68)	13 (11)	6 (5)	0 (0)
Heinlein	50 (36)	47 (34)	1 (1)	1 (1)
Asimov	59 (48)	36 (29)	4 (3)	1 (1)
Farmer	72 (52)	10 (7)	18 (13)	0 (0)
Brunner	46 (102)	15 (33)	35 (78)	4 (10)
Gibson	60 (70)	29 (34)	11 (13)	0 (0)
Sterling	41 (53)	44 (57)	15 (19)	0 (0)
Average of all words	57 (491)	27 (231)	15 (134)	1 (13)
Average of authors' percentages	60	28	12	1

I next attempted to determine which characters in these science fiction works most frequently used neologisms. After all, one function of language is to distinguish between insiders and outsiders, those who speak a certain language and those who do not. A thorough consideration of this issue would require careful classification of all characters in a novel and a tabulation of how many times they used neologisms in proportion to their total amount of speech—an investigation I did not pursue. However, as one indication of whether certain characters were or were not speaking the language of the future, I did first broadly categorize characters as sympathetic, unsympathetic, and neutral or undefined, and then I counted how many times each type of character *introduced* a neologism. Numerical results, presented in table 3, were not always significant because the presumably neutral narrator typically introduced most of the neologisms; nevertheless, a definite pattern did emerge.

In the first four works I studied, sympathetic characters introduced far more neologisms than the unsympathetic characters, suggesting a clear insider-outsider dichotomy. This difference reflects the fact that each novel's basic narrative can be characterized as a struggle between the past and the future. "Today it is not brute force that counts, but scientific knowledge" (153), Ralph proclaims as he goes forth to battle the representatives of brute force that have kidnapped his beloved Alice; he represents the new order, they the old. In Nowlan's novel the insurgent Americans are depicted as youthful and vigorous, in contrast to the stagnant, decadent Han Empire. Heinlein's protagonist in *Beyond This Horizon* is working to thwart an underground group that wants to overthrow a benevolent social order and return to a totalitarian state; while in *The Caves of Steel*, Asimov's hero opposes a similar group called the Medievalists, who seek to eliminate robots and other advanced technology and go back to a simpler life-style. Thus these works all feature sympathetic representatives of the future fighting against unsympathetic representatives of the past, and the heroes' and heroines' futuristic language marks this contrast.

A quite different picture emerges in the two New Wave works I examined. Here, most of the neologisms emerge from unsympathetic sources —broadcasters and advertisements, policemen and soldiers, and the superficial residents of a mind-numbing future society. The sympathetic spokesmen in these works—notably Grandpa Winnegan in "Riders of the Purple Wage" and Chad C. Mulligan in *Stand on Zanzibar*—explicitly denounce a new order that is dehumanizing, insane, and self-destructive, and call for a return to older modes of thought and behavior. Here, the dichotomy in neologisms reflects a struggle between an unsympathetic future and a sympathetic past.

Although their murky worlds of shifting realities and double-crosses make the delineation of sympathetic and unsympathetic characters in the cyberpunk novels rather problematic, there is nonetheless a reemergence of the older pattern. The sympathetic characters are again speaking the language of the future, while the unsympathetic characters are not. And the plots of the novels suggest the older struggle of the sympathetic future versus the unsympathetic past: Case and his cohorts are trying to bring about the creation of a new type of artificial intelligence, while their opponents seek to prevent this development; and Laura Webster in *Islands in the Net* is battling to maintain a peaceful world structure against a group of reactionaries trying to reintroduce nuclear weapons.

The difference between the New Wave writers and the cyberpunk writers is also marked by how three of these authors regard the continent of Africa—which, now revealed as the birthplace of the human race, serves as a symbol of return to humanity's primitive past. Both "Riders of the Purple Wage" and *Stand on Zanzibar* employ Africa as a positive icon: Grandpa Winnegan's final advice to his grandson, Chib, is "Go to Egypt" (143)—so he can retreat to a simpler society, escape from the madness of twenty-first-century Los Angeles, and pursue his desire to paint. In *Stand on Zanzibar*, the action of the novel gradually converges on the fictitious west African nation of Beninia—whose inhabitants carry a unique gene that essentially eliminates human conflict, offering a possible solution to all of humanity's problems. Indeed, the very title of Brunner's novel can be taken as a command—"stand on Zanzibar," "go back to Africa." In *Islands in the Net*, however, the headquarters of the reactionary movement is the African country of Mali—very close to the fictitious Beninia—and that is where Laura Webster endures two years of brutal imprisonment. Africa, a return to the past, is thus explicitly rejected as a possible path for humanity in Sterling's work.

Overall, the patterns of neologisms in tables 1, 2, and 3 suggest that the cyberpunk movement in fact represents a synthesis: Gibson and Sterling *write* very much like the New Wave writers—the divisions of words by part of speech and type of construction are basically similar—but they *think* like Heinlein and Asimov, as shown in the predominant use of neologisms by sympathetic characters. In his *Trillion Year Spree*, Brian Aldiss describes Gibson's *Neuromancer* as "a direct literary descendant of [the] kind of writing" in Samuel R. Delany's "Time Considered as a Helix of Semi-Precious Stones," a work he then likens to "Heinlein on speed" (472, 293)—a phrase suggesting exactly the kind of combination I found in cyberpunk works.

I finally sought to employ neologisms to illustrate and reinforce a traditional distinction between earlier and more recent science fiction works which I call the *pedagogical* and *nonpedagogical* models. In pedagogical works, a spokesperson is incorporated into the text to provide detailed explanations whenever they are necessary; this voice may be a character in the novel, the narrator, or the author adding helpful footnotes or appendixes to the main text—all devices, by the way, found in Gernsback's *Ralph*. The nonpedagogical work is defined by the absence of any of these features; its characters are all equally well informed, eliminating conversational explanations, and neither the narrator nor the author seems inclined to offer informative commentary. Here, exposition emerges in brief references, casual comments, and context clues. The two types were identified by John W. Campbell, Jr., in 1946 when he said that

in older science fiction—H. G. Wells and nearly all stories written before 1935— the author took time out to bring the reader up to date as to what had happened before his story opened. The best modern writers of science fiction have worked

Table 4. Expected Distribution of Neologisms in Science Fiction Works Divided into Ten Equal Parts

Part	Number of neologisms	Percentage
Pedagogical Work		
1	■■■■■■■■■■■■	12
2	■■■■■■■■■■	10
3	■■■■■■■■	8
4	■■■■■■■■■■■	11
5	■■■■■■■■■	9
6	■■■■■■■■■■	10
7	■■■■■■■■■	9
8	■■■■■■■■■■■■	12
9	■■■■■■■■■■	10
10	■■■■■■■■■	9
Nonpedagogical work		
1	■■■■■■■■■■■■■■■■■■■■■■■■■■■■■■	30
2	■■■■■■■■■■■■■■■■■■■■■	21
3	■■■■■■■■■■■■■■■	15
4	■■■■■■■■■■■	11
5	■■■■■■■■■	9
6	■■■■■	5
7	■■■■	4
8	■■	2
9	■■	2
10	■	1

out some truly remarkable techniques for presenting a great deal of background and associated material without intruding into the flow of the story. ("Concerning Science Fiction," ix)

If these two types of science fiction in fact exist, one can make a prediction about the distribution of neologisms in works of each type. Writers employing the pedagogical model would not have to worry about whether readers understand their neologisms; whenever one is introduced, the pedagogical voice is there to explain it. Thus one should expect to find neologisms distributed more or less evenly throughout the work. In contrast, writers employing the nonpedagogical model face a special problem; since their readers are obliged to deduce the meanings of neologisms through indirect references and context clues, such writers have to introduce most of the new words in the early part of their narrative so that readers can figure out their meaning by repeated use and gradual accumulation of information. In table 4 I show the two patterns I expected to find.

When I actually divided each work into ten approximately equal parts and counted the number of neologisms in each part, however, a dramatically different pattern emerged in all eight works, as indicated in table 5. In each case most of the neologisms are introduced in the early chapters of the work—suggesting the nonpedagogical model; yet at some point later in the narrative, usually around the halfway point, there is a sudden increase in the number of neologisms, indicating some use of the pedagogical model.

I draw two conclusions from these results: first, the distinction between pedagogical and nonpedagogical approaches to writing science fiction does not seem meaningful; as I reread these eight works, I found all authors employing both techniques. Thus, in the first chapter of *Ralph*, when Gernsback's hero tuned in to Alice speaking French, "He immediately turned the small shining disc of the Language Rectifier on his instrument till the pointer rested on "*French*" (26); without any elaborate explanation, the reader quickly understands that a *Language Rectifier* is a device attached to a picturephone which provides instant translations of foreign languages. In fact, Gernsback repeatedly stops his narrative to offer long-winded explanations not because he is too inept to convey information in any other way but because he *wants* to include detailed explanations, inasmuch as they are an important part of his theory of science fiction. And in the newer works, one is struck by how much time is spent in these allegedly nonpedagogical works in having somebody explain something to the protagonist; indeed, one moment of explanation in the early part of *Neuromancer*—Case accidentally tunes into a "Kid's show" explaining cyberspace—is as awkwardly intrusive as any lecture in *Ralph*.[6] In short, pedagogical and nonpedagogical models do not indicate, as Campbell suggested, two different types of science fiction, but two techniques for explaining matters that all science fiction writers employ at some point.

My second conclusion is more dramatic, for I contend that I have inadvertently discovered the fundamental narrative pattern of science fiction. To explain this pattern I must use the term *estrangement*—not to refer to the theories of Darko Suvin but simply to indicate that readers can find it estranging or irritating when an author uses words they do not under-

Table 5. Actual Distribution of Neologisms in Eight Science Fiction Works

Work (pp.)		Percentage (Number)

Gernsback, *Ralph 124C 41+*

Pages		Percentage (Number)
25–42	■■■■■■■■■■■■■■■■■■■■■■■■■■■■■■■■■■	36 (33)
43–60	■■■■■■■■■■■	12 (11)
61–78	■■■■	5 (5)
79–96	■■■■■■■■■■■■	13 (12)
97–114	■■■■■	5 (5)
115–132	■■■■■	5 (5)
133–150	■■■■■■■■	9 (8)
151–168	■■■■■■■■	9 (8)
169–186	■	1 (1)
187–207	■■■	3 (3)
TOTAL		98 (91)

Nowlan, *Armageddon 2419 A.D.*

Pages		Percentage (Number)
9–26	■■■■■■■■■	11 (9)
27–44	■■■■■■■■■■■	13 (11)
45–62	■■■■■■■■■■■■■	15 (13)
63–80	■■	2 (2)
81–98	■■■■	5 (4)
99–116	■■■■■■■■■■■■■■■■■■■■■■■■■■■■■■■■	38 (32)
117–134	■■■■■	6 (5)
135–152	■■	2 (2)
153–170	■■	2 (2)
171–190	■■■■	5 (4)
TOTAL		99 (84)

Heinlein, *Beyond This Horizon*

Pages		Percentage (Number)
5–19	■■■■■■■■■■■■■■■■■■■■■■	31 (22)
20–34	■■■■■■■■■■■■■■■■■■	25 (18)
35–49	■■■■■	7 (5)
50–64	■	1 (1)
65–79	■■■	4 (3)
80–94	■■■■■	7 (5)
95–109	■■■■	6 (4)
110–124	■■■■■■■■	11 (8)

Table 5. *(continued)*

Work (pp.)	Percentage (Number)
125–139 ▪▪▪▪▪▪	6 (4)
140–158 ▪▪▪	3 (2)
TOTAL	101 (72)

Asimov, *The Caves of Steel*

7–24 ▪▪▪▪▪▪▪▪▪▪▪▪▪▪▪▪▪▪▪▪▪▪▪▪▪▪	26 (21)
25–42 ▪▪▪▪▪▪▪▪▪▪▪▪▪▪▪▪▪	17 (14)
43–60 ▪▪▪▪▪▪▪▪▪▪▪▪▪▪	14 (11)
61–78 ▪▪▪▪▪▪▪▪▪	9 (7)
79–96 ▪▪▪▪▪▪▪▪▪	9 (7)
97–114 ▪▪▪▪▪▪	6 (5)
115–132 ▪▪▪▪▪▪	6 (5)
133–150 ▪▪▪▪	4 (3)
151–168 ▪▪▪▪▪▪▪	7 (6)
169–189 ▪▪	2 (2)
TOTAL	100 (81)

Farmer, "Riders of the Purple Wage"

70–76 ▪▪▪▪▪▪▪▪▪▪▪▪▪▪▪▪▪▪▪▪▪▪▪▪▪▪▪▪	28 (20)
77–83 ▪▪▪▪▪▪▪▪▪▪	10 (7)
84–90 ▪▪▪▪▪▪▪▪▪▪▪▪▪	13 (9)
91–97 ▪▪▪▪▪▪	6 (4)
98–104 ▪▪▪▪▪▪▪▪	8 (6)
105–111 ▪▪▪▪▪▪▪▪▪▪	10 (7)
112–118 ▪▪▪▪	4 (3)
119–125 ▪▪▪▪▪▪▪	7 (5)
126–132 ▪	1 (1)
133–144 ▪▪▪▪▪▪▪▪▪▪▪▪▪▪	14 (10)
TOTAL	101 (72)

Brunner, *Stand on Zanzibar*

1–65 ▪▪	42 (93)
66–130 ▪▪▪▪▪▪▪	7 (15)
131–195 ▪▪▪▪▪▪▪▪▪▪▪▪▪	13 (28)

(continued)

Table 5. *(continued)*

Work (pp.)		Percentage (Number)
196–260	▪▪▪▪▪▪▪▪▪▪▪▪▪	13 (28)
261–325	▪▪▪▪▪▪▪▪▪▪▪	11 (25)
326–390	▪▪▪▪▪▪	6 (13)
391–455	▪▪▪▪	4 (9)
456–520	▪	1 (2)
521–585	▪▪▪	3 (7)
586–650	▪	1 (3)
TOTAL		101 (223)

Gibson, *Neuromancer*

3–29	▪▪▪▪▪▪▪▪▪▪▪▪▪▪▪▪▪▪▪▪▪▪▪▪▪▪	26 (31)
30–56	▪▪▪▪▪▪▪▪▪▪▪▪▪▪▪	15 (18)
57–83	▪▪▪▪▪▪▪▪▪▪▪▪▪▪▪▪▪▪▪▪▪	21 (25)
84–110	▪▪▪▪▪▪▪▪▪	9 (10)
111–137	▪▪▪▪▪▪▪▪▪▪▪	11 (13)
138–164	▪▪▪	3 (4)
165–191	▪▪▪▪▪▪▪▪▪	9 (11)
192–218	▪▪	2 (2)
219–245	▪▪	2 (2)
246–271	▪	1 (1)
TOTAL		99 (117)

Sterling, *Islands in the Net*

1–40	▪▪▪▪▪▪▪▪▪▪▪▪▪▪▪▪▪▪	18 (23)
41–80	▪▪▪▪▪▪▪▪▪▪▪▪▪▪▪▪	16 (21)
81–120	▪▪▪▪▪▪▪▪▪▪▪▪▪▪▪	15 (19)
121–160	▪▪▪▪▪▪▪	7 (9)
161–200	▪▪▪▪▪▪▪▪▪▪▪▪▪▪▪▪	16 (21)
201–240	▪▪▪▪▪▪▪▪▪	9 (11)
241–280	▪▪▪▪▪▪	6 (8)
281–320	▪▪▪▪▪▪▪▪	8 (10)
321–360	▪▪	2 (3)
361–396	▪▪▪	3 (4)
TOTAL		100 (129)

Table 5. *(continued)*

Work (pp.)	Percentage (Number)

Average distribution of neologisms by percentage
Part

1	■■■■■■■■■■■■■■■■■■■■■■■■■■■	27
2	■■■■■■■■■■■■■■	14
3	■■■■■■■■■■■■■	13
4	■■■■■■■■	8
5	■■■■■■■■■	9
6	■■■■■■■■■■■	11
7	■■■■■■	6
8	■■■■■■	6
9	■■■	3
10	■■■■	4
TOTAL		101

stand. The function of language in designating insiders and outsiders works with writers and readers as well as with characters within works. Thus a writer who employs neologisms is consciously estranging the audience; but as he or she makes their meanings clear, the feeling of estrangement vanishes. It is widely accepted, I think, that many science fiction writers begin their stories by deliberately making their imaginary worlds appear extremely strange. My favorite example is Cordwainer Smith's "Scanners Live in Vain," a story whose first few pages are virtually incomprehensible; and part of the problem, of course, is that the reader has no idea what *scanner* or *cranching* means. Thus the fact that so many neologisms come near the beginning of works, which I have suggested is a technique for making those words more comprehensible, can also be interpreted as a purposeful strategy for making the story's setting initially seem as unusual and different from the present-day world as possible.

It is important to note that in this respect there is a dichotomy between the reactions of *readers* and those of the story's *characters*. Modern science fiction has largely dispensed with the device, seen in utopian fiction, of the befuddled visitor who represents the reader and wanders through the fictional world in constant need of explanation; while Gernsback's Alice and Nowlan's Anthony Rogers apparently fulfill this role, both become adjusted to their new worlds rather quickly and soon function as fully integrated residents of them. And in the more recent works there are not even vestiges of this old pattern;[7] all the main characters are thoroughly familiar with and comfortable in their future world as the narrative begins. Thus, at the start of these works, the *reader* is estranged from the fictional environment, but the *characters* are not.

All eight works, however, feature an abrupt change in mood: some event occurs, a new piece of information is added to the picture, and a world whose inhabitants thought it familiar and comforting, a world readers have become accustomed to, suddenly becomes strange and unsettling. This moment coincides with the second burst of neologisms seen in these eight works. In *Ralph*, the increase (around page 150) comes when Alice is kidnapped and taken into space—a development that transforms the placid Ralph into a furious rebel who disobeys a direct order from the Planet Governor, overpowers a guard seeking to detain him, and flies off into space to rescue Alice. In *Armageddon 2419 A.D.*, the sudden increase in neologisms (around page 110) occurs as narrator Rogers interrupts the story to provide some detailed scientific explanations, revealing that the ragtag guerrilla warriors actually possess amazingly advanced technology. Immediately afterward, Rogers is captured and imprisoned in a Han city, where he learns that these Asiatic invaders are in fact not all monsters; some of them are reasonably sympathetic characters who should be pitied more than hated. In *Beyond This Horizon*, the increase (after page 110) comes when the plot against the future society is thwarted and Felix and the readers gain new information about the Planners in charge of the society and their true natures and motives. In *The Caves of Steel*, the rise in neologisms (around page 160) comes when the robot Sammy is destroyed and Baley abruptly realizes that he is the logical suspect; the investigating detective finds himself cast as the criminal. In "Riders of the Purple Wage," neologisms increase (around page 105) when Chib learns that his girlfriend, Benedictine, is not going to marry him and bear his child; she actually hates him and is planning an abortion. In *Stand on Zanzibar*, the second surge in neologisms (after page 135) occurs when Donald Hogan discovers that he cannot take a walk in New York City without provoking a riot, right before he is called back to active duty to become a trained killer. In *Neuromancer*, the increase (around page 265) coincides with Case's anger when Wintermute kills his would-be abductors—his first moral reaction to anything in the novel—and his sympathetic reaction to Molly's long monologue about her life; suddenly, Case's world is something he cares about. And in *Islands in the Net*, the increase in neologisms (around page 190) occurs after the second attempt on Laura's life, when she first realizes that a truly powerful and malevolent force is arrayed against her and her company, and when she leaves her husband and baby to go on a perilous solo mission to Singapore, which ultimately leads to her imprisonment and an end to her marriage.

Thus we see in all eight works a pattern of *double estrangement:* at the *beginning* of the novel, *only the reader is estranged* from its future world, as indicated by the large number of neologisms; but at some point later in the novel, long after the reader's initial feeling of estrangement has been dissipated, *a second moment of estrangement occurs, when both the reader and the main character become estranged*, as marked by a sudden increase in neologisms. There are two things of special importance here: first, this pattern was completely unexpected—I chose these eight works not because I knew they would fulfill this pattern but because I knew they contained many neologisms, and I arrived at this pattern of double estrangement only after many efforts to shoehorn my results into the patterns I wanted to find. Second, if one accepts my hypothesis that the number of neologisms reflects the degree of estrangement felt by the reader, then I have uncovered a method, available only in science fiction, for *measuring and quantifying* estrangement. Thus the techniques I employed to (accidentally) uncover a fundamental pattern in science fiction narrative might well offer other new insights into the structure and functioning of science fiction works.

Perhaps I am reading too much into the use of neologisms in science fiction; but I argue in conclusion that they are by their nature unusually significant. In the talk he gave at the Eleventh Eaton Conference, Gregory Benford argued that the act of writing is largely a matter of the subconscious; the writer is not aware of why she or he is creating in a certain way. I know Benford was sincerely trying to convey what he sees as the essence of writing fiction; but his statement can also function as a convenient "cop-out." That is, when a reader asks Benford, "Why did you write it this way?" if he has an answer or wishes to give an answer, he can do so; but if he does not have an answer or does not wish to give an answer, he can simply reply, "I don't really know why—you'll have to ask my subconscious about that." Such a response is not possible in the case of neologisms; while combinations of existing words may well emerge without conscious thought, creations like *hypnobioscope, necrocosmetician,* or *eptify* do not mysteriously float out of the author's subconscious mind to magically appear on the printed page. That is, when we deal with neologisms, we confront unambiguous products of conscious intent and craftsmanship, and we can confidently analyze them as deliberate artistic creations. As examples of the sorts of additional study that might occur, Heinlein's repeated use of words beginning with *pseudo* in *Beyond This Horizon* must be a deliberate effort to undermine a fictional world he otherwise projects as utopian; and Gibson's fondness for words beginning with *micro* must be a deliberate evocation of the themes of shrinking and inwardness that permeate *Neuromancer*.[8] In short, when we ask of science fiction, "What's in a word?" the answer may be "quite a lot."

Notes

1. The many contributions of Gernsback and the reasons for regarding his work as the true beginning of science fiction are discussed in my articles "On *The True History of Science Fiction*" and "An Idea of Significant Import."
2. In choosing these works, I sought novels about a technologically advanced urban civilization of the future because I assumed that such works would yield the greatest number of neologisms, and I sought American writers, suspecting that works by British writers would introduce the needless complication of distinguishing unfamiliar British terms from actual neologisms. However, I ultimately made three exceptions: Nowlan's novel, which takes place in a technologically advanced but necessarily nonurban culture—since the cities in the world of 2419 A.D. are occupied by the Asian Han invaders; Farmer's long novella; and *Stand on Zanzibar*, by the British John Brunner, on the grounds that I could not envision a study of neologisms in the New Wave era without that seminal work, and I rationalized that Brunner has always written primarily for the American market.
3. This characterization of science fiction neologisms as borrowings from an imagined future language brings with it a prediction: in the science fiction written in languages that are historically not open to borrowings from foreign languages—French being an obvious example—one should find far fewer neologisms than in English-language science fiction. While I have no detailed information on this issue, two critics who have extensively studied French science fiction—George Slusser and Bradley Lyau—have told me in conversation that this hypothesis is essentially correct.

4. While not a particularly sympathetic critic of science fiction writers as linguists, Myers did acknowledge that "all the usual methods of word formation are represented in the coinages found in science fiction" (p. 138), an observation certainly supported by the neologisms shown in table 1. As for how authors manipulate their own words, writers first often create clipped or abbreviated versions of their own neologisms; thus, Gernsback's *Meteoro-tower* becomes a *Meteoro,* Nowlan's *disintegrator beams* and *repellor rays* become *dis beams* and *rep rays,* and Sterling's *Optimal Persona* becomes an *O.P.* In addition, writers sometime create not only new words but new bound morphemes used in a number of different words. Thus, Gernsback devised the prefix *Alo,* apparently derived from *aluminum* to mean "lightweight," as used in the words *Alohydrolium* and *Alomagnesium;* Nowlan derived from *ultron,* his posited smallest particle of matter, the prefixes *ultro* and *ultrono,* used in many words; and Asimov created the root *tex,* meaning "textile," used in words like *Plastex, celltex,* and *Textron.* Finally, a few neologisms undergo semantic change, like Nowlan's *projectoscope,* introduced as a noun but later used as a verb.

5. Two stories in this vein that immediately come to mind are Frederik Pohl's "The Midas Plague" and Robert Sheckley's "The Minimum Man."

6. I discuss these and other similarities between *Ralph 124C 41+* and *Neuromancer* in "The Gernsback Continuum."

7. An exception is in Heinlein's *Beyond This Horizon,* in which a minor subplot involves a man from the 1920s who was placed in suspended animation and awakes in the future; yet he functions primarily as a comic intrusion—he introduces the game of *feetball*—and otherwise seems out of place in the novel.

8. I discuss the theme of inward movement in Gibson's *Neuromancer* in my forthcoming book *Islands in the Sky: The Space Station Theme in Science Fiction Literature.*

Glossary: Neologisms from Eight Science Fiction Works

acceleratube n. Underground tube for urban rapid transit (Brunner, *Stand*)

appear n. A fruit, half-apple, half-pear (Gernsback, *Ralph*)

appleofmyeye n. A child (Brunner, *Stand*)

apt n. Apartment (Brunner, *Stand*)

ash vacuum n. An ashtray with a vacuum attached to draw in ashes (Asimov, *Caves*)

Bacillatorium n. A chamber people enter in which harmful germs are destroyed (Gernsback, *Ralph*)

business n. Fighting (Nowlan, *Armageddon*)

C/Fe [pronounced "see fee"] n. The concept that humans and robots can coexist and work together as equals (Asimov, *Caves*)

capillotomer n. A device that instantly shaves the face (Heinlein, *Beyond*)

Catalepsol n. A drug that induces instant paralysis (Gernsback, *Ralph*)

coffin n. A very small room rented for sleeping (Gibson, *Neuromancer*)

cosmetokit n. A device with several orifices for applying cosmetics (Asimov, *Caves*)

diet-negative adj. Low-calorie (Heinlein, *Beyond*)

dora n. The building that issues welfare money (derived from Pandora) (Farmer, "Riders")

electronorecordograph n. A device that stores records electronically (Nowlan, *Armageddon*)

emp n. Electro-*m*agnetic *p*ulse weapon (Gibson, *Neuromancer*)

eptify v. To prepare someone to perform a given assignment; derived from *e*ducation for *p*ar*ti*cular tasks (Brunner, *Stand*)

exchange n. Stranger (Nowlan, *Armageddon*)

fido n. A television screen (Farmer, "Riders")

food-oid adj. Pertaining to artificial food (Sterling, *Islands*)

fornixator n. A machine that stimulates sexual feelings (Farmer, "Riders")

fuzzy-wuzzy n. Policeman (Brunner, *Stand*)

go out v. To die by being disintegrated (Nowlan, *Armageddon*)

Helio-Dynamophore n. A huge solar power generator (Gernsback, *Ralph*)

housfit n. An outfit worn around the house (Brunner, *Stand*)

Hypnobioscope n. A device that transmits information directly to the brain during sleep (Gernsback, *Ralph*)

ice n. A guard against invasion of a computer program; derived from *i*ntrusion *c*ountermeasures *e*lectronics (Gibson, *Neuromancer*)

journo n. Journalist (Sterling, *Islands*)

Language Rectifier n. An instantaneous translation device attached to picturephones (Gernsback, *Ralph*)

lightworm n. A long, thin illuminated sign (Asimov, *Caves*) *macluhan* v. To show, to display (Brunner, *Stand*)

man-jam n. A traffic jam involving pedestrians on moving sidewalks (Asimov, *Caves*)

matron n. A genetically engineered woman with little intelligence (Heinlein, *Beyond*)

meat adj. Pertaining to the body and bodily experiences, as opposed to life in cyberspace (Gibson, *Neuromancer*)

Medievalism n. Future term for the beliefs and practices of the twentieth century; *Medievalist* n. Someone who is interested in or wishes to return to medieval practices (Asimov, *Caves*)

Menograph n. A device that converts thoughts into written symbols (Gernsback, *Ralph*)

Meteoro-tower n. A building that projects energy to alter the weather (Gernsback, *Ralph*)

microbot n. A very small moving robot (Sterling, *Islands*)

microlight n. A small, light flying vehicle (Gibson, *Neuromancer*)

mind-absent adj. Not alert, not thinking; antonym: *mind-present* (Brunner, *Stand*)

necrocosmetician n. Cosmetician who prepares corpses for public display (Heinlein, *Beyond*)

offyourass n. Assertiveness; spunk (Brunner, *Stand*)

orthowife n. Regular, legal wife (Heinlein, *Beyond*)

OTEC n. Offshore power station; derived from Offshore Thermal Energy Converter (Sterling, *Islands*)

pay-restaurant n. A restaurant where one must pay for food, as opposed to the free government restaurants of the future (Heinlein, *Beyond*)

Personal n. Public bathroom (Asimov, *Caves*)

popskull n. A strong alcoholic beverage (Farmer, "Riders")

premillennium n. Twenty-first century term for the twentieth century; *premillennial* adj. (Sterling, *Islands*)

projectoscope n. A long-range observation device; v. To transmit by projectoscope (Nowlan, *Armageddon*)

protoveg n. A type of synthetic vegetable (Asimov, *Caves*)

pseudo-dactyl n. A mechanical finger, attached to a wall, used for personal massage (Heinlein, *Beyond*) *psycho field* n. One's field of reference or mental world (Heinlein, *Beyond*)

psycho-pediatrician n. Child psychologist (Heinlein, *Beyond*)

puppet n. A woman who has had her consciousness turned off to work as a prostitute without truly experiencing or remembering what she is doing (Gibson, *Neuromancer*)

razorgirl n. A female bodyguard with built-in retractable blades in her fingers (Gibson, *Neuromancer*)

sammer n. Someone who works for the American government (Uncle Sam) (Farmer, "Riders")

scientific restaurant n. A restaurant that serves only liquid, easily digestible food (Gernsback, *Ralph*)

scop n. Artificial yellow substance used to make food; derived from *single-cell* protein (Sterling, *Islands*)

sense free adj. Senseless (Heinlein, *Beyond*)

silicon adj. Possessing sockets and microchips in the brain for computer access; "He was the first person the Finn had known who'd 'gone *silicon*' " (Gibson, *Neuromancer*)

stationary n. Future term for a nonmoving sidewalk (Asimov, *Caves*)

steelonium n. An alloy of steel and aluminum used in the future instead of steel (Gernsback, *Ralph*)

stereosculp n. A sophisticated device used in plastic surgery (Heinlein, *Beyond*)

tanglegun n. A gun that shoots out strands of plastic to entangle victims (Sterling, *Islands*)

teemager n. Active teenager (Farmer, "Riders")

tempoxy n. A powerful temporary glue (Farmer, "Riders")

travolator n. A large moving walkway (Brunner, *Stand*)

video rouge n. Makeup used when appearing on television (Sterling, *Islands*)

virgin n. A man with no bionic parts or sensing devices (Gibson, *Neuromancer*)

zeck n. Executive (Brunner, *Stand*)

zock n. A popular dance of the future (Brunner, *Stand*)

zymoveal n. A type of synthetic veal made out of yeast products (Asimov, *Caves*)

Works Cited

Aldiss, Brian W., with David Wingrove. *Trillion Year Spree: The History of Science Fiction*. New York: Atheneum, 1986.

Asimov, Isaac. *The Caves of Steel*. 1953. New York: Pyramid Books, 1962.

Benford, Gregory. "Style, Substance, and Other Illusions." Paper presented at the Eleventh Annual Eaton Conference on Science Fiction and Fantasy, Riverside, California, 1989.

Brunner, John. *Stand on Zanzibar*. 1968. New York: Ballantine Books, 1969.

Campbell, John W., Jr. "Concerning Science Fiction." In *The Best of Science Fiction*, edited by Groff Conklin. New York: Crown Publishers, 1946.

———. "Science-Fiction." *Astounding Science-Fiction* 21 (March 1938): 37.

de Camp, L. Sprague, and Catherine Crook de Camp. *Science Fiction Handbook—Revised: A Guide to Writing Imaginative Literature*. New York: McGraw-Hill, 1975.

Delany, Samuel R. "Time Considered as a Helix of Semi-Precious Stones" (1968). In *World's Best Science Fiction 1969*, edited by Donald A. Wollheim and Terry Carr. New York: Ace Books, 1969.

Ellison, Harlan. "Brinkmanship." In *Over the Edge*, by Harlan Ellison. New York: Belmont/Tower Books, 1969.

———. "Science Fiction: Turning Reality Inside Out." In *Sleepless Nights in the Procrustean Bed: Essays by Harlan Ellison*, edited by Marty Clark. San Bernardino, California: Borgo Press, 1984. Essay originally published in the October 1974 issue of *New Times*.

Etchison, Dennis. "Style, Literature, and the Imagination." Paper presented at the Eleventh Annual Eaton Conference on Science Fiction and Fantasy, Riverside, California, 1989.

Farmer, Philip Jose. "Riders of the Purple Wage." 1967. In *Dangerous Visions #1*, edited by Harlan Ellison. New York: Berkley, 1969.

Gernsback, Hugo. *Ralph 124C 41+: A Romance of the Year 2660*. 1911–12. New York: Frederick Fell, 1950.

———. "Science Fiction Week." *Science Wonder Stories* 1 (May 1930): 1061.

Gibson, William. *Neuromancer*. New York: Ace Books, 1984.

Heinlein, Robert A. *Beyond This Horizon*. 1942. New York: Signet Books, 1960.

Kipling, Rudyard. *With the Night Mail, a Story of 2000 A.D. (Together with Extracts from the Contemporary Magazine in Which It Appeared)*. 1905. New York: Doubleday, Page, 1909.

Myers, Walter L. "The Future History and Development of the English Language." *Science Fiction Studies* 3 (July 1976): 130–42.

Nowlan, Philip Francis. *Armageddon 2419 A.D.* 1928. New York: Ace Books, 1962.

Poe, Edgar Allan. "Mellonta Tauta" (1840). In *The Science Fiction of Edgar Allan Poe*, collected and edited with an introduction and commentary by Harold Beaver. New York: Penguin Books, 1976.

Pohl, Frederik. "The Midas Plague" (1954). In *The Science Fiction Hall of Fame*, vol. IIB, edited by Ben Bova. New York: Avon Books, 1974.

Sheckley, Robert. "The Minimum Man" (1959). In *The Fifth Galaxy Reader*, edited by H. L. Gold. New York: Pocket Books, 1962.

Shelley, Mary. *The Last Man*, with a new introduction by Brian Aldiss. 1826. London: Hogarth Press, 1985.

Smith, Cordwainer [Paul Linebarger]. "Scanners Live in Vain" (1950). In *The Science Fiction Hall of Fame*, edited by Robert Silverberg. New York: Avon Books, 1971.

Sterling, Bruce. *Islands in the Net*. New York: Ace Books, 1989.

Suvin, Darko. *Metamorphoses of Science Fiction: On the Poetics and History of a Literary Genre*. New Haven: Yale University Press, 1979.

Wells, H. G. *When the Sleeper Wakes*. New York: Harper and Row, 1899.

Westfahl, Gary. " 'The Gernsback Continuum': William Gibson in the Context of Science Fiction." In *Fiction 2000: Cyberpunk and the Future of Narrative*, edited by George Slusser and Tom Shippey. Athens: University of Georgia Press, 1992.

——— . " 'An Idea of Significant Import': Hugo Gernsback's Theory of Science Fiction." *Foundation* 48 (Spring 1990): 26–50.

——— . *Islands in the Sky: The Space Station Theme in Science Fiction Literature*, preface by Gregory Benford. San Bernardino, Calif.: Borgo Press, 1992.

——— . "On *The True History of Science Fiction*." *Foundation* 47 (Winter 1989–90): 5–27.

Chapter 18

Styles of Invisibility:

Sustaining the Transparent in

Contemporary Prose Semblances

Brooks Landon

It is, I confess, with considerable diffidence that I approach the strange narrative which I am about to relate. The events which I purpose detailing are of so extraordinary a character that I am quite prepared to meet with an unusual amount of incredulity and scorn. I accept all such beforehand. I have, I trust, the literary courage to face unbelief.
—Fitz-James O'Brien, "What Was It?"

By the time Alice declares that a grin without a cat is the most curious thing she has ever seen in all her life, we can hardly share her surprise, much less accept her superlative. After all, by the time she encounters the Cheshire cat she has already fallen down a rabbit hole, experienced a couple of alarming size changes, been swimming in a pool of tears, gotten advice from a stoned caterpillar, and had a human baby transform in her arms into a small squealing pig—each fantastic development supporting her claim that affairs in Wonderland were growing "curiouser and curiouser." [1] But if familiarity does not necessarily breed contempt, neither does it necessarily breed progressively more fantastic fantasy, and I suspect most readers find Alice's adventures "curious and various" or even "curious and then less curious" rather than "curiouser and curiouser." And this may be true for Alice herself. Her narrator does consider some of the jading impact of too much novelty, explaining that "Alice had got so much into the way of expecting nothing but out-of-the-way things to happen, that it seemed quite dull and stupid for life to go on in the common way." And once we acknowledge the leveling influence of the fantastic on the ordinary, isn't the inevitable next step to ask when the sustained or familiar fantastic becomes merely the ordinary?

A corollary to this consideration, it seems to me, might possibly apply as well to the reading adventures of Alice's early audience, late nineteenth-century readers of the fantastic, soon to be joined by more and more readers of the developing genre of science fiction. For example, some thirty years after readers first shared Alice's encounter with an invisible cat, another noteworthy example appeared in print, this time "a pair of eyes without a cat," although this cat was most certainly not grinning as it lay invisible and drugged on Griffin's invisible pillow in Wells's *The Invisible Man*.[2] And among Wells's early readers there could have been one or two who had *already* experienced a range of plausibly presented invisible creatures in various fictions by Fitz-James O'Brien (1859), Edward Page Mitchell (1881), Guy de Maupassant (1887), and Ambrose Bierce (1893)—a list that in another few years would include invisibility narratives by Jack London (1903) and Jules Verne (1910). Who knows—such hypothetical readers might even have also actually witnessed Bulwer-Lytton parading before the eyes of visitors in his study, acting as if he apparently believed *himself* invisible. Strained as it may be, my point is that by the time Wells had finished appropriating invisibility as one of his subjects, definitively mapping territory that had until then been only tentatively explored, invisibility had been pretty well identified as a literary theme and had already undergone a number of significant transformations. Originally a gift of the gods (the Helm of Hades delivered by helpful Hermes), by the end of the nineteenth century—long before it had been reduced to a humorous special effect of Carroll's canny uncanny cat—invisibility had come to represent disastrous hubris more than crafty knowledge, alienation more than innovation, problems more than power.

For all his genius, Wells codified these changes rather than causing them. For, having peopled its world with invisible spirits ranging from gods to ghosts before literature began its subtly faithless investigations, humanity could only drain its original myths of power (even if only by the thimbleful) through the relentless investigations of literature as it sought to clarify those myths and extend them more and more to mortal agents. First an attribute of the gods, then one of their marvelous gifts to favored mortals, then a stock-in-trade for children's stories, and finally represented as even attainable through diligent scientific research, the idea of invisibility has gradually evolved through increasingly normalizing stages. Surely the other side of the shiny new and increasingly secular coin of mortal invisibility is an increasing skepticism about the operating assumptions of a world of unseen spirits. At the same time literature was representing invisibility as progressively easier to achieve, its originating invisible potencies were growing progressively harder to credit. In other words, once man got his hands on invisibility, there went the old mythic neighborhood. And between our first myths of invisible gods and the emergence of invisibility along with ugliness as the two primary modernist metaphors for alienation and despair, some fascinating conceptual corners must have been turned.

But the declining fortunes of invisibility as a myth are not my main concern. Instead, I want to hazard a very rough prolegomenon to an alternative line of inquiry in which invisibility is considered an intensely self-reflexive and metaliterary metaphor, a conceptual pressure point we can use to organize or reorganize some of our thinking about prose narratives and prose style. I can't pretend to shape my discussion toward any particular thesis, but I do want to suggest that the current—apparently quite healthy—status of invisibility as a literary subject has more to do with the nature of literature itself than with the more conventional explanation of the appeal of invisibility narratives as adolescent power fantasies, metaphors of alienation, or links to the numinous.

To begin with, I'm struck by several fascinating semantic convergences, even if they are no more than coincidental. The historical discussion of prose style as the dress of ideas (a dualistic approach most stylistic theory has long since rejected) establishes a style-as-clothing metaphor that can only make me remember that most mythologies associate the power of invisibility with items of apparel—magical caps or capes or rings. I note this because probably the second-best-known, and also firmly repudiated, chimera in the historical discussion of prose style is the idea of a transparent or invisible style, either as a writer's self-effacing option (Stealth style?) or as the norm from which variations define the writer's uniqueness. And in more rigorous terms, if we posit any discourse unit, say, a sentence such as "Great and strange ideas transcending experience often have less effect upon men and women than smaller, more tangible considerations,"[3] and then ask for its stylistic features, we soon realize the crucial role played by context, a kind of invisible pattern, in any stylistic analysis. Invoke the concept of style, and the rhetoric of invisibility is almost sure to follow.

Chiastically, the invocation of invisibility in the semblance of a prose narrative seems to be attended by several metaliterary implications.[4] For instance, one way of describing the starting point of literary semblance building would be to say we start from nothing—from the unimagined, from the unseen, from the invisible. A counterproposition would cast semblance formation in terms of conceptually chiseling fiction's illusional worlds from some dense, granitelike block of sensory overload, but insofar as I can interrogate my own imagination, I think I start from nothing and build up. And a folklore index I consulted reminds us that medicine men often claim to be able to see invisible beings whom ordinary mortals cannot see. Not a bad summary of the phenomenon of semblance formation by gifted readers and writers alike.

Indeed, only through the most delicate and complex conceptual negotiations between our sense of the seen and the unseen can literature work its basic magic. More specifically, invisibility seems inherently pertinent to our understanding of most narrative schemes, arrangements that routinely present narrators as if they were invisible characters. Until first-person narrators look in the mirror or otherwise have their features inventoried, we cannot "see" them, and omniscient narrators closely approximate invisible observers who completely realize invisibility's voyeuristic potential. And finally, what is the reader's involvement in a literary semblance if not invisible? Just as surely as seeing is believing, believing in a literary semblance is seeing, but seeing secure in the necessary knowledge that we remain unseen. The visually charged lexicon of our reading, a rhetoric in which textual phenomena "appear" or "come into focus," in which we "look" at issues, scramble for "insights," "observe" characters or "see" signs, and gain new "perspectives" or "lose sight of" distinctions, has been much remarked. What has remained unremarked, however, is the unseen nature of our vantage point, one that makes an invisible man or woman in a semblance a ready model for our mode of encountering and realizing the semblance of a literary text.

But again, I want to fall back from these admittedly crudely formed and very tentative propositions and turn to a more conventional consideration of some different ways in which invisibility is represented in prose narratives—what I call styles of invisibility. But first a necessary—if somewhat suicidal—definition of style. When I refer to styles of invisibility I do so within a larger concept of prose style shaped by my belief that *prose style is what the writer writes, what the reader reads, or both.*[5] Whether it is considered an attribute of a writer or a group of writers, of a text or a group of texts, or of a reader or a group of readers, prose style exists in the interaction among the writer's purposes, the reader's purposes, the general cultural backgrounds both writer and reader bring to the creation of a text, and in the more specific linguistic and literary traditions—such as those involving invisibility—that inform both the writer's and the reader's understanding of the text's semblance, or illusional world. More important, and much more ephemeral, style is indeed a gift, in the quite literal sense brilliantly explored by Lewis Hyde. As Hyde points out, the essential attribute of a gift is that *it must always move:* the gift of style is what can and must be passed on, whether to readers or writers, embodied in traditions, formulas, concepts, semblances, or sentences.[6] And in turning to that phrase "the gift of style" I am once again struck by the coincidence that invisibility enters our myths and our literature as a *gift* of the gods; I can only suspect that our first concept of style must have had a similar origin.

When I refer to contemporary prose semblances, I have in mind both texts that offer some plausible pseudoscientific explanation for the phenomenon of invisibility and texts that without explanation posit essentially realistic semblances in which invisibility constitutes the primary disruption of our expectations about the way the world of the text works. Traditional distinctions between SF and fantasy simply don't fit my needs here, because my concern is not with whether the phenomenon of invisibility can be rationalized—in terms of pigmentation bleaching, molecule rearrangement, or refractive index manipulation—but with ways in which the sense or feel of invisibility can be sustained in our experience of the literary semblance. Likewise, my title specifies transparency as a key attribute of invisibility to suggest the requirement that invisible objects and characters must be "actually" present in the semblance and not otherwise fantastic: ghosts are often invisible, as are gods, demons, and Jack the Giant Killer, but my interest is not with them. Alice, Jack, and Frodo appear in narratives that challenge much more than my expectations about sight, and I leave it to others to look at, focus on, or critically eyeball their kinds of invisibility. *My* kind appears and disappears in works by Edward Page Mitchell, H. G. Wells, Jack London, Jules Verne, Philip Wylie, Ralph Ellison, Thomas Berger, H. F. Saint, Christopher Priest, and Robert Cormier—an assemblage meant to be indicative rather than exhaustive.

Of particular interest to me are Thomas Berger's *Being Invisible* (1987), H. F. Saint's *Memoirs of an Invisible Man,* (1987), and Christopher Priest's

The Glamour (1984),[7] because each represents investigations of invisibility as primarily a moral, a physical, or an intellectual phenomenon. Moreover, each work recasts the style of the invisibility narrative in terms selfreflexively concerned with writing and reading (as does Robert Cormier's 1988 novel *Fade*).[8] Each of these works explicitly invokes the intertext of invisibility by referring to specific previous invisibility narratives. That four significant invisibility novels should be published within four years in the 1980s, by four writers so little alike, strikes me as a pretty good sign that the literary dimensions and implications of invisibility are deep and wide ranging enough to support much more than my cursory investigation.

I start my discussion with Christopher Priest's *The Glamour*, which most strongly supports my contention about the inherent metaliterary resonance of invisibility narratives but least follows the tradition of Wells. Priest's title—at first a necessary obfuscation or misdirection—eventually comes to remind us of the etymology of *glamour,* a word whose original sense of having to do with illusion, enchantment, or delusive beauty, a look that deceives the eye, has itself become transparent, yielding to connotations of substantive excitement charged with celebrity status. In positing a small population of glamorous people so visually inconsequential that they have faded from public consciousness as well as from sight, Priest continues a major strain of invisibility narratives, particularly in folklore, which claim not physical but psychological or intellectual invisibility caused by the clouding or deception of sight—more an issue of camouflage than of transparency. I won't detail the intriguing arcana Priest creates for his invisible "glams," because the most fascinating aspect of his novel is a nidified narrative structure so perversely crafted that it quite distracts a reader's attention from the issue of invisibility—in effect extending the cloaking cloud of glamour to our experience as readers. Our "view" of the story is deceived just as completely by Priest's narrative scheme as is the sight of the nonglamorous characters in his semblance.

What seems to open as a story about the efforts of a celebrated former BBC cameraman to recover a portion of his memory lost when he was gravely injured in a London car bombing unfolds through a series of Akutagawa-like shifts of point of view, each presenting a different version of recent events. After what initially seems to be a brief two-page reminiscence of childhood by an unidentified first-person narrator, this narrator abandons the field, announcing that what follows will be his story but told in different voices. Then Priest's novel seems to get down to business in its lengthy second section. There, a traditional limited omniscient third-person narrator fills us in on the cameraman, Richard Grey, whose convalescence is marked by attempts to penetrate the retrograde and possibly traumatic amnesia that has robbed him of any recollection of the several weeks before the bomb blast. A young woman visits Grey in the rehab center and claims that she had become his girlfriend during the blank period in his memory, a fact Grey finds plausible and appealing but cannot confirm. Point of view then shifts to Grey as he laboriously reconstructs his memory of the missing weeks and of his missing relationship with Susan. It later turns out that much of his thoroughly compelling reconstruction is compensatory fantasy and quite inaccurate, the first of a series of fraying narrative threads.

The next section returns to the original third-person narrator, who, 143 pages into the narrative, suddenly describes a scene in which Susan also demonstrates to Richard that—by the way—she can become invisible. Next comes a section narrated by Susan in which she frequently refers to her very possessive former lover, Niall, also a glam, and in which she reveals that she had recognized in Richard himself strong glamorous potential, and had informed him of that potential before the bomb blast. Narration then reverts to the third person once again in a section in which the jealous rival Niall comes to seem more and more ominous and psychopathic. His relentless invisible presence wherever Susan and Richard go is the explanation for her increasingly nervous behavior—only we finally discover that the third-person narrator *is* Niall and that both Susan's and Richard's narratives were but masks he had previously adopted.

The story "told in different voices" we had simply assumed to be Richard's has been Niall's all along, a possibility always before our eyes but completely overlooked. As Niall smugly announces to characters and readers alike, "I am indeed invisible to you, but not in the sense you mean" (298). In Priest's deft hands, invisibility stunningly disappears into narrativity.

While *Being Invisible* does have its invisible protagonist admit to himself on the book's final page that his invisibility might have been no more than self-delusion, Thomas Berger's invisibility narrative surprises us in much smaller increments than does Priest's. Berger has acknowledged that Wells's *The Invisible Man* is among the few books he has read more than twice, parenthetically adding, "I also admire my friend Ralph Ellison's novel of almost the same title . . . but that is an unseen horse of a different color."[9] However, Berger's *Being Invisible* seems to be more in the spirit of Kafka's *Metamorphosis* than in the more ideological tradition of either

Wells or Ellison. For just as Gregor Samsa gradually realizes his humanity precisely through his "bugness," Berger's protagonist, Fred Wagner, becomes morally visible only through his experience with physical invisibility. Like Kafka, Berger simply predicates his protagonist's fantastic situation in the first sentence: "Fred Wagner began his career of public invisibility in a large midtown post office" (3). Moreover, like Kafka's, Berger's narrator quickly moves to normalize this new imaginative territory, casually assuring us in the novel's second sentence that "one does not become invisible without carefully studying one's reflection."

What both authors' characters most desperately seek is *nourishment,* a matter of the spirit rather than of the flesh. Berger's truths are essentially also Kafka's, but the world of his fiction runs according to more complicated and more familiar rules, and Fred Wagner's metamorphosis proves much less costly and much more humorous than Gregor's. Along the way, while addressing the salient issues of the invisibility formula as codified in both film and literature, Berger's novel provides a wry investigation of the petty tyrannies of quotidian life. Indeed, Berger's gift to the invisibility narrative may be the suggestion that before the onslaught of banality, even invisibility proves powerless.

A chrestomathic index to petty humiliations, Fred Wagner is "the sort of man who could lose face by the return of a letter with postage-due charges," just as he can feel embarrassed when forced to make an ungrammatical response to the greeting of a doorman. Indeed, "losing face" may have been the figurative first step in Fred's literal discovery that he can simply will himself to become invisible, the ultimate stage in the disintegration of self-image. Yet, Fred's fantastic ability confers neither fantastic power nor maddening delusions: when invisible he remains a disappointed novelist, his wife has still left him, and the world that barely noticed him in the first place now sees him not at all.

Relentlessly, Berger subjects his protagonist, seen or unseen, to the exquisite gamut of painful humiliations possible in post offices, restaurants, public restrooms, doctors' offices, and elevators—recasting these spaces as the banal torture chambers of modern life. What emerges from Fred's misadventures in these arenas is Berger's sense that victimization by a surly postal clerk or arrogant waiter is just as instructive of the dynamics of power as the more dramatic examples of physical or psychological abuse. In the world of Berger's fiction, small indignities debilitate even more inexorably than do large injustices; whereas the latter are sometimes subject to redress, the former usually are not. Fred himself announces what could be an initial assumption of Berger's interest in invisibility—that "the shift of power is always a fascinating process." And just as "through being invisible Wagner learned many truths that otherwise would have been inaccessible," Berger's readers soon realize the pervasive power of the unreasonable in invisible just as in visible life.

The creative faculties that fail Fred as a novelist also fail him as an invisible man, and he initially thinks of his ability only as "a device to avoid inconvenience or embarrassment, not as a means of shirking responsibility" (54). When Fred finally applies his invisibility to robbing a bank, he returns the money as soon as he realizes that the young woman bank teller from whose drawer he had taken the money will undoubtedly be blamed for its disappearance. As is true of almost all of Berger's earlier protagonists, Fred remains the captive of a relentless awareness of responsibility, both personal and intertextual.

Thus, despite his extraordinary gift, Wagner is still as much at the mercy of events as he ever was. Perhaps he lacks the basic stuff to be a legendary invisible personage, one of the pioneering titans of the tradition on whose shoulders all future unseen practitioners would stand. Perhaps he is a poetaster, not a poet of invisibility, his experiences a mere doggerel of the ability to elude the eye (221).

More properly, Fred's failures assure him and Berger's readers of an investigation of the arcane philosophical implications of invisibility. For example, he admits to himself that his ability would not count for much in his ex-wife's practical aesthetic because it could neither be appreciated for its style nor evaluated: "To Babe that would be a trick, not a talent; an ingenious trick to be sure, but if *She* could have learned how to do it, so could others. Whereas talent was unique" (241). Discovering that being invisible has no effect on the "fundamental way" the world works, the previously unnoticed Fred now finds it impossible to get people to notice his invisibility: "In all the world there was no one who would willingly and with more than a polite interest serve as his audience" (248).

But that's not exactly the case, is it, since we, Berger's readers, watch Fred's every move. For, whatever his failings, Fred *is never invisible to us;* he is always center stage, frozen in the spotlight of Berger's narrative scheme. Fred may be a marginal character in his fictional world, but he remains the main character in our reading, his thoughts equally open to us whether he is invisible or visible. And here is Berger's final ironic twist to the invisibility formula. Fred's prominence in the narrative almost ensures that we will sentimentalize our response to him, the narrator's point of view ever directing our attention toward Fred's invisibility and away from the otherwise clear evidence that *others are as invisible to Fred as he is to them.*

Fred's story can be viewed in terms of a sequence of characters initially as overlooked or misperceived by him as he is by them, and the action of the novel consists largely not of Fred's exploits but of the other characters forcing themselves into his sight. As these characters come into better focus for Fred, they also come into better focus for Berger's readers, presenting the nagging prospect that they may turn out *to be more interesting than Fred,* even if he is Berger's point-of-view character. Through this subtle process Berger reminds us that social or moral invisibility, after all, is a mass rather than an individual threat, and the phenomenon inheres fractally within the conventions of the novel just as surely as it does within the conventions of society. It is to this final irony that Berger's title directs our attention—to the universal processes of invisibility rather than to the sentimental uniqueness of a single invisible personage. Explaining one of Fred's many surprises, Berger's narrator philosophizes that "whatever the milieu, at any given time someone must always be the most newly arrived" (223). In the milieu of Berger's fiction, the most newly arrived, of course, is always the reader.

The style of Berger's representation of invisibility promotes our ultimately problematized identification with Wagner in much the same way that Wells ensured *against* such identification by having his narrative scheme offer virtually every point of view *but* that of his invisible man. H. F. Saint plays against that aspect of Wells's style even more radically by offering his invisibility narrative completely in the first person—a nice twist that invites us to consider the novel distinctions between a first-person, invisible narrator and the range of other narrative options. "If only you could see me now," deadpans the opening sentence of Saint's *Memoirs of an Invisible Man.*

Nick Halloway, Saint's narrator and protagonist, is a successful, reasonably satisfied securities analyst who neither wills nor discovers invisibility, but suffers it as a random bystander caught in a "minor but altogether extraordinary scientific mishap" which "rendered a small spherical chunk of New Jersey utterly invisible." (I should add that with a clear tip of the old Helm of Hades to Wells, Saint remembers to throw a cat, as well as his protagonist, into the initial sphere of invisibility.) By making Halloway neither a scientific investigator nor an alienated casualty of the social and economic system, Saint frees his protagonist from any moral responsibility

for his plight, shifting the novel's emphasis to the detailed physical implications of invisible life and to the literary and linguistic ironies that beg to
be exploited in invisibility narratives. Trying to survive his own invisible
odyssey, Saint's narrator has time to stumble across a copy of *Ulysses* to
find the motto for Saint's style in Joyce's reference to Turko the terrible: "I
am the boy/That can enjoy/Invisibility." [10]

Accordingly, Saint's novel has the feel more of playfully following pro-
cedural formulas and of pursuing literary jokes than of anything else: Halloway must cope with updated versions of Griffin's physical problems, but
the commodified existence denied Griffin is made accessible to Halloway
because he manages to appropriate all kinds of invisible supplies from the
disaster area. Correctly perceived by the government as a strategic weapon
too dangerous to be at large, and incorrectly perceived by a young woman
who is attracted to him by her belief that he is really an incubus, Halloway
confirms a number of our received truths about contemporary culture but
actually learns little apart from the peculiar logistics of invisible survival,
owing as much to the examples of Robinson Crusoe or any Ludlumesque
paranoid thriller protagonist as to Griffin, with whom he seems to share
only the visibility of ingested food and drink. Costume parties he attends
in the guise of James Whale's Invisible Man offer him a certain social satisfaction, and he decides, of course, that Halloween is his favorite holiday.

In short, Saint relentlessly exploits the humorous linguistic aspects of the
invisibility narrative (inevitably, Halloway tells his lover, "What you see is
what you get"), devoting great portions of his 458-page novel to detailing
the mechanics of hyper-insider trading and invisible style, offering us the
archetypal Yuppie power fantasy. And that he inexorably normalizes invisibility as a condition by sustaining his semblance for so long and with
such densely textured details is an irony Saint embraces. Along with Halloway's lover, Alice (an interesting choice of a name), readers must surely
grow very used to the once-marvelous evidences of invisibility—pencils
and wineglasses floating in the air, already special effect commonplaces in
invisibility films. Halloway realizes that "these things had become part of
her daily life and no more miraculous than the kitchen table or the view
from her window or anything else in creation" (423).

If Berger's approach to invisibility serves to establish the sovereignty of
banality even in an invisible life, Saint seems determined to exhaust the
novelty of invisibility in a literary semblance. And it is precisely this exhaus-
tion of novelty that Saint offers as his metaliterary gift to the invisibility
narrative: invisibility may grow old, but its self-reflexive literary implica-

tions do not. In language strikingly applicable to the generally perceived role of the writer in society, Saint's narrator acknowledges:

I should have liked to be able to sum up the whole experience for you, to offer you, from my unique vantage point, some valuable insight into the human condition—or at least some greeting more poignant than "You can't catch me!" The trouble is, I have grown so accustomed to my vantage point that its uniqueness is lost on me, and although you might hope that an invisible man could offer you some intelligence of an invisible purpose in the world, if it is there, I have not yet found it. No doubt I am looking right at it and just can't see it. Like the pattern in the carpet. Like me, for that matter. If I ever work it out, I'll be sure to let you know. (457)

Saint's final tweak to the reader's sensibility is the fact that Alice does figure things out, at least to her own satisfaction, in a fashion strongly reminiscent of Nabokov's *Transparent Things*. On the book's final page she tells Halloway: "I think you've misunderstood everything that's happened. You're a ghost after all. You died in that accident, and you've been sent back to accomplish certain very important things." In the courtroom of literature, where most of the evidence is itself invisible, who can prove her wrong? And, as Wells himself so effectively noted some ninety years before Saint: "It is so much easier not to believe in an invisible man." [11]

Notes

1. Lewis Carroll, *Alice's Adventures in Wonderland* (New York: Heritage Press, 1941).
2. H. G. Wells, *The Invisible Man* (New York: Bantam Books, 1987).
3. Ibid., p. 43.
4. My use of the term *semblance* derives from Gordon Mills's discussion in *Hamlet's Castle: The Study of Literature as a Social Experience* (Austin: University of Texas Press, 1976), in which he identifies a literary semblance as "the illusion of human experience in its totality." A semblance is more than only a *visual* illusion, but my comments address only its visual aspects.
5. My tentative definition of prose style attempts to recognize that the perception or description of style will always be strongly influenced by the reader's degree of literary sophistication, critical purposes, aesthetic preferences, and

so on. The rigorous discussion of prose style must acknowledge the role of the reader in isolating characteristics of style.

6. Lewis Hyde, *The Gift: Imagination and the Erotic Life of Property* (New York: Vintage, 1983), p. 4.

7. Thomas Berger, *Being Invisible* (Boston: Little, Brown, 1987); all references are to this edition. H. F. Saint, *Memoirs of an Invisible Man* (New York: Dell, 1987); all references are to this edition. Christopher Priest, *The Glamour* (London: Jonathan Cape, 1984); all references are to this edition.

8. Robert Cormier, *Fade* (New York: Delacorte, 1988).

9. Berger mentioned this in a letter to me dated March 2, 1983.

10. I am indebted to my colleague Cheryl Herr for providing the context for these lines in her *Joyce's Anatomy of Culture* (Urbana: University of Illinois Press, 1986), pp. 118–20.

11. As ever, I am tremendously grateful to Jay Semel and Lorna Olson for their encouragement and support services provided by the Center for Advanced Studies of the University of Iowa. Without their invisible but very tangible assistance this invisibility article would not have been written.

Contributors

GREGORY BENFORD is professor of physics at the University of California, Irvine, and the Nebula Award–winning author of *Timescape* and *Great Sky River*.

DAVID BRIN holds a Ph.D. in astrophysics and is the award-winning author of *The Postman* and *The Uplift War*. His recent novel, *Earth*, deals with ecological dangers in the near future.

PAUL A. CARTER is professor emeritus of history at the University of Arizona and author of the classic study *The Creation of Tomorrow: Fifty Years of Magazine Science Fiction*.

ROBERT CROSSLEY is professor of English at the University of Massachusetts at Boston. He writes widely on science fiction and is literary executor for the estate of Olaf Stapledon.

SHARON DELMENDO teaches English at the State University of New York at Buffalo and is completing a dissertation on nineteenth- and twentieth-century American literature.

PETER FITTING is professor of French at the University of Toronto. He writes on literary theory and on utopian fiction and film.

CARL FREEDMAN teaches English at Louisiana State University. He is the author of one book and more than twenty articles on science fiction and on other aspects of modern culture.

STEPHANIE HAMMER is an assistant professor of comparative literature at the University of California, Riverside, and is currently working on an anthology of East German science fiction.

KAREN A. HOHNE teaches English at Moorhead State University in Moorhead, Minnesota. She has written on Stephen King and has edited a collection of essays on feminism and Mikhail Bakhtin.

BROOKS LANDON is professor of English at the University of Iowa.

REINHART LUTZ is an assistant professor of English at the University of the Pacific in Stockton, California.

JOSEPH D. MILLER teaches neurobiology at Stanford University and moonlights as a science-fiction critic.

SUSAN J. NAVARETTE teaches English at the University of North Carolina at Chapel Hill.

PATRICK PARRINDER is professor of English at the University of Reading in Reading, England. A noted Wells scholar, he is vice-president of the H. G. Wells Society.

JEFFERSON PETERS is a graduate student in English at the University of Michigan. He is completing a dissertation on science fiction.

CHARLES PLATT is author of thirty-five books, among them *Dream Makers* (profiles of science fiction writers) and novels such as *Free Zone* and *The Silicon Man*. He has also been a science-fiction editor.

GEORGE SLUSSER is professor of comparative literature at the University of California, Riverside, and directs the newly formed Eaton Program for Science Fiction and Fantasy Studies.

GARY WESTFAHL teaches reading at the University of California, Riverside. He has recently completed a study of space stations in science fiction and is at work on a book on Hugo Gernsback's influence on science fiction.

Index